# DICK COLE'S WAR

The American Military Experience Series
John C. McManus, Series Editor

The books in this series portray and analyze the experience of Americans in military service during war and peacetime from the onset of the twentieth century to the present. The series emphasizes the profound impact wars have had on nearly every aspect of recent American history and considers the significant effects of modern conflict on combatants and noncombatants alike. Titles in the series include accounts of battles, campaigns, and wars; unit histories; biographical and autobiographical narratives; investigations of technology and warfare; studies of the social and economic consequences of war; and in general, the best recent scholarship on Americans in the modern armed forces. The books in the series are written and designed for a diverse audience that encompasses nonspecialists as well as expert readers.

# DICK COLE'S WAR

## DOOLITTLE RAIDER, HUMP PILOT
## AIR COMMANDO

### DENNIS R. OKERSTROM

UNIVERSITY OF MISSOURI PRESS
COLUMBIA

# CONTENTS

Illustrations follow page 149

# FOREWORD

I remember very well reading the book *30 Seconds over Tokyo* when I was in high school. What a story! It impressed me and many of the young men and women in my generation. So it is no surprise that many of us wanted to grow up and be just like those brave men who flew back in World War II. That's how I found myself as a young ROTC (Reserve Officers' Training Corps) cadet at Manhattan College in the Bronx more than forty years ago. I too wanted to join them "Up in the Blue." My dream: to fly, to wear the wings of an Air Force pilot, and to serve in the tradition of those airmen who had saved the world in the 1940s. In my mind, none stood taller than those eighty brave men who volunteered for the raid on Tokyo in April 1942.

I finally earned those wings, and late in my career when I was the assistant vice chief of staff of the Air Force, I finally got to meet some of those gallant fliers at a Doolittle Raiders reunion celebration held at the National Museum of the US Air Force. I felt like a little kid looking at my heroes. Among them was a quiet man with a ready smile who, however reluctantly, seemed to serve as an unofficial spokesman for the group. Lt. Col. Richard E. Cole, I learned, was among the oldest of the Raiders. He had been Gen. Jimmy Doolittle's copilot on that fateful day when they took off in the first B-25B from the heaving, sea-soaked deck of the USS *Hornet* and flew into history.

Dick was friendly but taciturn. I soon learned that he had strong opinions regarding service, duty, and sacrifice. I was enthralled when I listened to them talk about how they toasted those who had gone before them. Tradition had it that when there were only two of the aviators left, they would open the special bottle of Hennessy cognac and toast General Doolittle and all the crew members who flew that mission, and then there would be no more reunions. At the end of the explanation, Dick Cole shouted out, "I want to know who the *other* person doing the toast will be." I knew then that he was a rare individual with spirit, resolve, and a good sense of humor.

Over the next several years, I attended more of the Doolittle Raider reunions and was proud to consider myself a friend of those extraordinary men. I learned something else about Dick Cole: when the conversation turned to deeds and exploits, he always managed to turn the talk to focus on someone else. Humble beyond the normal meaning of humility, he always downplayed his role in the war, despite the fact that he was the only man in the US military to have served as a Doolittle Raider, a Hump pilot in the dangerous first year of that operation, and then as a 1st Air Commando pilot in Burma.

As commander of Air Mobility Command, I held up Dick Cole as a hero for those serving in our outfit. You can imagine my surprise when I learned that one of the young tanker pilots serving in our command was Dick's grandson Nathan Chal, who was assigned to Fairchild Air Force Base, flying our venerable KC-135s. The part that wasn't surprising to me was learning that the tradition of flying and serving continued in the Cole family—it's in their genes.

I am pleased that Dick has finally consented to have his story told for posterity. Future generations deserve to know this great man and what he and his comrades did in that largest of wars to save the world from fascism. I am blessed to have gotten to know him, and I am proud to call Dick Cole my friend.

**Gen. Arthur J. Lichte, USAF (Ret.)**

# PREFACE

Writing about someone's life is a risky business and incredibly presumptuous, and particularly so when that person is living. No book can possibly capture the actions, thoughts, and emotions of a human being throughout that person's life; in the case of Richard E. Cole—Dick to his friends and family—that life has spanned nearly a century, and it has been incredibly rich, filled with adventure, terror, honors, and the joys of everyday existence as a son, a husband, a father, and a grandfather.

I therefore have not tried to present the complete life story of a man who never sought the limelight. Instead, this book focuses solely on his involvement in the global war that dragged America into the conflict some two years after much of Europe was aflame.

At twenty-six, Dick Cole found himself blinded by the glare of the powerful spotlight of fame; that fame has followed him since his B-25 was launched from a Navy carrier and flown toward Japan just four months after the attack on Pearl Harbor. Adm. William "Bull" Halsey called the mission "one of the most courageous deeds in military history," and the public seemed to agree. Dick and all of the Raiders were idolized, the subject of magazine articles, books, and Hollywood movies. For nearly three-quarters of a century, the survivors held reunions, which at first were raucous affairs but over the years mellowed to include wives, families, and the public. A final reunion was held in April 2013 in Fort Walton Beach, Florida, and hundreds turned out to meet the remaining three Raiders who were able to attend. A final toast—a tribute to the seventy-six men who had passed since that April day in 1942—was held at Wright-Patterson Air Force Base in November 2013. Dick Cole, Ed Saylor, and David Thatcher opened the bottle of 1896 Hennessy cognac and raised their silver cups in a moving ceremony.

Bob Hite, who was a prisoner of the Japanese for three and a half years, was too ill to attend. In May 2014, the Raiders were awarded the Congressional Gold Medal, and Dick was on hand for the signing of the bill by President Barack Obama.

But the intense publicity for the Doolittle Raid has tended to overshadow the rest of Cole's experiences in the largest, most destructive war in history.

Dick went on to fly for a year as a "Hump" pilot, flying supplies from India over the Himalayas to Kunming, China, one of the most dangerous assignments of World War II. The United States lost nearly six hundred aircraft flying over the most forbidding terrain on the planet, in the world's worst weather, flying inadequate airplanes with few navigation aids and inaccurate maps. He survived, came home for three months, and then volunteered for the 1st Air Commandos in the aerial invasion of Burma, one of the most daring missions of the war. He is the only man to have participated in all three of those events.

After the war, he remained in the Air Force (there was a short separation following the end of the war; he had decided on a career in forestry when the Air Force called him back) for thirty years, with a variety of postings. He was forever defined as a Doolittle Raider, but despite the adulation, the yearly reunions, the bright illumination from a nation that did not want to forget, those few minutes over Tokyo in the darkest hours of the war were not the sum total of Richard Eugene Cole.

Born in Dayton, Ohio, the exact center of the aviation universe in 1915, Dick Cole was the quintessential youngster mesmerized by airplanes and those who flew them. He went to college for two years, was accepted for aviation training before America's entry into the war, and then found himself sitting in the right seat of a B-25 beside his boyhood idol, James H. "Jimmy" Doolittle.

Following his career as a military officer, Dick moved to Texas and raised oranges, selling them to area markets in partnership with a former P-38 pilot. It is doubtful that any of his customers ever knew that the smiling, balding man who sold them fruit had been one of the most valiant fliers in the biggest war in human history. He was, and remains, intensely unwilling to ballyhoo his contributions to a free world.

I got to know Dick when I was researching material for my book *Project 9: Birth of the Air Commandos in World War II* (University of Missouri Press, 2014). Dick Cole, I learned, had been an Air Commando. The summer of 2012 he was going to be at Oshkosh, Wisconsin, where he and David Thatcher, another Tokyo Raider, would speak. I went to the air show and met his daughter Cindy Cole Chal. Explaining that I was writing about the Air Commandos brought a squeal of delight from her: "No one ever writes about the CBI [China-Burma-India] theater!" She invited me to the final reunion of the 1st Air Commandos that fall in Fort Walton Beach, where I was able to interview several of the remaining veterans, including Dick. He was very helpful in my efforts to learn all I could of the aerial invasion of Burma. Later, when I first brought up the idea of writing the wartime story of her father, Cindy was enthusiastic but doubtful. Writers had tried for a half century to chronicle his exploits, but Dick had always turned them away, except for those who wanted simply to tell of his involvement alongside his flying buddies. "I was just doing my job, and there were lots of others who were heroes."

After a few months of trying, Cindy had been unable to convince her father to open up and have his story told. She called me in early 2013 to report "no joy" in her mission; she gave me Dick's telephone number and told me to call early in the morning (by nine he was in his barn, where he would work the rest of the day) and talk loudly. He was, after all, ninety-seven years old.

I called the next morning. Dick answered, his voice strong. "Yes, I remember you." Sure you do, I said. "I'll prove it. Just where is Park University?" In a small town just across the Missouri River from Kansas City, I explained. "Well, I went through some pilot training at Parks University near St. Louis," he said.

"Well, you probably know why I am calling. Cindy has been talking to you about my possibly writing a book . . ." Dick cut me off. "No, I don't think so. I was just doing my job—"

Now it was my turn to stop him. "Sir, this call is on my dime, so I get to finish before you say no. Look, I know you were just doing your job, but in truth you did a hell of a job with what they gave you. And I know you're not a hero. But you served with a lot of young guys who were, and many of them didn't come home." I let that hang for a couple of seconds. "So who is going to tell their stories? I think, sir, that you have an absolute obligation to speak for those men who can't speak for themselves."

This was followed by a pause that was probably only a couple of seconds, but it seemed an eternity. "Well, I think that would be appropriate," he said. "When do you want to come down?" We made arrangements for me to travel from Independence, Missouri, to the Texas hill country over my spring break and to spend the week with him.

He was open, funny, and generous. After several days of taping interviews, he brought out two scrapbooks. "I don't guess there's anything here, but I thought you might be interested. . . ." One was his boyhood clippings, newspaper and magazine articles about anything related to aviation. It was a fascinating look at another time, when every flight, it seemed, set a new record or resulted in a new technique or upgraded equipment; many of the clippings were from the *Dayton Daily News* and focused on the activities at McCook Field, the Army's aviation test center that was almost in downtown Dayton, Ohio.

The second was a treasure trove: Cole's letters home from the time he left for flight training in 1940 through his return from the war in 1944. His voice, unfiltered by political correctness, lacking the soft patina of time, and absent the tricks of memory, came through the intervening seven decades as fresh as when he wrote the letters as a twentysomething young man. I have included many passages from those letters in this work, hoping to allow readers access to the man I have come to know, a man sometimes naive, sometimes joyous, always devoted—to his family, his work, his friends—who went off to war in 1941.

It has been a full, rich life for Dick Cole. His beloved wife, Mart, passed a few years ago, and he spends his days on a small ranch near Comfort, Texas, with a zebra and a couple of buffalo. "If you mention that, the important thing to know is that they are all for sale," he says, laughing.

But don't think Dick Cole is going gentle into that good night. He is still fiercely protective of the legacy of his own personal hero, Jimmy Doolittle, and he appears regularly at flight-related events, raising money for college scholarships for aviation-minded students. When my book on the Air Commandos was released in June 2014, he traveled to the Kansas City Public Library and the Eisenhower Presidential Library in Abilene, Kansas, to participate in programs about the elite group. He is closing in on one hundred now, and Dick might decide to stay for another century. I hope he does. We won't see his like again.

This is the space in which authors publicly thank the people who made a book possible. It is small repayment, but heartfelt, for writers know that their work would not be possible without the encouragement, advice, information, and enthusiasm of a host of people who, we hope, will be listed here. We live in fear that we will unintentionally neglect to mention someone whose contribution was significant. To begin, none of this would have happened if Dick Cole had not agreed, after seventy years, to talk about his roles as an aerial warrior in the world's most destructive conflict. His gentle good humor, recall of details, and generous giving of his time in numerous interviews over a couple of years are much appreciated by the author. His daughter Cindy Cole Chal has been a remarkable archivist and researcher of material related to Cole's wartime service and was beyond generous in making material available to me. Keith Roberts, son of Maurice Ray Roberts, Cole's flight engineer in the Burma campaign, was enthusiastic in providing photographs and flight logs from that period. I am grateful to Lt. Col. Jim Lunsford for his explanation of airborne training and parachutes and to the Lloyd I. Samp family for their information about Samp, the pilot who located the wreckage of Maj. Gen. Orde Wingate's bomber. John Bartlett was helpful in providing information on his father, Mickey Bartlett, a glider pilot, and Charles Turner, another glider pilot, provided me with valuable stories about the invasion of Burma. James Segel, who flew with Cole during the early days of the Hump, was gracious and generous with his stories and his memoirs. Maranda Gilmore, of the Air Force Historical Research Agency at Maxwell Air Force Base, was a blessing to me as she located material on the Doolittle Raid, and Doug McCabe at the Alden Library of Ohio University was extremely helpful in locating material related to Cole in that university's special collections. Wen Hsin, a colleague at Park University, eagerly provided translations of some material written in Chinese. Clair Willcox, executive editor of the University of Missouri Press, offered valuable advice on the text itself, and Annette Wenda was supportive and helpful in her excellent copyediting. To all of these friends and colleagues and strangers who became friends, I am grateful. As usual, any mistakes herein are solely the responsibility of the author.

# PROLOGUE

The mahogany cabinet was beautifully crafted of hard red-tinted wood, dense and richly figured; three piano hinges allowed it to fold into a neat trunk or to open wide to display its contents. It was a bit battered now, after more than a half century of being crated and carted around the country. But it was what it held that captured the gaze of those in a hangar at Wright-Patterson Air Force Base on 9 November 2013: nestled into niches lined in purple velvet were small sterling silver goblets, eighty of them, polished, gleaming, lustrous. Hand engraved, each displayed a name twice, once in the upright position and again upside down. All but four of them had been turned onto their rims. The cabinet sat on a white-draped table atop a dais, tended by two young men in cadet uniforms; on the table in front of the goblets was a red box, holding what was arguably the most famous bottle of cognac in the world.

Three men, all in their nineties and dressed alike in dark-blue blazers and gray slacks, were escorted onto the small stage by other men wearing expensive suits or blue uniforms with rows of colorful ribbons. In the hangar at the National Museum of the US Air Force, just outside Dayton, Ohio, a small crowd had gathered to witness the end of an era and to pay tribute to men with firm ideas about duty and honor.

The men—Ed Saylor, Dick Cole, and David Thatcher—were clearly not intimidated, perhaps not even overly impressed, by the glitz and the status of those around them. They had lived too long, been through too much, to be concerned with such things. The three were seated in burgundy leather button-tufted chairs beside the table that bore the cabinet and the silver cups.

1

On 18 April 1942 these men, along with seventy-seven other young men—none of whom had ever before flown a single combat mission—had taken off from a Navy carrier in Army twin-engine bombers on their way to Tokyo and into history. They were the last survivors of that group forever known as the Doolittle Raiders, and the occasion was the final toast: they would open the bottle of 117-year-old cognac and salute their friends who had passed. Not in attendance was Lt. Col. Bob Hite; too ill to travel, he watched the ceremony on closed-circuit television from his home in Nashville, Tennessee.

Around the hangar a variety of aircraft, some modern, others from an earlier era, were parked. Overhead hung an MQ-9 Reaper, a drone, a lethal flying machine requiring no flight crew. It represented the future of aerial warfare, a reminder that the days of pilots and navigators and aerial gunners might well be limited.

The acting secretary of the Air Force, Eric Fanning, was present; so was the Air Force chief of staff, Gen. Mark A. Walsh. There were other generals, many others, and perhaps a hundred or so civilians. The ceremony began, and soon C. V. Glines, a retired officer and author of many aviation-themed books, began a roll call of eighty men, listed by crews of sixteen aircraft. As their names were called, the men on the stage answered "Here!" Silence was the only answer to the other names; relatives in the audience stood quietly. This was followed by proclamations from politicians—members of Congress, the governor of Ohio—and the three men on stage endured it all stoically.

Curiously, an official from a liquor company commanded the most interest to that point. Rodney Williams, senior vice president of Hennessy, talked about the bottle of 1896 cognac that had been presented to Lt. Gen. James H. Doolittle in 1956, on the airman's sixtieth birthday. It now rested in a red box, a one-off bottle that would represent, in just a few minutes, the end both of an era and of a mission. A replica bottle had been given to the National Museum of the US Air Force in recent years to display alongside the mahogany cabinet and its silver goblets, but the original bottle had been carefully guarded, in secret, by several of the men whose names were engraved on the cups, Williams revealed to the audience.

The mission to the very heart of Japan nearly three-quarters of a century earlier had electrified a shell-shocked nation, still reeling from the attack on Pearl Harbor in December 1941. Just four months after the surprise attack, while the Japanese army and navy seemed invincible in a march across the Pacific, Doolittle and his seventy-nine men had launched their B-25 medium bombers from a Navy carrier, bombed Tokyo in broad daylight, crash-landed or bailed out of their planes in China, and were aided in escaping by courageous Chinese. Three men were killed that day; others were captured and three executed; one died in captivity; still others would die in other actions during the war. Books were written about the raid, movies were produced, magazine articles and journal pieces were written, and an adoring public idolized the Doolittle Raiders, as they were known.

Following the war, the survivors held reunions each year on 18 April, the date of the raid, and cities vied for the honor of hosting them. In 1959 the city of Tucson, Arizona, presented the Raiders with the case and the silver goblets, and a local booster, Charles C. Arnold, floated the idea of a "last man" club. The idea was that the last two surviving Raiders would open the bottle of cognac and toast those who had passed. A final public reunion was held in Fort Walton Beach, Florida, in April 2013. The three survivors who attended agreed that they would meet later that year to open the bottle of cognac for the final toast; they didn't want to wait any longer.

The Air Force arranged the private, invitation-only event at the National Museum of the US Air Force. The Raiders had long ago achieved near-legendary status, and it was inconceivable that the survivors should meet privately to honor their friends and brothers-in-arms. No, the raid had been a very public action, and the final toast would be done with great ceremony and dignity.

So, after the speeches, the readings of proclamations, the presentation of silver eagle statues to the three men on the stage, it was time. The bottle of cognac was removed from its red box beside the goblets, and ninety-eight-year-old Dick Cole, copilot of the first plane to launch, was asked to open it. He rose, picked up a sommelier's knife from the table beside the bottle, and began to cut the wax seal, carefully slicing around the top. Grasping the cork top, he tried to twist it from the neck. It wouldn't budge. "It's a tough one," he said with a laugh, and the audience chuckled. After a bit of coaxing from his strong hands, the stubborn stopper came out. Relief from the audience was palpable.

Cole returned to his chair, and two Air Force Academy cadets, in uniform and wearing crisp white gloves, carried the appropriate silver cup to each of the three men, rendering a salute before they straightened and marched in square corners back to the table.

Tom Casey, the longtime manager for the Doolittle Raiders Association, poured cognac into each of the three goblets. No one else was served; none would have dared presume. Cole rose and raised his goblet.

"Gentlemen, I propose a toast—to those we lost on the mission, and those who have passed away since. Thank you very much, and may they rest in peace." The men drained the cognac from their cups.

With that, the Doolittle Tokyo Raiders quietly passed from public view. For Dick Cole, he had come full circle. Born in Dayton, he had grown up almost in sight of Wright-Patterson; as a boy, he had watched his boyhood idols, the early aviation pioneers, as they flew in and out of McCook Field in what is now downtown Dayton. He had often seen Orville Wright as the inventor of the powered airplane went around the city. Cole had dreamed of flying and left for the Army Air Corps from here.

The Doolittle Raid had been pivotal in Cole's life. It defined his attitude toward duty—he always insisted he had only been doing his job—and secured his place in World War II history. For more than seventy years, reunions and presentations about the raid had dominated a part of his life despite the fact that the single mission to Tokyo had been only a small fraction of his service during the war. After the raid, he would be involved in other actions that were as dangerous as the brief operation against Japan.

# PART I
# THE RAID

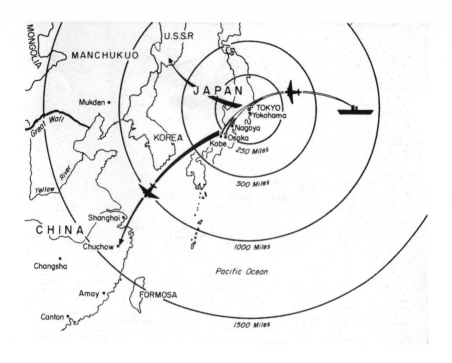

Map showing the location of the USS *Hornet* when the sixteen B-25Bs of the Doolittle Raiders were launched in the mission against targets in Japan. The bombers hoped to land at safe fields in China, but they all eventually crashed except one, which landed in Russia, where the crew was interned. (US Army Air Forces illustration)

IT was an improbable mission, born out of a desire for revenge.

The surprise attack by Japanese naval torpedo bombers against the American naval base at Pearl Harbor on the Hawaiian island of Oahu had stunned Americans; the long string of Japanese victories across the Pacific that followed had demoralized them. President Franklin Delano Roosevelt, who had shepherded the nation through the gaunt years of the Great Depression, understood symbolism and the importance of psychological victories. Within weeks of the attack on December 7, 1941, the president was relentlessly pressing his military leaders for a retaliatory strike, a headline-making poke in the eye that would raise spirits in the United States and send the Japanese a clear message that they were not safe from American military might, not even in their home islands.

But how to achieve such a goal? The Pacific fleet was badly damaged. America's industrial might, which by the end of the war would produce hundreds of thousands of aircraft, ships, tanks, bombs, and guns, had yet to gear up for war. No US airfields were close enough to allow bombers to strike. Military minds considered a host of possibilities and finally settled on a couple of options: a land-based strike from secure fields in western China and another, seaborne, attack from the east. Neither would be easy; success was uncertain.

The general of the Army Air Forces (AAF), Henry H. "Hap" Arnold, tapped a short, pugnacious lieutenant colonel to plan the mission that would necessarily involve the Navy. Jimmy Doolittle was a well-known racing and test pilot from the 1930s; he also had a doctorate in aeronautical engineering from the Massachusetts Institute of Technology (MIT). The raid was simple enough on paper: sixteen twin-engine Army bombers would take off from a Navy carrier and bomb Tokyo. But there were many impediments to success. Eighty men, five per plane, would fly in this first strike; none had ever flown a combat mission before. Even with a clamp on all possible sources of leaks regarding the mission, it was nearly inconceivable that the Japanese would not learn of it. The enemy city, site of the emperor's palace, a large naval base, and numerous military facilities, would be heavily defended by aircraft and antiaircraft artillery. Barrage balloons floated over key installations, and a line of picket boats was stationed six hundred miles out from the home islands, searching for any sign of an enemy attack.

Doolittle led the raid himself, taking off in the first B-25B from the deck of the USS *Hornet* on 18 April 1942. Sitting beside him was a young Army flier from Dayton, Ohio, who had graduated from flying school less than a year earlier. Lt. Richard E. Cole would have a front-row seat for what would become one of the most celebrated military actions of World War II.

# CHAPTER 1

If, in the first decades of the twentieth century, a young boy enamored of aviation—and they all were—could choose a city in which to live and grow up, there was really only one candidate: Dayton, Ohio.

Dayton was in some respects an unlikely suitor for a boy's attention, especially one whose mind was in the clouds or otherwise tuned to adventure. No mountains, no seashore, no large expanse of wilderness. It did have the Miami River coursing through its center, a fact that would mean death and heartache when it flooded in 1913, destroying large swaths of downtown and leaving up to four hundred dead. But other distinctive physical attributes were few, and it resembled scores of other cities in the Midwest that had grown where boosters and pioneers had decided to halt their wagons. The city grew on the site of a skirmish in 1782 between Indians and troops of Gen. George Rogers Clark; over the years it had its share of scandals and political scalawags, and it laid claim to one of the first accepted African American poets, Paul Laurence Dunbar.

Dayton boomed in the nineteenth century after a canal was built connecting it to Cincinnati and later expanded to Lake Erie (it was later eclipsed, in the manner of such things, by the railroads). Companies such as Dayton Rubber, National Cash Register, and Aetna Paper made Dayton their headquarters, and the city grew exponentially. It was vibrant, alive, and fairly bursting with creative energies. A film produced by the National Park Service boasts that Dayton in the early twentieth century had more patents per capita than any other city in the United States.[1]

9

But of course, neither the early history nor the physical setting of the city was what made Dayton the exact center of the universe for all things related to the young field of aviation. Dayton was the home of the brothers Wright, Orville and Wilbur, and the eyes of the world were focused on the former printers and bicycle-shop owners who had successfully flown a powered aircraft and transformed the globe in doing so. It was also home to the Army Air Corps testing and evaluation laboratory known as McCook Field, a fact that would influence the life course of at least one young man.

In 1915 the great war in Europe was in its second year of mass slaughter. But while hundreds of thousands of young men were being ground into fertilizer in the fields of France and Belgium, life in Dayton and generally across the United States went on in the way of countries not at war and insulated from the horrors of state-directed carnage.

The front page of the *Dayton Daily News* on 7 September 1915 asked in inch-high black letters: "Hesperian Sunk by Mine or Torpedo?" A subhead proclaimed, "Commanding Officers Say British Liner Was Hit by Enemy's Torpedo." A black-and-white photo in the center of the front page above the fold showcased two children, with the caption "Their first day of school finds these youngsters eager to begin life study." The first graders were surrounded by war news, but it was Fair Week in Montgomery County, which includes Dayton, and merchants were eager to accommodate the shoppers. Traxler's ad on page 3 promised "This store welcomes Fair-Week visitors" and offered new women's fall suits for $14.95 and "new and clever" high lace-up shoes for $4.98 or Axminster rugs for $1.95. Baseball was very much the national sport, and the sports page listed Philadelphia atop the National League, Boston topped the American League, while Minneapolis led the American Association and Pittsburgh was ahead of St. Louis by a single game in the Federal League. Roy Melson, a former Dayton city pool champion, challenged all comers to a friendly game of billiards at the Royal Billiard Parlor, beginning at 8:00 p.m. that evening; a cash prize would be given to the challenger with the highest score against him. In the society column, no doubt readers were breathless to know that Mr. and Mrs. Harry Croninger, accompanied by Miss Helen Croninger and Miss Mary Hatch, motored down to Cincinnati on Monday, where they were entertained by Mr. and Mrs. Campbell McDonald at the Hyde Park Country Club. Apparently, some whispers of impropriety regarding the Sisters of St.

Mary had been making the rounds, for a two-column headline on page 18 exclaimed, "We're Serving Humanity." A revealing subhead is also in quotation marks: "When We Tell Others of the Value of Father John's Medicine as a Tonic and Body Builder and for Colds." The Sisters of St. Mary had written to the newspaper from Masson, Quebec, to set the record straight.

The obituary column noted the passing of Ferdinand Unger, age sixty-four, and Maude Maxton, age twenty-seven. More than one hundred local Caledonians attended the Dayton and Middletown Scottish Society Meeting—the first annual, according to the newspaper—and evidence of a kind of smug, paternalistic racism was found on an inside page. The Colored Baby Show, which had been scheduled for the county fair, had been canceled. E. T. Banks, chair of the commission setting up the event, declared that the baby contest would be held instead on Emancipation Day in protest against a reference to "pickaninnies" in a news article about the show in a local newspaper. Dayton may have claimed Paul Laurence Dunbar as a native son, but it resembled the rest of the country in its language regarding other people of color.[2] In short, Dayton was a city not so very different in most ways from cities across the country. Babies born on 7 September 1915 in New York, in Los Angeles, in Austin or Minneapolis, or in any other city of America were all products of their milieu, bathed in all of the prejudices, ambitions, worldviews, shortcomings, strengths, and foibles of their time. But only those born in Dayton considered themselves inheritors of the gift of flight.

On that Tuesday, while much of Dayton was still breaking its fast and reading the news of the previous day, activity related to the birth of its newest citizen was occurring at 747 Faulkner Avenue, in one of the middle-class neighborhoods on the city's northwest side. There, in an upstairs bedroom at 9:00 a.m., the Cole family welcomed Richard Eugene into the fold. He would be called Dick and later would offer to punch anyone who called him Eugene. The house still stands, neatly painted and with flowers on the front porch in season, a domestic monument to middle-class dreams. Dick Cole grew up to live the dream of flight.

And to fight a war.

Fred and Mabel Louise Cole formed a hardworking couple. Mabel was a country girl, knew about cooking and canning and cleaning before she married, and bore Fred six children in the course of their marriage. Fred was perpetually serious—Dick couldn't remember ever seeing him laugh, although he had a quiet sense of humor—but provided for his family through sheer grit and physical exertion.

In 1890, when he was about twenty-one, Fred Cole was hired as a fireman on the Erie Railroad. It was good work but physically challenging and incredibly dirty. It was also dangerous: Fred lost his right eye in a train accident, and he also lost his job in those days before workers' compensation and disability insurance. Many years later, neighborhood children would shriek and scream when Fred removed his glass eye—and then beg him to do it again.

Out of his railroading job, Fred bought a team of horses and set up an excavating business, contracting with builders to dig the holes for the basements that were a common feature of Dayton homes. Eventually, together with a young civil engineer, the elder Cole set up a company called Foster Engineering; in 1929, the two men obtained a large business loan to expand the company. Their timing was terrible. The stock market crashed, the country's economy went south, and Foster Engineering went bankrupt. Once again, Fred Cole was out of a job.

The city of Dayton hired Fred as a sidewalk inspector. Fred was forty-six years old when Dick was born, the fifth of six children. The first three were girls (Martha Elizabeth, Josephine Bowen, and Mary Catherine) followed by three boys (Fred Dryden, Dick, and Thomas Franklin).

In time, Dick went to Jefferson Elementary School, then on to Colonel White Junior High before entering Steele High School. What he remembered most about school years later was the enormous effort by his teachers to convert him: born a southpaw, they were determined that left was wrong and right was right. So he stayed after school—that was the worst part—as his teachers painstakingly tried to force his right hand to do what his left had done so effortlessly. He eventually was converted, sort of. He was able to sign his name in cursive, a neat, compact signature: R. E. Cole. But for anything longer, such as a letter, he printed each word.

When he graduated from Steele, he was the second smallest young man in his class. (That wouldn't last. He grew six inches, to five foot ten, in the next two years.) Dick was not a gifted student, by his own admission. He was far more interested in the outdoors, swimming, tennis, and, above all else, aviation. As a boy, he joined the Airplane Modeling League of America and began to construct balsa-wood-and-tissue-paper models of the biplanes of the day. He was about ten years old when he completed his first model. John Patterson, inventor of the cash register and founder of National Cash Register Corporation, had built a large auditorium in downtown Dayton. Each Saturday he opened it to youngsters to fly their rubber-band-powered models inside, out of the wind that was a daily feature of Dayton weather. Until he graduated high school, Dick was an avid modeler.

He also was a voracious reader of the local newspaper and of the many aviation-themed adventure magazines of the day. The lurid covers of *Air Trails* and *Eagles of the Air* tempted thousands of youngsters to part with a quarter and read the breathtaking "true" accounts of eagle-eyed pilots in aerial imbroglios that often featured fisticuffs at five thousand feet, with the hero narrowly escaping falling to his death at the hands of an ex-German pilot or a Russian spy. Exciting reading, to be sure, but not nearly so thrilling as what was going on across the Miami River at McCook Field. There, the Army Air Forces had established its first test station, and young Dick Cole would watch from the riverbank as real-life heroes came in and out of the field.

Jimmy Doolittle was a frequent visitor to McCook. In the 1930s, he was among the most famous of the aviators, setting speed records and winning virtually every national aviation trophy. Flying was a romantic adventure, and men like Charles Lindbergh, Wrong Way Corrigan, Wiley Post, and Doolittle were bigger-than-life figures to an adoring public. Even a woman was granted admission to the club, as Amelia Earhart was unrelentingly pushed into the limelight by her publisher husband, George Putnam.

For Dick Cole, McCook was a magnet too powerful to resist. Aviation-related sites were all around the city and in Dayton proper; it was impossible not to be cognizant of the city's most famous brothers, Orville and Wilbur. The Wright mansion, Hawthorn Hill in Oakwood, sat on seventeen acres on a rise that dominated the area. Huffman Prairie, east of town, was renowned as the field where the brothers had tested their first gliders. Their sister, Katherine Wright, was a teacher at Steele High School, and one of their bicycle shops on West Third Street had been converted to Monbeck's barbershop, where Dick got his hair cut. Dick's sister Mart was friends with Katherine, and it didn't seem all that extraordinary to Daytonians; everyone knew, or knew someone who knew, the Wrights. Among one of Dick's earliest jobs was mowing Mrs. Spinning's lawn, on Broadway across from the Wright laboratory. Often as he was pushing the rotary mower, a car would pull up to the laboratory and Orville would emerge from it and enter the brick building. It all seemed perfectly normal; the Wright brothers may have invented the powered flying machine a mere dozen years before Dick's birth, but they were just folks around Dayton, after all.

Besides, all that Wright business seemed like ancient history next to the up-to-date, ongoing, and exciting activities at McCook Field.

The aeronautical testing site had been built in 1917 with the advent of the United States into World War I, at the confluence of the Miami and Mad Rivers, virtually in the heart of the city itself, or so it seemed. Cole and some of his boyhood friends rode their bicycles five miles to the levee and sat to watch the aircraft come in and depart. The levee was too far from the runway to make out individual pilots, but the newspapers the next day carried photos of Doolittle, Carl Spaatz, and other daring airmen.

McCook was an aerial laboratory, developing and testing dozens of new techniques, instruments, and equipment over the years, until the field closed and the testing facilities moved east to Patterson Field, outside of town. Night aerial photography was perfected at McCook, as were radio-beacon navigation, pressured cockpits, and high-altitude engine equipment such as the supercharger. For Cole, perhaps the most important development personally was the parachute. It would save his life in the years to come.[3]

So young Dick Cole spent his early years in and around Dayton, in love with the outdoors and aviation equally. On paydays at Wright Field (it became Wright-Patterson in 1948), an Army flying field northeast of the city, he could look up and see a Curtiss P-6 Hawk biplane circling over the paymaster's truck as it made its way from Dayton to the air base. Fueled by exciting tales of adventure and derring-do in his twenty-five-cent aviation magazines, Dick imagined himself as the fearless flier overhead, waiting for the bad guys and ready to dispense swift justice to them. Flying was the ultimate adventure.[4]

And why not? Aviation was a fledgling endeavor, with new records set weekly, new heroes wearing leather helmets and goggles featured in the newspapers. Nothing seemed impossible; flights across the country, across the Atlantic, at night, in foul weather, by instruments alone, farther and faster than yesterday; planes could refuel from other aircraft in the air and remain in flight for days; pilots could save their lives by using parachutes to safely descend from crippled airplanes. Young Dick Cole kept a scrapbook of planes and aviators; one photo from 1934 was of the daredevil Doolittle, outfitted in leather helmet and goggles, with cavalry breeches and knee-length laced boots.[5]

But it was a long and uncertain road for youngsters in Dayton and across the country before they could emulate their heroes, slip into a cockpit, and begin their own conquests of the air. As we shall see, the hazards of boyhood play nearly ended Dick's flying career long before it ever got off the ground.

When he was ten or eleven years old, he and his buddies on Faulkner Avenue made their own fun after school and on weekends when they were not working at odd jobs. The street was full of kids—ninety-seven in the single block where the Cole family lived—and they found ways to entertain themselves. On this day, he and Ralph Sells and George Pullman and others were gathering for a game of street hockey; it was cold, below freezing, and Dick was bundled against the low temperatures. He stepped from the sidewalk onto the brick-paved street—and went down hard. He hadn't seen the ice, and his feet slipped from under him. He landed on his face on the top edge of the curb. Dick was stunned momentarily. He reached for his nose and wiped away a bit of blood, and then his tongue played over his lips. But the real damage was to his two upper front teeth, both chipped, leaving ragged edges that formed a shallow, inverted V.

He felt his teeth, tried to wriggle them, and couldn't. That was good. The other boys were calling for him to play. He shrugged off the incident, although his tongue wouldn't stop worrying the rough new edges of his teeth. When he went home later that evening, his mother shook her head. "You know those are your permanent teeth. You won't get any more." One of his sisters had suffered a similar injury and had opted to have her teeth capped. Within two years, they had turned black. Dick elected to just live with his broken front teeth. It would have repercussions later.[6]

Dick took a job delivering the *Dayton Daily News* when he was in the eighth grade. At first, the paper was delivered in the afternoon, so when school was out he had plenty of time to walk the route and still have a few hours for homework and play in the evening. That changed when the publishers decided that a morning paper would be better for circulation, so Dick arose at five to throw the newspaper before school. At first, he pulled a wagon loaded with rolled-up papers and used a sled in the winter. Eventually, with his savings he purchased a used red Schwinn. It cut down his time considerably and allowed him to range farther afield for boyhood adventures, including rides out to McCook Field.[7]

There were other activities that allowed him to enjoy the outdoors. Along with Ralph and George, Dick took up hunting in the fall for rabbits, or pheasant, or whatever was in season. Riding their bikes on dirt roads—outside the city they were nearly all dirt—they would gather black walnuts, cherries, blackberries, and raspberries and take them back to their mothers to can. It usually only took asking the farmer. As the Depression deepened, most were happy to share with the youngsters. The outdoors called to him nearly as strongly as flying, and it was far more accessible. Dick made a decision early to be either a forest ranger or a pilot in the Army Air Corps. That was years away, he knew, and school didn't seem very important. In fact, it seemed a lot like prison.

Dick should have graduated in 1933 from Steele High, but at the start of his senior year he learned of a six-month course in aviation mechanics being offered at Parker High, a primarily vo-tech school in Dayton. He wanted that course, enough to delay graduation by a year. At Parker, the seven students in the class disassembled a Liberty aircraft engine and then reassembled it. To pass the course, the engine had to work when they finished. The instructor used a hand crank to rotate the engine's crankshaft, and the students tested each spark plug. They passed, and Dick graduated in 1934.

It was the depth of the Great Depression. All that summer he tried unsuccessfully to find work. Finally, he went to labor on the farm of his mother's sister, Bonnie, about forty miles north of Dayton. The farm was fairly large, at 360 acres, with about half heavily wooded with sugar maples. He learned to tap the trees and make maple syrup, in addition to caring for the livestock, milking cows, plowing, planting, and harvesting. The seasonal nature of the work left him with time to hunt and fish. He stayed two years, receiving seventy-five dollars a month plus room and board.[8] In the summer of 1936 Dick and George Pullman borrowed George's brother's old Ford sedan and drove to Minnesota to camp and fish for walleye pike. It was a glorious week, and Dick reveled in the freedom of the outdoors. It was a Hemingway kind of summer, the sort that Nick Adams would have loved. Cole resolved to get on with his life: both of his career choices—a pilot or a ranger—required college degrees, but he had no money to pay for education. When he returned from the last great camping trip of his youth, he applied for a job at National Cash Register, one of the biggest corporations in Dayton.

Dick was hired, at forty-five cents an hour. His title and, he assumed, his actual performance would be apprentice toolmaker. In practice, he was a gopher, running for coffee for this worker, more rags for that one. He was disgusted and after a few weeks went to his foreman to say he wanted to do something more productive. In the area known as Drill One, he had watched as a giant multiheaded drill press bored holes in the sides of the heavy metal cash registers being manufactured. That looked like actual work, and it didn't hurt that Drill One workers cleared thirty to thirty-five dollars a week. The foreman looked at Dick for a long minute without speaking; the young man expected to be fired. But the next day, he was assigned to Drill One and at the end of two years had saved six hundred dollars. He enrolled at Ohio University in Athens for the fall of 1938 and listed his major as forestry. Dick would be a forest ranger.[9]

But flying still played a siren tune in his mind. Just to learn if it was even remotely possible to become a pilot, Dick drove out to Wright Field to try to enter cadet flight training in the Army Air Corps. The minimum education requirement at the time was two years of college; Dick knew this but wanted to know if he could pass the stringent physical and academic tests. If not, he would abandon his boyhood dream and go into forestry for a life outdoors.

He passed the written portion of the cadet test but failed the physical. He still had his tonsils, and his two front teeth were too badly broken, he was informed. The childhood hockey accident came back to hurt him once more. The Air Corps was so underfunded in the late 1930s that it did not want to spend unnecessary money on tonsillectomies or dental work. Far from being deflated, Dick was ebullient. He had passed the written; he would have his tonsils removed, see what could be done with his front teeth, and get in two years of college at Ohio University. It just might still be possible to follow in the footsteps of his boyhood idols.[10]

Two years at Ohio U were largely pro forma. Young Cole as college student was no more inspired than he had been in high school. At best, he was an average scholar, with his eyes more on the skies than on his studies. He had little time for the storied social life of college students: he rented a room with Mrs. Lulu Posten but worked in lieu of cash payment, firing the furnace in the large rooming house as well as doing yard work. To eat, he worked as a short-order cook at the Bobcat Restaurant four hours a day, and to earn a bit of extra money he fired furnaces at the Methodist church, the parsonage, and a sorority house, in addition to cleaning windows and doing janitorial work at Miss Kathryn Figg's dress shop.[11]

And then came one of those opportunities that seem tailor-made for some people. Between his sophomore and junior years, he was accepted into the Civilian Pilot Training (CPT) Program, a government-sponsored and -funded plan to train several hundred thousand pilots for what most now assumed would be another war involving the United States; it was already raging across Europe. That summer of 1940 he went to work for Bill Lear in Vandalia, Ohio; Lear, later famous for his business jets, was a prolific inventor, including designing many aviation systems (the automatic direction finder, or ADF, was one that revolutionized aerial navigation). When Cole told Lear that he was enrolled in flying training through the CPT program, Lear allowed him to take time off for his flight lessons without docking his pay. The ground-school portion of the training program was at Wittenberg University in Springfield, Ohio. Cole bought a derelict Model A Ford coupe for fifty dollars, restored it to running order, and drove to the evening ground-school classes each night after work.

Flight lessons were in a Taylorcraft with side-by-side seating (Taylorcraft models produced for the Army were tandem seaters). Cole seemed to take to flying; he soloed in about nine hours. On that morning in July 1940, his instructor, Mr. Kastner, took him up, and they completed S-turns, steep turns, and stalls, before Kastner instructed Cole to return to the landing field.

The instructor climbed out of the tiny airplane and, turning to Cole, said, "Take it up by yourself. Give me three takeoffs and landings." And that was Cole's first time to exercise the gift of wings bestowed by the Wright brothers. Every pilot remembers his first solo. It is an experience unlike any other.

By August 1940, Cole was a licensed civilian pilot. As the time to re-enter the university approached, he was undecided what to do. He had already applied to transfer to Michigan State University to complete a degree in forestry, but the skies were now calling him more loudly than ever. He finally made up his mind to enlist in the Army Air Corps. He drove to Fort Thomas in Kentucky, across the Ohio River from Cincinnati. He once more passed the written part of the air cadet examination and sweated out the physical exam. Eyes, perfect. Hearing, good. Heart, lungs, range of motion of each limb, fine. Tonsils, absent. Teeth…minimal standards, but okay. Dick Cole was accepted into the Aviation Cadet Corps and sent to Parks Air College, in East St. Louis, Illinois, for primary flight training.

The trajectory for his life was set. He would fly.

## CHAPTER 2

Cole had sweated his selection at Fort Thomas and then waited an agonizing month before he was sent on to Parks Air College in East St. Louis on 23 November 1940. At twenty-five, he was two or three years older than most of his cadet classmates. He dropped his mother a quick note from the railroad station: he would be one of twenty-four selected for flight training from Fort Thomas. After another physical exam, which they all passed, thirteen were sent to Parks, nine to Dallas, and two to a training facility in Georgia. He promised to write again when he reached East St. Louis.[1]

The letters home during his time at Parks Air College were upbeat, nearly joyous, expressing his delight at finally being in a position to realize his dream of becoming a pilot in the Army Air Corps. His first message home was sent the evening he arrived; it was obvious, he wrote, that Parks might be a civilian facility, but the discipline would be strictly military and stringently enforced: "*We have to shave every day, make our bed, shine shoes, belt buckle, coverall and flying suit buttons. They cut your hair short but they feed you good and give you a good bed.*"[2]

The diversity of young men chosen for cadet training, and their lack of travel experience, was evident to Cole as well. He notes that they traveled from Fort Thomas to East St. Louis on a Pullman car with sleeping accommodations that most had never seen. It was all good fun for the youths, many of whom had never traveled beyond their state borders before.

Fun, perhaps, but the curriculum and standards were strict. Flying was not an endeavor for the fainthearted, the weak of spirit, or the in-

20

decisive, or even for the too confident. Everything pertaining to a flying machine owned and operated by the United States would be done
strictly according to established procedures. They would fly by the
numbers or be sent packing. As well, the process of taking away individual identity began in earnest; Richard Eugene Cole, known as Dick
his entire life, was about to assume a new identity. He wrote his parents
that cadets must always address each other as "Mister," and if asked by
an upperclassman to "Sound off!" his only acceptable response must be
"Flying Cadet Cole, R. E., Sir!"[3] Individualism was not a highly regard-
ed character trait in the Army.

Oh, and one more thing. Cole and his fellow cadets wouldn't be home
for Christmas.

In two weeks, the rigorous schedule and exacting standards had begun to take a fearsome toll. Flying Cadet Cole wrote his mother on 4
December, a determined and sober young man. The class immediately
ahead of his and still at Parks had started with 128 aspiring aviators;
they were down to 60. The one immediately before that started with
124, and only 28 graduated. His own class was thinning; one of those
washed out was a roommate of Cole's who could not conquer his air-
sickness. Cole described the training aircraft, Fairchild PT-19s, to his
mother: at 1,734 pounds, it cruised at 110 to 115 and landed at 65 mph.
The sky was filled with them, flown by instructors and students: *"Boy,
flying around here is like belonging to a hornet's nest. There are 82 planes
total and they all take the air 3 times daily. It is a very pretty sight to see
them take off one after another then disappear and about an hour or so
later they appear again and land one by one."* When they were not flying, the cadets were in class. *"We don't have much time to idle around.
We go to ground school from 8 till 11, 1 hour of engines and 2 hours math.
In the afternoon we go to the field and fly. Next week we will fly in the
morning and go to ground school in the afternoon."*[4]

And, of course, there were those iconic uniforms and flying togs. *"You
ought to see me in my flying suit, I look like the 'man from Mars.' They gave
us 3 pairs of overalls, 1 sweater, 1 pair shoes, 1 laundry bag, 4 Air Corps
towels, and two dress uniforms and cap. They are slate gray and have Air
Corps insignia on hat and shirt arm."*[5]

A postscript to this letter reveals Cole's dislike for nonsense: *"We must
sign our names and be referred to as Flying Cadet so&so. If they catch you
talking like 'Hi Dick' or the like it means 1 demerit. We gotta say 'Hello
Flying Cadet Dale' etc. It's a lot of baloney, I think."*[6]

But Flying Cadet Cole was savvy enough to keep those thoughts to himself. He noted that so far, he had no demerits. And he had accumulated two hours and three minutes of flying; one lesson was cut short because of poor visibility.

Two weeks later, he sent a postcard to his mother with a brief note that declared in large, bold letters: *"Solo."* He underscored this: *"This is the 1st step up the almost rungless and unseen ladder."* And then some elaboration: *"Well it finally came. Tuesday at 3:15 I started and put in 25 minutes solo. My time was 9:06 plus my 25 minutes make total time of 9:21."* If baseball is a game of inches, flying is a game of hours and minutes, neatly tabulated and entered in columns denoting solo, dual, night, cross-country, instrument, multiengine, and other categories. Cole's flying clock had started, and he would carefully note flight time throughout his career in the air, recording hours and minutes as faithfully as an accountant.[7]

On 20 December, he wrote again. Flying weather had been good, and he was up to sixteen hours and sixteen minutes of flight time, with six hours solo. He had taken his first Progress Checkride and passed; failure of the P-Check meant a follow-up check ride; failure there meant washing out. It was a constant winnowing, and the fear of failure permeated the very air they flew in.

And it was official: the US government was providing the cadets with turkey dinner on Christmas Day. *"Merry Christmas to you all. Hope you all are well and happy so you can enjoy it,"* he wrote.[8]

He made it through the primary course at Parks and in late January got a few days home. The washouts had continued right to the end, with one cadet removed on his graduation flight from primary. The military pilot training program played no favorites. If you couldn't convince your instructors that you could safely fly, there were thousands more eager to take your place. Jack Sims and Bob Meder were two of his Parks classmates who survived the chopping block, and he would grow to know them both very well in the months and years to follow.

By the second week of February, he was on a train to Randolph Field, northeast of San Antonio. Like most midwesterners, his image of Texas was flat prairie and a lot of cactus. He was favorably impressed: *"The further south you come the better it gets. It's really very nice country down here."* The land, he told his mother, *"isn't as flat as one thinks. It is gentle rolling, green and wooded, very nice."*[9] Later, the former forestry student admired the trees: *"Palm trees, cactus and nearly every kind of trees grow all around. The spruce, pine, and fir trees are the prettiest I have ever seen."*[10]

At Randolph, he and his classmates became forever known as the class of 41-E. There, Cole would fly the BC-1, a more complicated and sophisticated trainer than the open-cockpit PT-19s of primary training. The BC-1 had an enclosed tandem cockpit and resembled fighter airplanes of the day, then still called pursuit planes. Randolph was the pinnacle of forward-thinking military architecture of the day; roads were laid out in a circular pattern, and the most recognizable building was the administration center. With its tall central tower topped by a dome, it was called the Taj Mahal, or simply the Taj. The entire base was a showcase, it seemed to Cole, who referred to it as a *"country club"*: *"It is about the nicest place I have ever seen, excels most college campuses. . . . Beautiful homes, swimming pools, tennis courts and about anything you could wish for."*[11]

Cole settled into room 40, Company B, at Randolph. He was tickled at the amount of uniform gear he was issued: *"I could have come down here without a stitch of clothes. They gave us six pairs of socks, six shirts, two pair pants, two hats, 2 pair gloves (white & gray), 1 pair of shoes, all flying equipment we need, rain coat, overcoat, foot powder, underwear, handkerchiefs, belts, towels and coveralls."*[12]

What Cole and his classmates of 41-E thought was rigid discipline at Parks paled in comparison to what they found at Randolph. Two hours after arriving, they were in uniform and drilling. *"Boy! This place is tough with a capital 'T'. They say 'take a brace' they mean 'take a brace.' Sixteen wrinkles in your chin, chest out, arms down your sides straight and hold it! Pretty soon your face begins to turn purple and they say 'Fall out Mr.' which means return to normal position of attention, which is bad enough."*[13]

Surprisingly, despite his innate distaste for meaningless ritual such as the artificial form of addressing each other as "Flying Cadet Cole," he didn't mind the discipline at Randolph. He told his mother that it wasn't as bad as it sounded: *"We are all enjoying it because it is good for us and is valuable training for later years, but most of us would go through anything in order to get to fly."*[14]

And fly they did, in planes that Cole thought were *"to[o] nice for student training."*[15] Cole loved flying, reveled in the precision called for in formation flying, and declared night flying the best of all. But there were other activities at the jewel of the Air Corps bases. On 22 March, he told his mother, the premiere of *I Wanted Wings* would be shown at the base theater. *"It will be quite a big affair. In the afternoon there will be an air show of about 300 airplanes, and there will be all kinds of 'big shots' as our guests. At night they will have a dinner and the show afterwards."*[16]

She was lithe, blonde, and sensual. Her long hair fell over one eye, lending her perfect, beautiful face a carefully planned air of seduction.

Veronica Lake was only nineteen, but her hairstyle was copied by millions of young women around the country, and her face was on movie billboards everywhere. She moved effortlessly as she danced with Dick Cole, all the while maintaining a fixed smile as they glided across the polished floor.

With this gorgeous woman in his arms, Cole could think of only one thing: don't step on her feet. He sweated out the glide around the large ballroom and mumbled something that was in the neighborhood of gallant, but the young film actress and Hollywood star probably didn't hear a word as she went on to the next aviation cadet at Randolph Field. Much of the filming of *I Wanted Wings* had been shot at Randolph using government-issue aircraft, officers, and enlisted men. Despite the lurid and inane plot of the movie, the Army Air Corps at that time was more than willing to support any project that made America's young men clamor to fly. When the film premiered at Randolph, Veronica Lake along with Ray Milland, William Holden, Wayne Morris, and Brian Donlevy were on hand to thank the cadets and officers for their unpaid roles.

The shy and occasionally awkward Cole was possibly the only one at the large air base near San Antonio who wished Lake and her cohorts had stayed in Hollywood. He made it through the dance without stepping on her feet, and now he just wanted to get on with the business of learning to fly. Women could wait. It had been a long journey, this arduous task of earning wings, and he didn't appreciate the break.[17]

A few months later, Cole advised his mother: *"If you saw I Wanted Wings don't believe all you saw 'cause it all isn't true. We are here for one purpose and that is to learn to fly. All that playing around and drama is just typical movie stuff."*[18]

The high rate of attrition—washouts—continued at Randolph; Cole believed the rate was higher than at Parks. Four in his flight had gotten the ax the week of March 15. *"I had a check ride, whether it was my 'twenty hour check' I don't know but I'm still flying so guess they haven't caught up with me yet."*[19]

By mid-March he had twenty-eight hours of additional flying time and had been introduced to instrument flying. The cardinal rule of flight by instruments is to always—always!—trust your instruments and not your senses. That point was brought home to Cadet Cole in the most basic and graphic of ways. Flying in the rear cockpit of his trainer, with a canvas hood over Cole's portion of the canopy, his instructor put the trainer through a series of maneuvers before turning control over to Cole. What attitude? the instructor asked. *"I told him I was making a right turn and it was a falling left turn—well! He just proved to me that instruments are right and you're wrong. I was wrong 5 times out of 5."*[20]

Cole and his classmates were also introduced to night flying. Cole loved it. *"Night flying is* [sic] *really got everything beat,"* he told his mother in early April. *"On my first trip they take you up dual and show you how it is done. They shine flood lights across the field, the beam is about 50 feet wide. You must break through the beam and land in the light. Well, the natural tendency is to try to land on top of the beam which is about 20 ft. up in the air. I got on to it after 4 landings."*[21]

By the middle of March, Cole's address changed. He hadn't moved far physically—from room 40 to room 15—but the symbolic difference was great. Room 15 was on the ground floor, reserved for upperclassmen. He had survived long enough to begin to dole out to incoming dodos— the underclassmen—some of the misery and hazing inflicted on him by the former lords of the roost. Cole, like all cadets before him, quickly abandoned his former distaste of ritual and rank-induced privileges and embraced his new status.

While Cole was in basic, his instructor one day requested something that the acolyte flier found odd: he wanted him to do power landings at an auxiliary field, leaving the throttle partly open throughout the approach instead of cutting power completely on short final and gliding in. Power landings were usually done in multiengine aircraft. Was he to be a bomber pilot? The question went unasked and unanswered.[22] On 15 April, he wrote his mother that orders for his class had been received, but no individual orders had arrived. The breakdown for life after Randolph called for fifty cadets to go to Barksdale Field in Louisiana, where they would likely receive multiengine training; one hundred would go to Brooks Field, just south of San Antonio, and two hundred to Kelly Field, immediately west of San Antonio.[23] In the sometimes hard-to-figure ways of the military, after graduation those students who received multiengine training at Barksdale were assigned to a P-39 squadron, a single-engine fighter unit, based in the Philippines.[24]

Cole was hoping to be trained as a transport pilot, he said, making transition to an airline job much easier if he should leave the service.

By 15 April, he wrote his mother, he had a total of sixty-one hours, of which fifty minutes were aerobatics, one hour and thirty-five minutes were night-flying hours, two hours of check rides, two hours and thirty minutes of cross-country flying, and one hour and thirty minutes of formation flying. That day he had done his first solo formation flight, with his instructor leading him and another student. *"Boy this is more fun than anything yet so far. You really have to keep on your toes and you really have to fly the airplane, you sweat blood but it is lots of fun,"* he told her.

Ground school was complete; he had passed everything except Morse code. He was scheduled to retake the exam the next Friday and had been taking additional training in order to receive eight words a minute. He was not worried, he said.[25]

The graduation dance was scheduled for the last week of April. Cole would go but find his own date. *"I don't care much for these Cadet Widows,"* he wrote on 15 April. *"Think I'll get some girl from San Antonio College. They are pretty nice girls."*[26] The young local women who attached themselves to a cadet in each succeeding class were of no interest to Cole.

By the end of April 1941, Cole was at Kelly Field—the barracks were air-conditioned!—facing only the last few obstacles to achieving the dream he'd held since he was a small boy watching those rickety, kite-like flying machines take off and land at McCook Field. Others in 41-E had gone on to other advanced flight schools. There was less pressure now; flight school at this stage was a bit like medical school. Early in the training course, the inept, the timid, the too confident, and the lazy had been trimmed from the cadet corps. Now, only the best of the best remained, and very few would be eliminated now. The government had too much invested to lose them at this point. More formation flying was on the schedule—Cadet Cole described it as "fun"—and night cross-country flying. These were flown solo. The Army Air Corps had established courses marked every ten miles by a red light: one went from Kelly to Dallas; another ran to Navasota.

Cole and his classmates flew AT-6 Texans, appropriately enough, as well as BC-1s, a similar advanced trainer (AT stood for "Advanced Trainer"; BC was "Basic Combat"). They were similar to the basic trainers in outward appearance, but had retractable landing gear and a few more instruments—"gadgets," as Cole called them—and were capable of cruising at 180 to 200 mph. The flying cadets became proficient in the complex airplanes, and soon the cockpits of the AT-6s seemed a bit like home. Airspeed indicators, altimeters, compasses, rate-of-climb gauges, artificial horizons, turn-and-bank instruments, engine oil pressure and temperature registers, outside air temperature gauges, light switches and radios and throttles and flaps and carburetor heat controls and mixture controls and propeller pitch adjustments, in addition to fuses and cockpit locking levers and seat adjustments—all of the controls that pilots use to have mastery of their machines, all of the "gadgets" that made a cockpit seem so intimidating, now seemed very familiar, their secrets unlocked, their uses known. They were feeling less like cadets, more like pilots. And so they were.

Cole remained the loving son as well. He was chagrined and heartbroken to have missed doing something for his mother for Mother's Day in early May. Not totally his fault, he explained in a subdued letter: "*I am really sorry.*" He had saved his money to make a call, but in those days of operators and cranked telephones, he had placed his call but was told by the operator that the exchange through St. Louis was closed; she would call when it was open. He waited three hours and then left and tried again starting at 7:50 p.m. Still, no lines were open. "*The fact remains that I laid aside some money just for this purpose. I saw something in town you would like, so I will get it instead. It might be a little late but you know the meaning is greater than ever before.*"[27]

Cole and his classmates were getting plenty of flying. Although it seemed to rain nearly every day, it cleared quickly and allowed them to get airborne at some point during the day. By 12 May, Cole had added 17 hours to his flight log, which now totaled 196 hours; he needed another 50 before completing the advanced course. Included would be an eight-hundred-mile round-trip cross-country flight to Barksdale Field in Louisiana and return, which Cole was looking forward to eagerly.

Car dealers around San Antonio were in seller's heaven with the increase in flying cadets at airfields in every direction around the city. They made it easy for advanced student pilots to purchase cars, knowing that soon they would be making good, steady money as officers; by buying as a group, they could take advantage of bulk-buying discounts. Cole told his mother that he had purchased a Pontiac coupe—black, with no options except a radio—"*suits me fine*." Clothiers also did a booming business, making bespoke uniforms for the soon-to-be newly minted lieutenants. They were told early in the Advanced Flying Course to purchase their dress uniforms for graduation and service beyond. Cole dutifully followed the directive but was unimpressed with the outcome: "*Boy! I'll never be comfortable in one of those monkey suits. They fit like a glove and really look nice, on some people.*"[28]

What would happen when the class of 41-E turned out? Speculation was rife, and rumors were everywhere. In early May the rumor was that half of the graduates would become instructors, and the other half would be deployed overseas, probably to the Philippines.[29] Events in December would change all that, but at midyear the country was still at peace and hopes for good assignments were still alive.

But, of course, the cadets themselves still needed to stay alive and make it through Advanced. Accidents could yet happen to end the dreams of wings held by each member of 41-E. In June Cole had a scare on a three-hundred-mile cross-country flight: "*Almost had a forced landing. Motor quit on me, I didn't know what was the cause so just switched tanks and used fuel pump and she caught and kept running o.k. Probably dirt or water in gas.*"[29] Three weeks later he wrote again, saying a major advised them that their class was "the best and safest and fastest class that ever went through Kelly." Minor accidents did occur: "*One guy busted a wing, one pulled up his wheels instead of his flaps while still on the ground, and while night flying a guy landed with his wheels up.*" Experience presumably would limit those incidents, but Cole noted that "*an instructor landed with his wheels up and a ferry pilot with a new ship did same. It's not hard to do—just have to keep on the ball.*"[30]

It came at last, graduation day. On July 11, 1941, the class of 41-E lined up in crisp formation on the tarmac at Kelly Field to receive their golden bars and silver wings. They were now officers, commissioned as second lieutenants and rated as military pilots in the Army Air Corps. With all the pomp and ceremony, the marching and the bands and the speakers, it all seemed a bit overblown to Dick Cole. Until he looked down and saw those silver wings above his left pocket. He smiled broadly.

Cadet Cole was now Lieutenant Cole and rated a salute.

Despite receiving only single-engine training, Cole and many of his classmates were assigned to multiengine bomber squadrons. He would be joined by William G. Farrow and Richard A. Knobloch. Jack A. Sims and Robert J. Meder, from Cole's days at Parks, had graduated at the same time at nearby Brooks Field, in addition to J. Royden Stork and Griffith P. Williams. They would all become as close as brothers in a combat mission as important as any flown during World War II. But in July 1941, they had no thoughts or emotions except joy at being the newest—and to their minds the best—pilots in the Army Air Corps.

Cole was given ample travel time to report to his new home: the 17th Bomb Group (BG) in Pendleton, Oregon. He headed out by way of Dayton, Ohio, which as any pilot can tell you is the most direct route from San Antonio to Oregon.

# CHAPTER 3

A Douglas B-18 is arguably one of the ugliest bombers ever produced. It is awkward and graceless—2nd Lieutenant Cole described it as "a big whale"—as well as slow. The Bolo, as it was named by Douglas, was the result of an attempt to build a bomber from a commercial airliner, the DC-2. The end product was marginal at best.

The Martin B-10 had been a mainstay bomber of the Army Air Corps since 1934, and in those heady, fast-moving days of technological advancements it was obsolete almost before the first one was accepted into the military stable. In the race to develop a successor to the Martin, Douglas modified its twin-engine airliner: to accommodate an internal load of bombs, it deepened the fuselage, giving it the appearance of being pregnant; it retained the airliner's wings, albeit lengthening them; and it added very puny defensive armament by sticking in three .30-caliber machine guns. Despite its inadequacies, it was approved by the Air Corps, and deliveries began in 1936.

Cole reported to the 34th Bombardment Squadron of the 17th Bombardment Group in Pendleton, Oregon, in early August 1941. The 17th was composed of four squadrons: the 34th, the 37th, and the 95th Bomb Squadrons and the 89th Reconnaissance Squadron. It had the distinction of being designated the first "medium" bomb group in the Army Air Corps in 1939. (In the time period through World War II, a medium bomber was a twin-engine aircraft capable of carrying three to four thousand pounds of bombs; heavy bombers were four-engine machines such as the B-17 and B-24 that could carry five to eight thousand pounds of bombs.) In February 1941 the 17th Bomb Group had been the first unit to receive a few of the hot new North American B-25

30

Mitchells, although the majority of aircraft in the unit were still the outmoded and outclassed Douglas models. The 17th had been a pursuit group in the 1920s, commanded by then major Hap Arnold; the 34th Squadron had been led by then captain Ira Eaker. Both Arnold and Eaker were now senior commanders; Arnold was general of the entire Army Air Corps.

Along with Jack Sims, Bob Meder, William Farrow, Griffith Williams, Royden Stork, and Dick Knobloch, the brand-new pilots of 41-E (from several different training fields) formed the nucleus of a new flood of butter bars—second lieutenants—who would slip into the right seats of twin-engine B-18s and B-23s without having a single hour of multiengine instruction. The plan, apparently, was for them to be trained on the job.

Pendleton was a remote field, inland about halfway across the state and just south of the Washington line. It was west of the Umatilla Indian Reservation on the Columbia Plateau; the Blue Mountains could be seen puncturing the sky in the east. Cole drove his black Pontiac coupe through the front gates at his new station and found the administration building; there he learned that the entire 17th Bomb Group was on TDY (temporary duty) to Felts Field, near Spokane. Cole had driven from Dayton to Seattle with his sister Jo, who wanted to visit friends there, and then motored south and east to Pendleton. He would now drive on to Spokane.

Capt. Alvord Rutherford commanded the 34th Squadron. A West Point graduate and a bit stiff, he seemed to be overwhelmed by the flood of new personnel, but he did his job and Cole, at least, had no complaints. At Felts, the 17th Group was practicing live bombing runs, dropping their bombs in the remote area of Ephrata, east of Seattle. Cole and the other brand-new pilots were scheduled as fill-ins, not assigned to a single complete crew that functioned as a unit but simply as they were needed. For about three weeks, they acted as the "other guy" in the cockpits of the squadron's B-18s, mostly observing how the pilot did his job, raising the gear when signaled to do so by the man in the left seat, and trying to absorb as much of this multiengine business as they could. In three weeks, it all changed. Now, the 34th Squadron was to be totally reequipped with the latest Mitchell, the B-25B. The B-18 and B-23 were already warplanes of the 1930s; the B-25B was state of the art, a flying ship for the next decade. The first six arrived in late August, and the fliers of Cole's squadron were ecstatic.

The first Mitchells off the line were straight-wing models, with the wing coming out of the fuselage at a slight upward angle (called dihedral) and continuing at the same angle to the wingtip. This caused some stability problems in flight, so later versions had a pronounced downward bend from the engines to the fuselage. The addition of the gull-wing configuration made the twin-engine bomber more stable, and the bent-wing characteristic became an easily recognized feature of the soon-to-be-famous warplane, as distinctive as its twin tail. Cole noted other changes in a letter to his mother from the bivouac at Felts Field, a site he denoted as "Tent City": "*We got 6 new ships today, B-25B. Not much difference except the tail gunner on B-25A is replaced by a power gun turret. It's a little faster too.*" He was interrupted in his letter writing to fly a load of bombsights to Tacoma, Washington. Flying at eleven thousand feet, with the tops of the clouds at seven thousand, Cole was clearly touched by the view: "*It was quite a pretty sight to be flying over all those billowy cotton clouds with Mt. Rainier and Mt. Adams poking their tops through it. Mt. Rainier is even prettier than the pictures. Just out of Spokane we had snow, ice, and rain. It was just local, sun shone the rest of the way.*"[1] He didn't know it at the time, but he would soon be flying over much higher mountains, in much worse weather.

For Cole and the other brand-new pilots, their posting to the 34th could not have been a better assignment. In just weeks, they had transitioned from flying school where they operated single-engine trainers to sitting in the cockpits of the Army Air Corps' newest, fastest, most advanced medium bomber. They were getting plenty of flying time, real flying, as they practiced bombing runs and made periodic flights down to Riverside, California, to pick up another new Mitchell. They were flying three or four times a week, each time with a different pilot, which had positive and negative implications for the copilots. One pilot would want his right seater to do things in a particular way, and the next would want something different. But all in all, it was a good education. The new fliers quickly grew intuitive about the men they flew beside; with some you could relax and be at ease, others only half so much, and still others left them with the question, "What's up with this guy?"[2]

The flying part of their new assignment, then, was as good as it got for young pilots eager to learn on the newest, most up-to-date equipment. As copilots, their jobs varied with each pilot with whom they flew. Some wanted them only to operate the radio; others wanted the copilot to raise and lower the landing gear on a hand signal from the pilot.

Still others allowed them "stick time" when they were safely in the air, and some eventually allowed the right-seat newbies to do takeoffs and landings with the pilot ready to take over instantly if things began to go badly. And a few simply wanted the copilot to sit, observe, and be quiet.

The accommodations side of the assignment was a bit less glamorous than the flying. Cole had left Kelly and Randolph Fields, two of the most modern airfields in the Air Corps inventory, with clean and air-conditioned barracks, immaculate grounds, and eye-catching architecture. Life at Pendleton would have been a tick less luxurious, but he didn't have a single night there before reporting to Felts Field, where the crews were living in tents. By 28 August, the "tent city" was down to two hundred men, including Cole. More than six hundred had already returned to Pendleton, but he would remain another week.

*"The weather has been dark, cold, rainy and dreary. Tues. nite it began to snow a bit but soon changed to rain. My shoes have been wet for a week—no place to dry them."*[3] Cole would be one of the last to leave Felts. Still, Cole was able to look on the positive side. Bad weather meant more instrument flying, and he recalled that he had been copilot on a run to Pendleton the previous day, when the weather had closed in. *"The pilot made an instrument approach and letdown and came out right over the field. It was better than some when the weather is good. It sure proved the value of confidence in those instruments and the ability to use them."*[4]

And he was looking forward to the fall and some time to explore and hunt in the Pacific Northwest. On the last day of August 1941, he had taken a solitary drive up through some of the rugged country about sixty miles northwest of Felts Field. *"It's really wild and rough country,"* he wrote his mother. He had stopped at a general store and struck up a conversation with an old man there who invited him to deer hunt when the season opened. *"We were sitting on the porch and three [deer] came out of the underbrush onto the road but soon disappeared. I never saw so many squirrels, gray and red, and fox. Also lots of pheasants and partridge plus all this beautiful country."*[5]

But Cole wouldn't get to enjoy the country or the hunting. On 5 September the entire bomb group would leave for Jackson, Mississippi, for a long war-game exercise known as the Louisiana Maneuvers. Cole made arrangements to store his car on blocks for four dollars a month, which included having the radiator drained and the tires and battery periodically checked and filled. After the group was alerted, however, they departed nearly a week late because of weather and some aircraft maintenance and repair issues.

Cole wrote his mother on 13 September from Lowry Field, Denver, raving about the B-25: "*We just breezed in here from Spokane, 1,111 miles in 5 hrs. 5 min. An average of 220 miles per hour and we were just loafing along to save on gas*." They would leave Lowry the next morning at 9:00 a.m., stop in Tulsa for gas, and arrive in Jackson that night. The stop at Denver was unplanned. They had crossed over Snowy Range in Wyoming at fourteen thousand feet and flew a course that took them over Rawlins, Laramie, and Cheyenne, where they had intended to land and spend the night. Fog and rain had closed the field, however, so they diverted to Lowry.[6]

The luck of the draw for pilots placed Cole with 1st Lt. Harold F. "Doc" Watson, with whom Cole was immediately comfortable. He later described climbing into the cockpit of the B-25B with the first lieutenant as "like getting into a car." Watson told him with a smile that he would do the first takeoff, then he wanted Cole to take over the controls and stay in the traffic pattern at Pendleton. After Watson did a third takeoff, he let Cole take it off himself. It was a mark of confidence in his copilot, one that Cole appreciated.[7]

The Louisiana Maneuvers, as they were called, were the largest mock battles ever conducted by the US military. From 15 to 28 September 1941, Lt. Gen. Ben Lear's "Blue" army of 123,000 men fought Lt. Gen. Walter Kreuger's "Red" army of 219,000 across the bayous of Louisiana and the hills of eastern Texas. The war raging across Europe had prompted some "America First" isolationist responses, but military leaders were generally convinced that the country would eventually be drawn into the conflict. The maneuvers were designed to test not only battle strategies and tactics but leaders as well. For two days, many motorists found themselves sitting in traffic while troops "fought" door to door in towns and cities across the region.[8]

One bit of equipment tested at the time was the light plane for use as an artillery spotter and liaison vehicle; Taylorcraft, Aeronca, and Piper made available to the military numerous tiny two-place, fabric-covered airplanes that could take off and land in short grass fields. They proved to be extremely valuable; the Air Corps ordered thousands of them, and they would be an important element later in the wartime flying career of Cole, although he did not personally fly one.

Cole and the rest of the 17th Bomb Group fliers were kept busy during the maneuvers, and they got very little sleep; Cole's roommate throughout the maneuvers was Lt. Bob Hite. Fate would dictate different paths for Cole and Hite when the war began in earnest. Ted Lawson later wrote that they were on alert twenty-four hours a day and wore helmets and carried .45 pistols when they were not flying.[9]

"*We have had about one day all totaled in time off I guess and not much sleep while we're on alert*," Cole wrote his mother on 25 September. "*Tomorrow is a full day. We have 10 missions to fulfill, starts at 3 a.m. and ends* ———— *don't know. Maneuvers aren't exactly a picnic as you can see. Lots of flying, though. We bombed Houston, San Antonio, Beaumont, Texas and Shreveport, New Orleans, Lake Charles, and Baton Rouge, La. Hope we never have to do it actually. I didn't learn to fly for that reason.*"[10]

The happy flier and reluctant warrior would soon be deeply involved in missions that were not games. Years later, Cole said that he believed the greatest value of the maneuvers for the 17th Bomb Group was establishing communications between the Air Corps fliers and the ground troops, since the majority of missions for medium bombers were tactical, that is, ground support. Clear and unequivocal communication would be critical for the safety of the good guys on the ground and the successful elimination of targets in the years ahead.[11]

When they finally left Jackson in late September, the 17th Group didn't head straight back to Pendleton. Instead, they took off for Westover, Massachusetts. Cole wrote his mother that they would be stopping to refuel at Patterson, and he would try to call while there. From Dayton, they would be going to Jacksonville, Florida, and by November would be in Augusta, Georgia, for more maneuvers. He plainly was tired of the itinerant life. Of the planned fuel stop at Patterson, he wrote his mother: "*Pray for some bad weather after we land and maybe we'll have to stay there all night. Sure would like to get a good meal, the food, meals down here are lousy.*"[12]

The new maneuvers were scheduled from 15 to 30 November. Before they started, Cole and a major from headquarters squadron of the 17th flew to Los Angeles to pick up another new B-25B. They then flew that ship to Augusta, by way of Albuquerque, and then to Barksdale, Louisiana. On 12 November, he wrote: "*We arrived back here in Augusta yesterday noon. We covered 2807 miles in 11 hrs. and 17 minutes, close to 260 mph.*"[13] Something delayed the start of maneuvers, and Cole shed no tears. On the fifteenth, he wrote a quick note on a postcard to his mother: "*Maneuvers delayed till 6:30 a.m. tomorrow. Can call 'em off for all I care. Gonna end Dec. 1. Suits me to a tee.*"[14]

On 18 November, Cole wrote his mother again from Daniel Air Base in Augusta. The group had been "bombing" bridges and airports regularly, but the "war" this time was set up for the fliers differently than during the Louisiana Maneuvers. This time they were on duty for ten hours, then off for ten, giving them a breathing spell and making it so they had to arise before sunup only every other day. It was a large-scale "war," with ten to thirty bombers sent on every mission. Cole sympathized with the local residents: "*I bet these people will be glad to see us leave. We always run a 'Dawn Patrol' and the number of planes averages 15 ships, so you can imagine the noise. We take off right across town, 4 a.m. to 6:30 a.m.*"[15]

Noise was one reason for wishing them gone. There were others. Being young, mostly single, and adventurous, the airmen spread out across Augusta on their time off to experience local culture. One evening Cole and another flier, Bruce Bass, were playing pool in a local establishment downtown, while another group of pilots was apparently taking in the sights. No one remembered what was said, but a scuffling match occurred between a copilot, Lt. Robert M. Hackney, and another flier. Words were exchanged, there was some shoving, and then the other man took a swing at Hackney. A sometime boxer, Hackney had quick reflexes and ducked. A police officer who had walked up to see what the commotion was about took the blow in the face; he promptly called for assistance, and the entire group of fliers was arrested and thrown in the city jail. When the group commander, Lt. Col. Walter Peck, heard about it, he marched to the jail and demanded the release of his men. Peck was a no-nonsense career officer, and no one argued with him; the men were let off.[16]

While Cole's letters home were chatty and upbeat, he did not include everything that happened. He wrote nothing about the loss of one of the group's B-25Bs and the entire crew when both engines quit on takeoff and the bomber went straight into a grove of pines. Five men were killed, including the copilot, who had been a classmate of Cole's. Other accidents occurred at a rate that might have been alarming in other circumstances but in the event closely duplicated the accident rate that would occur later in combat; sometimes, it seemed that Allied pilots damaged nearly as many aircraft as enemy action. Ted Lawson, Richard O. Joyce, and William M. Bower all had noninjury accidents during the exercises. Bower's Mitchell went off the end of the runway as he hydroplaned following a rain on the new blacktop surface. He struck a pile of blacktop and ripped off his nosegear. Capt. Karl Baumeister, an older experienced pilot and a squadron commander, had the same loss of braking and hydroplaning when he landed behind Bower. As he approached the end of the runway and still was too fast to stop, Baumeister hit the left rudder hard and increased the throttle to the right engine, turning the Mitchell 180 degrees and saving it from a similar accident, as well as preventing a collision with Bower's plane.[17]

There was an interesting bit of news from a general officer who addressed the group. Cole wrote his mother that the general told them the 17th, because it was on maneuvers, had just missed being deployed to Iceland. Instead, the 22nd (Medium) BG from Langley, Virginia, had gone. As to the future of the 17th, "*He said that we would go back to Pendleton, and have 4 months intensive bombing practice and then foreign duty . . . where? He didn't say. If we're gonna have to go I would just as soon go to South America instead of Panama, China, Hawaii, British West Indies or the Philippines.*"[18]

There was some small-scale positive news as well. When the fliers returned to Pendleton, there were enough rooms in the BOQ (bachelor officers' quarters) to allow each officer two rooms, they had been told. "*I can't fill one let alone two. Guess I'll rent one out, or buy a goat.*"[19]

The "war" continued. On 25 November, Cole noted that the weather in Georgia had been mild, with an Indian summer: "*Warm days and cold nites. Swell.*"[20] That morning the second phase of the war started at 0400, with the 34th sending fifteen bombers in the first mission and fourteen the second. They "lost" two of their aircraft but were credited with shooting down five enemy fighters, one bomber, and an observation plane. Plus, they received credit for destroying their target, a bridge. Hopes for a return to Pendleton when the maneuvers were over were dashed, however.

"*As the wind changes so changes our plans,*" he wrote his mother. On the twenty-first, the group had received orders "*to pack up and move to Winston-Salem, N.C. Lock stock and barrel. Well, we got all packed and then—some more orders saying the 34th and 89th would stay here (Augusta) and the 37th, 95th, and headquarters would move. All's well. Flash—more orders—we will proceed from Augusta to March Field, Riverside, California to participate in some more maneuvers, Dec. 8 to 16, and then, who knows? I got a sneaking hunch there will be no Christmas leave, but there is still a chance.*"[21]

# CHAPTER 4

When the maneuvers in Augusta ended on 1 December 1941, the men of the 17th were more than ready to leave for their home base at Pendleton. They had been gone for months, living in tents, eating on the run, getting up long before the sun, and flying mission after mission each day for the simulated war. It would be good to be back home. All of them looked forward to a peacetime routine and the promise of a twenty-day leave.

But first, one more week of "war" at new maneuvers on the West Coast. They began packing up for the transcontinental flight, servicing the planes, making minor repairs. In a couple of days, they were ready, and on Friday, 5 December 1941, they landed at March Field, south of Los Angeles. This would be their home for the scheduled exercises slated to begin Monday, 8 December, and to end on the sixteenth. Lt. Col. Walter Peck, the group commander, recognized the need for his men to have some time off, so he declared "open post"—the men could leave the base, but had to be back on the airfield by midnight Sunday. Cole and several of his buddies wanted to see Hollywood, so they checked into the Hollywood Plaza Hotel.

Hollywood was what they had expected, and the jubilant fliers wandered the streets and stared in the windows of expensive shops. Lt. Bruce Bass had an uncle who lived in the area, and he took Bass, Cole, and a couple of buddies on a tour of the fabled city. He "*showed us some homes so beautiful that you could hardly believe your eyes*," he wrote his mother. Additionally, they saw "*the movie stars' homes, CBS, NBC, radio studies, motion picture studios. Sure is a big town.*"[1] They ate well, splurging on steaks and seafood. All day Saturday they experienced the glories of one of the most decadent capitals of the world of extravagance and overindulgence.

Cole awoke Sunday morning, 7 December 1941, around seven o'clock. He showered and shaved and was getting into his uniform when there was a knock at the door. One of the pilots from another room announced that the Japanese had attacked Hawaii. A few minutes later, a young man in the uniform of the hotel greeted him, looking somber. All military personnel were to report to their bases, immediately. The former business partner of Cole's father in Dayton now lived in Los Angeles. Fred Cole had given his son the phone number and told him to call him up if he was ever in LA. Now was the time, Cole reasoned, since several of the pilots were in the hotel and needed a ride back to March Field. The man was surprised but eager to drive the young fliers back to the base, about twenty miles away. Cole, Bass, and Robert Harry were grateful for the lift.[2]

No, there would be no leave at Christmas, as Cole had suspected. And there would be no relaxing period of peacetime routine—or the scheduled weeklong West Coast maneuvers. The balloon was up—it was a real war. Cole was apprehensive, a bit numb, but accepting of the new reality. He was a pilot in the Army Air Corps; it was his job to fight. But it was a subdued group that reported back to their unit. Each man was lost in his own thoughts, with only a few quiet speculations of where they would be sent. That evening he wrote his mother: "*Well! That 20-day leave was a good idea anyway, but 'tain't no more, the lid's off. . . . The first message of the attack really set this post to work. They worked like a clock, dispersed our ships, set up machine guns, anti-aircraft, search lights, aircraft warning devices, and etc. Guards are bumping each other and everybody is on the alert. Even me!*"[3]

The future was uncertain, but he promised to write or telegraph at every opportunity. "*I don't want you to worry cause there is really no reason for it, so don't start now.*"[4] If they had only known what was to come, the words would have been cold comfort.

The attack on the military installations around Pearl Harbor in Hawaii was brilliant in its complete surprise, its devastation to the Navy's Pacific fleet, and the relatively minor losses to the aircraft of the Japanese Imperial Navy. It also dealt a major blow to the country's sense of insularity; with an exclamation point, the attack ended any thoughts that the wars in Europe and Asia would rage on without the United States. In the smoldering devastation left in the wake of the bombs and torpedoes at Pearl Harbor and nearby Hickam Field, 2,403 Americans lay dead, and another 1,178 were wounded; four battleships were sunk and four others damaged; three cruisers, three destroyers, a minelayer, and an antiaircraft training ship were sunk or damaged; and 188 aircraft were destroyed.

*Time* on 15 December called the attack "premeditated murder masked by a toothy smile"; the *New York Times* on 8 December said, "The Japanese aggression yesterday did more than start a Pacific war. It broadened the conflicts already raging into a world-wide struggle whose end no man can know"; and in an editorial on 9 December, the *St. Petersburg (FL) Times* approved of the swift declaration of war by Congress: "We have answered the defiance of a cowardly, back-stabbing foe who talked peace even while plotting undeclared war."[5]

From the attack at Pearl Harbor until the end of the war, Americans engaged in an unremitting campaign of racism directed against the Japanese. Cartoons from Hollywood depicted large-toothed Japanese—called Japs or Nips even in mainstream magazines and newspapers—wearing thick glasses. Movies invariably showed them as evil, baby-killing monsters. Posters produced by the War Information Office depicted hideous creatures—snakes, spiders, or monkeys—with the cartoon heads of Japanese. In February 1942, President Roosevelt signed an executive order moving 120,000 residents of Japanese descent to relocation centers—internment camps—in ten remote locations. No such order was issued regarding those of German or Italian heritage, nor were the caricatures of those foes as extreme as those of Japanese.

Lieutenant Cole, who up to now might have been considered an eager flier but a reluctant warrior, was himself transformed by the Japanese surprise attack. "*We have a lot of valuable training and the best of equipment,*" he wrote his mother on 10 December. "*And the Japs better watch out cause we're a fighting outfit and the worry is all theirs. Watch the 'Thunderbirds.'*"[6] Of course, he had no inkling at the time just how right he would be.

Pride in their squadrons took a major uptick among all the fliers of the 17th Bomb Group, and soon their leather flight jackets all bore colorful patches on the left front: a Thunderbird for the 34th Bomb Squadron, a prowling lion for the 37th, a kicking mule for the 95th, and a winged helmet for the 89th Reconnaissance Squadron. They would become iconic, among the most recognized emblems of aerial warriors of the largest war in history.

At 4:00 a.m. on 8 December, they departed March Field for Pendleton, where the bomb racks in the Mitchells were changed to accommodate 300-pounders for their new duty; there would be no need for 100-pound practice bombs. One week later, they began flying submarine patrol duty along the Oregon and Washington coast, operating out of a small field near Portland. Another group covered the north half of the Washington coastline, and a third group patrolled the southern part of the Oregon coast. They lived on the auxiliary field: *"Have been living and sleeping in a big hangar, not so bad, good beds and I brought my sleeping bag. Someone brought lots of magazines and a radio so all is well,"* he assured his mother.[7]

The patrols were tiring and boring, on the days they could fly. Each morning when the weather allowed Cole and his crew arose early, attended a briefing that included their assigned section of a prepared grid as well as weather reports, and then flew back and forth at thirty-five hundred feet, endlessly watching the gray-green ocean below for any signs of a Japanese submarine. Some missions were as far as three hundred miles off the coast, others closer in. They had no formalized training or sophisticated equipment, just the advice to look for small wakes that might be telltale signs of a raised periscope or dark, elongated shapes just below the surface. Waves crashing white against the dark rocks of the coast would be the last sight of interest before they left for the vast expanse of water beyond, water that held no promise of easy victories, water that seemed to stretch on forever, water that promised only a cold, wet grave if things were to go wrong.

For four hours each mission the men of the 17th BG patrolled America's shores, staring at the sea below with binoculars at the ready. The attack on Pearl Harbor had raised general fears of an invasion of the mainland, and rumors were constant of landings by parties of Japanese saboteurs and agents. The antisubmarine patrols were taken seriously by the fliers, but the constant scanning of the waves below produced headaches and eyestrain and very little in the way of information or sightings. At the end of each patrol, the crews were debriefed: Did you see anything? The answer was almost always, No. Nothing.

The weather in the Pacific Northwest in December is hardly ideal for flying. There were days that no one could take off, others when the missions were cut short. On 20 December, Cole wrote his mother: *"Today we saw the sun for the first time in about 10 days. . . . Never in my life have I seen it rain so much. Has rained day and night continuously, hence we haven't done much flying as it was accompanied by some London fog."* On one occasion, he wrote, they were able to take off and begin their scheduled patrol: *"Went out to see the sea. Boy, there is a lot of it there. Weather was bad so we had to turn back, saw a few boats."*[8]

Just days later, on Christmas Eve, the situation changed, and the need for the patrols was made abundantly evident. Lt. Everett W. "Brick" Holstrom and his copilot, Lt. Ross R. "Hoss" Wilder, from the 95th Squadron, were operating out of another small and remote airfield along the coast. They took off about noon and flew their assigned location on the grid, about sixty-five miles west of the mouth of the Columbia River. Accompanying him in two other bombers were Lt. Ted W. Lawson and Lt. Robert W. Witty. The weather, as usual, was bad; rain clouds covered all of the sky and were lowering. Holstrom descended to about five hundred feet over the gray sea in an effort to stay below the cloud base and be able to see the ocean. The sea was dotted with lumber, possibly from a freighter that was sunk, and several times a crewman thought he saw a periscope.

The flotsam and the lifeless gray water made a hard task far more difficult. Monotony changed to frustration. Then Wilder shouted that they were right beside a submarine that was surfacing, its bow just breaking through the surface, white ribbons of seawater coursing back from the blunt nose. Orders for the airmen were to destroy any submarine that was not escorted; American subs would all have a surface escort. The crew looked around quickly. No surface vessels were in sight. Because the submarine was on Wilder's side of the airplane, Holstrom ceded control to Wilder, who banked sharply to come around and line up with the sub. They released one bomb, which missed. They came around again in a steep bank and dropped two more, one of which struck the bow, the second one exploding on the deck just forward of the conning tower. The submarine went down, and a large oil slick spread over the area. To be certain of the kill, the crew dropped its remaining bomb in the center of the slick.

Ted Lawson later wrote that he saw Holstrom dropping his bombs and flew to the site; by that time, "oil was coming up in greasy bubbles, as if some awful thing was throwing up under water."[9] Weather closed in rapidly, and Holstrom, out of bombs, headed back to base. Lawson and Witty, their adrenaline up, continued to search for additional submarines until low on fuel. Witty ended up landing on a Washington beach; Lawson put in at an emergency field at Ilwaco.[10]

Holstrom was a native of Oregon. He was born in Cottage Grove, graduated from Pleasant Hill High School, and attended Oregon State University before entering the Army Air Corps. He should have been an instant local hero. But when he and his crew landed at Boeing Field in Seattle, they were met by officers of West Coast Command, who ordered them to keep quiet about the mission. The country was close to panic over the possibility of another Japanese attack, and the report of a Japanese submarine sunk off the coast would fuel the fires of hysteria.

Cole felt no such hesitation about informing his mother, however: *"We have been doing a lot of flying, but still no excitement except on one occasion,"* he wrote on 2 January 1942. *"A ship of the 95th saw, bombed and sunk a Jap sub fifty miles out to sea last week."*[11]

He was pleased to be back at McChord Field near Tacoma *"after thirteen days of living in another hangar and our flying suits."* The weather had cleared in the past two weeks, but the temperatures had dropped to twenty below zero and it had snowed more than a foot at the auxiliary field they had been using. The next day, he reported, they would be moving to Portland. The country in the Northwest is spectacular, but dangerous. The rugged terrain and horrible flying weather made a bad combination: *"This country is the most picturesque I have ever flown over. Lots of virgin spruce forests, trees 200' to 300 ft. high. Ole Mt. Rainier, Mt. Adams, Hood and St. Helena, Cascade Range and up along the Canadian Coast, the Olympia Range and the Vancouver Range all snow covered, but treacherous obstacles when the fog rolls in."*[12]

Three weeks later, Cole wrote his mother about the latest rumor regarding the 17th: they would be moving permanently to Savannah by the first week in February. *"At Savannah we are to get new ships of Heavy Bombardment Type—B-24—made by Consolidated. 4 engines tricycle landing gear. It's about the best of heavy bombardment class."* But he was unconvinced. *"I got to see all this before I believes it!"*[13]

Doubt was a good reaction. Rumors continued to swirl, and by 7 February the group's move to a permanent base was still a mystery. The fliers had begun referring to their next duty station as "Bango-Bango," which was as good a guess as any. Some personnel were being transferred—Bruce Bass went to a pursuit squadron, another officer to a heavy bombardment unit, and four were sent to a point of embarkation bound for somewhere in the Far East.[14] Cole was making his own preparations, having sent all of his civilian clothes in a footlocker to Dayton via a freight company, along with the keys and receipt to his mother. He sold his black Pontiac—with the optional radio—and now kept only the bare necessities he would need for flying duty.

When his family heard from him again two weeks later, Cole was at New Lexington Air Base in Columbia, South Carolina. What he and his flying buddies in the 17th did not know was that the new group commander, Lt. Col. William C. Mills, had received a telegram on 3 February directing him to transfer the entire command to Columbia without delay. He was also instructed that word should be passed among his men that volunteers were needed for an extremely hazardous mission.[15] At Columbia, virtually every man volunteered without knowing any details and without knowing they would be leaving Columbia almost immediately.

"*After so long here comes a letter again, and from the deep, deep South,*" he wrote on 22 February. "*It seems that the 17th Group is a builder of air bases, for once again we have moved into a new base. Once again we are living in tents. All have stoves and floors, oh yes! Hot water and electric lights. The weather has been warm by day and cool at night and it's really not half bad.*" He closed his bank account in Texas and asked his mother and sister Mart to open a joint account, so "*in case something happens to me, you could have access to the money.*" He also arranged for his base pay of $125 a month to be mailed to his mother for deposit in the joint account.[16]

So after many false rumors and delays, Columbia, South Carolina, would be the home of the 17th Bomb Group. "*Pendleton is 'Home on the Range' no more, this is our permanent base till we leave.*"[17]

Cole's permanent base lasted only about two or three weeks. He was selected, along with 139 others, for the unknown hazardous mission, a project that would come to define his life for the next three quarters of a century.

# CHAPTER 5

Unknown to Lt. Dick Cole and the other airmen of the 17th Bomb Group—as well as the rest of the world, for that matter—the Japanese attack on Pearl Harbor had set into motion an American response that would electrify the nation, alter the course of the war in the Pacific, and achieve a legendary status that inspired movies, books, and countless articles and theses. It would be studied from every angle, dissected, and praised, and move Admiral Halsey to declare: "In my opinion, their flight was one of the most courageous deeds in military history."[1] Cole would disagree, but one thing cannot be disputed: he would have the best seat in the house for one of the most famous missions flown by the Army Air Forces in World War II.

Within two weeks following the attack, President Franklin Delano Roosevelt was pushing his military chiefs for an attack on the home islands of Japan. Gen. George C. Marshall, Army chief of staff; Gen. Henry H. "Hap" Arnold, head of the Army Air Forces; and Adm. Ernest J. King, chief of naval operations, met with the president regularly to map out an overall strategy for the conduct of the war. By Christmas they were meeting as well with their British counterparts to plan a coordinated Allied vision for winning the war. It was determined fairly early that the focus would be on defeating the German and Italian forces in Europe and North Africa before turning their attentions on Japan. For the next few months, it appeared that the Japanese Imperial Navy and Army were unstoppable in any event: within a couple of months, Wake Island, the Philippines, Hong Kong, Singapore, Burma, and the Dutch East Indies had all fallen under the flag of the Rising Sun, and Australia was under threat as well. The soldiers, sailors, and airmen of Japan appeared to be supermen, and the militarists there had promised the population that the home islands would never be attacked by the Allies.

The idea for a strike on key targets across Japan took root gradually. A week before Christmas, Texas newspaper publisher Amon G. Carter had raised the possibility of an air strike against Japan—using five hundred airline pilots—in a letter to Maj. Gen. Edwin Watson, the president's military aide, who then forwarded the suggestion to Arnold. Several memos in early January reveal that Arnold was considering the idea. That was not the wildest proposal. That prize might have gone to a scheme first articulated by Harvey Davis, director of the Stevens Institute; in a speech to the Century Club in New York, he suggested that bombing some of Japan's nine hundred semiactive volcanoes might trigger eruptions across the islands. The idea was sent to the president, who forwarded it to the Army Air Forces. Arnold told the president he would look into it.[2]

What came to be the Doolittle Raid was one of several plans set in motion nearly simultaneously. One involved a proposed raid by B-17s to be led by Col. Caleb V. Haynes out of China, known as Operation Aquilla, which began to take shape in February 1942. This would be followed up in strength by a bomber force of twenty-three (original plans called for fifty) B-24s under Col. Harry A. Halverson.[3] However, the Haynes mission arrived in India after the Doolittle Raid, and the Halverson project, known as HALPRO, was diverted after it reached Egypt for the raid on the Ploesti oil fields and never arrived in China.[4] Neither of these missions, using four-engine bombers, would have been possible from a carrier.

Admiral King had suggested that Navy carriers might be able to transport Army cargo planes and bombers to North Africa to participate in a campaign there against Axis forces, envisioning that they would be loaded by crane in the States and unloaded the same way at ports in Africa. General Arnold, however, envisioned that certain planes—B-18s, perhaps, and C-47s—might be flown off the carriers. He told his staff to find which aircraft might be good candidates for such a project.[5]

Arnold's curiosity was met with equally creative thinking by a naval officer—a submariner on King's staff—Capt. Francis S. Low, who while on a flight to Norfolk, Virginia, to check on the readiness of the Navy's newest carrier, the *Hornet*, had seen Navy planes practicing takeoffs on a field painted with the outline of a carrier deck. He also observed Army planes making simulated bombing runs on the same painted outline. Would it be possible, he asked King, that pilots of Army bombers could be trained in taking off from extremely short distances, say, the length of a carrier deck? If so, the range of aircraft leaving a carrier would be greatly increased, and the chances of conducting a bombing raid on Japan itself likewise would be increased. With the attack on Pearl Harbor, the Japanese navy had demonstrated what aircraft carriers could do with single-engine dive bombers and torpedo bombers. If larger multiengine aircraft, capable of carrying several thousand pounds of bombs and flying much farther distances, could be operated from ships, the strategic value of such operations would be increased exponentially. King told Low to talk with Capt. Donald B. Duncan, King's air operations officer, and cautioned him to speak to no one else about the idea.

When Low met with Duncan the next day, he asked about the feasibility of an army twin-engine medium bomber taking off and landing on a Navy carrier. Landing, Duncan said unequivocally, was out of the question—particularly for the newest aircraft in the Army's arsenal, the B-25 and B-26. Both, he explained, had tricycle gear—that is, a nose-wheel instead of a tail wheel in addition to the main gear—and that configuration meant the tail sat far too high for use of a tail hook to arrest the landing. Additionally, they landed too fast for safe operations on a carrier.

Taking off was a different story. It might be possible that either airplane could be taken off from a carrier deck, provided the crews were properly trained. Duncan agreed to study the matter further. In five days, he had written a thirty-page analysis of the problem, taking into consideration the published operational limitations of the two aircraft and the dimensions and other data of Navy carriers available at the time.

It could be done, he concluded, but only by B-25Bs. Only the Mitchell had the ability to safely take off from a carrier deck, carry two thousand pounds of bombs, and with additional fuel tanks fly several hundred miles to a target. A target such as Japan.

The B-26 Marauder at this time had a shorter wingspan than the Mitchell, making it easier to clear obstacles on a flight deck, but it required higher takeoff speeds and longer runways. Duncan and Low presented the report on 16 January to King, who read it immediately and directed them to go see General Arnold. If he thought it would work, they were to ask him to contact Admiral King. Arnold did indeed like the idea, and he agreed to work with King on a joint Army-Navy project. King wanted Duncan to coordinate all of the Navy logistics; Arnold looked around and determined that there was only one candidate for the Army side, a recently promoted lieutenant-colonel who had been recalled to active duty and was working down the hall in the Munitions Building.

In the meantime, Duncan made arrangements to see if his calculations were correct. He asked Arnold to make three B-25s available when the *Hornet* arrived in Norfolk, Virginia. One of the bombers had an engine problem and was not available, but on 2 February a Mitchell piloted by Lt. John E. Fitzgerald successfully flew off the deck of the *Hornet*, followed by one flown by Lt. James F. McCarthy. Both bombers were lightly loaded, but the question had been answered: an Army medium bomber could indeed be launched from a Navy carrier.[6.]

Cole wrote his mother in late March from the visiting officers' quarters at Eglin Field, in Valparaiso, Florida, in the western panhandle, just a few miles east of the naval flight training center at Pensacola. Cole and his mates from the 17th Bomb Group had been transferred to Eglin, along with their B-25s, arriving in late February. It was a chatty letter, upbeat. His stay at Columbia had been very short, he explained, because of a call for volunteers "*to come down here and run some navigation and load tests so here I am.*" Five crews had been selected from each of the four squadrons of the 17th, he explained. (Actually, six were chosen.) But enough of that, on to some really exciting news: "*Yes! We are still flying B-25s. I thought I told you about getting 'checked off' early in December, anyway I have been a first pilot since then.*" He sent her a photograph of a 34th squadron Mitchell taken at Patterson Field, "*Thunderbird and all.*" Eglin Field, he said, was "*a very interesting place as it is an Air Corps parade ground, lots of funny gadgets around.*" And they had "*barracks to live in and not 'tents.'*" And oh, yes, one other thing: "*Our commanding officer is none other than Jimmie [sic] Doolittle, the famous speed demon—he flys a B-25 the same way. We have learned a lot of new data about our ships and from the looks of things we will be needing all of it.*"[7]

Cole wasn't totally dishonest with his mother. There had been, to be sure, plenty of navigation and load tests done over the past three weeks. He also had not mentioned that long-distance fuel tanks were being added to their planes, they were learning some new takeoff techniques, and bombing practice and gunnery practice were being conducted along with honing navigation skills.

He was shorter than Cole imagined as a boy pasting his photo in his scrapbook. Probably no taller than Cole himself had been when he graduated from high school, the second smallest boy in his class. But Doolittle had shoulders, wide and thick, that betrayed his early boxing career. He had been good, with a devastating right fist. He had a large head with blunt features, a cleft chin, and eyes that seemed to take in everything at once. At forty-six, Lt. Col. James Harold "Jimmy" Doolittle was a no-nonsense guy; something about the way he carried himself and spoke commanded respect. The assembled fliers of the 17th listened carefully, some craning to see more of the man who was already a living legend in the flying community.

Doolittle had been an Air Service pilot in the First World War, but despite his many attempts had been unable to get overseas before the fighting ended. In the intervening years, he had been a test pilot at Mc-Cook, received the first doctorate of science in aeronautics from the Massachusetts Institute of Technology, set numerous speed records, been awarded the Mackay Trophy in 1926, and performed the first outside loop. In 1929 he had made significant contributions to instrument flying—so-called fog or blind flying—by successfully taking off, flying, and landing an airplane solely by reference to his cockpit instruments, using the newly developed artificial horizon and directional gyro. For this feat he was awarded the Harmon Trophy. In 1930 Doolittle resigned his regular commission, accepted a reserve commission as major in the Air Corps, and went to work for Shell Oil Company, where he helped develop high-octane aviation fuel. In the decade of the 1930s, he continued air racing, winning the Bendix Trophy in 1931 in a race from Burbank, California, to Cleveland, Ohio, and the Thompson Trophy flying the unstable Gee Bee, before retiring from racing.

He had been recalled to active duty by Hap Arnold in July 1940 and was placed in charge of several production projects involving automotive manufacturers converting to the building of aircraft and aviation components. The Pentagon had not yet been built; his office was in the Munitions Building, near the Lincoln Memorial, just off the Mall. Doolittle had continued to fly and by March 1942 had more than seventy-seven hundred flight hours. He knew a little something about flying.

On 3 March, Doolittle had assembled the volunteers of the 17th Bomb Group together at Eglin. He got right to the point. "My name's Doolittle. I've been put in charge of the project that you men have volunteered for." There was only a small buzz; word had already made the rounds about who their new commander would be. Cole watched and listened intently to his boyhood idol. It was strange to see him in the flesh after following his early career so avidly a decade earlier. The speed demon was now a wartime leader, and Cole was to follow him. The job, Doolittle explained, was going to be extremely dangerous, and only volunteers would serve. At any time, he said, anyone could drop out and nothing would ever be said, and there would be no marks against him, ever. No one moved. Someone asked if he could be more specific about the project, and Lieutenant Colonel Doolittle said he could not. But he stressed, and would continue to stress, the secret nature of the mission. Tell no one, he warned, what you are doing here. Not your wives, your mothers, your sweethearts, your family. No one. Not a word, including discussion or speculation among yourselves. And if anyone seeks to question you, the Federal Bureau of Investigation will have a conversation with the interrogator.[8]

Doolittle introduced the officers chosen to head up various functions during training. They were, of course, all fliers from the 17th: Maj. Jack Hilger, an intense perfectionist who was commander of the 95th Bomb Squadron, would be Doolittle's executive officer, in charge when Doolittle was off base for his frequent trips back to Washington; Maj. Harry Johnson, adjutant; Capt. Edward J. "Ski" York, operations; Capt. David M. "Davy" Jones, navigation and intelligence; Capt. C. Ross Greening, gunnery and bombing; Lt. William Bower, engineering; Lt. Travis Hoover, supply; and Lt. Royden Stork, photography.

Eglin Field had been chosen for several reasons: it was relatively remote, it had numerous auxiliary fields where the men could practice away from curious eyes, and it was on the ocean, so navigation over open water could be perfected.

In Cole's estimation, Doolittle the fearless flyer turned out to be Doolittle the extraordinary leader of men. He recognized immediately the need for cohesion and the importance of flight crews functioning smoothly and seamlessly as a team, nearly anticipating the requirements of the others on the crew. Previously, throughout Cole's short career in the 34th, flight crews had been assembled as the need for a test hop, a ferry run, or a mission came up. At Eglin, permanent crews—pilot, copilot, navigator, bombardier, and engineer-gunner—were assigned and would train as a single unit. Cole was teamed with Capt. Vernon L. Stintzi as his pilot, Lt. Henry "Hank" Potter as navigator, Sgt. Fred Braemer as bombardier, and Sgt. Paul Leonard as engineer-gunner. He would come to know them all well, but as it turned out Stintzi would not be his pilot for the coming assignment.[9]

Potter was tall, about six-foot-four, easygoing but extremely compe-tent. He reminded Cole of Jimmy Stewart, already well known for his roles in *Mr. Smith Goes to Washington* and *Destry Rides Again.* (Stewart would later become a highly decorated bomber pilot in Europe.) Brae-mer was quiet, steady, eager to do his job; he had completed navigator as well as bombardier training. Leonard, a bit older than the rest of the crew, was a father figure to many in the squadron. Doolittle character-ized him as an outstanding, intuitive mechanic. Stintzi was a veteran pi-lot, extremely competent, but with an undetected ulcer that would soon knock him out of the lineup for the mission.

Cole observed that Doolittle, despite his fame and his position of com-mand of this special unit, was modest and always open to questions or suggestions about alternate ways to proceed. "Any question or anything like that, he listened to you. It didn't matter whether you thought it might be foolish, or if you had a comment that you felt might improve something, you could pitch it out without any kind of ridicule," Cole said years later.[10]

Doolittle always called everyone—officer and enlisted men alike—by their first name, an act that seemed very personal while also establishing a sense of egalitarianism. And, Cole learned, Doolittle rarely gave direct orders, but preferred suggestions: "Do you think that if we . . . " was a common phrase at Eglin; those serving under Doolittle learned that almost always, the suggestions turned out to be good ones. Time was in short supply and the assembled crews needed to get started in their training for this unknown mission, but suggestions and modifications to improve equipment or a task continued throughout the weeks at Eglin.

Each crew member had a specific job, and for the pilots it was learn-ing how to take off in distances no Army pilot would have thought pos-sible. At the start of the training at Eglin, as Doolittle prepared to return to Washington, Jack Hilger suggested that a Navy instructor would be valuable in teaching techniques for carrier takeoffs. Lt. Henry L. "Hank" Miller (later Admiral) was assigned from nearby Pensacola, where he had been instructing student naval aviators. When he arrived at Eg-lin, he met with York, Jones, and Greening; when he told them he was there to teach them how the Navy did takeoffs from carriers, they were surprised. It was clear to Miller they had not been told that their work would involve floating runways. When they asked the Navy flier how much time he had in a B-25, his answer left them equally surprised: he had never even seen one.[11]

Army pilots flying a B-25—or any heavily loaded military plane, for that matter—are taught to hold it on the runway until the aircraft virtually flies itself off and to use as much of the paved surface as they need. The Mitchell had proved to be fairly easy to take off, compared to the group's earlier B-18s and B-23s. That was because of the tricycle landing gear, that is, the addition of a nosewheel and the elimination of the older-style tail wheel. Aircraft equipped with nosewheels sit level with the runway when parked; a tail wheel means the fuselage and hence the wings sit at a nose-high angle when parked or taxiing or at the start of a takeoff run. To reduce as quickly as possible the extreme drag produced when the entire bottom surface of the wings is exposed to the relative wind, or oncoming air, pilots must push forward on the control stick or yoke at the start of the takeoff roll to lift the tail as quickly as possible and reduce the drag inherent in the nose-high attitude. When the speed is sufficient, the tail will begin to rise, at which point the pilot must pull back the stick or yoke to neutral; as the plane builds speed rushing down the runway, the pilot applies slight back pressure on the controls and the plane will fly itself off the runway. In a nosewheel-equipped aircraft, the pilot need only keep the stick in a neutral position and pull back slightly at a predetermined speed.

Various factors determine how much runway any given aircraft will use; things such as temperature, wind speed and direction, type of runway, and the weight of the airplane will all influence the length of a takeoff run. Higher temperatures mean the air is less dense, and thus a longer takeoff run will be required; a wind coming directly at the airplane will shorten the run, directly proportional to the wind velocity; a rough or grass-covered runway will necessitate a longer takeoff distance; and the heavier the airplane, all other conditions being equal, the longer the takeoff run.

An Army bomber, on a wartime mission, would ordinarily be loaded with fuel, bombs and other ordnance, and a full crew. Prior training thus emphasized using as much of a runway as possible and letting the airplane fly when it was ready. Hank Miller had other ideas, and the pilots of the 17th were clearly not ready to buy what he was selling. The pilot's manual for a B-25 was explicit regarding takeoff speeds: "As soon as you have good control (at approximately 85 mph), lift nose wheel slightly; then as speed picks up, allow airplane to fly itself off. Normal take-off speed is . . . 120 to 130 mph for combat-equipped B-25Js."[12]

Miller said they would be airborne with far less speed. He explained the procedure: pilots would stop their bomber on the centerline of the runway, set flaps in the fully down position, and stand on the brakes while full power was brought to both engines. The yoke would be held back, clear into the pilot's chest; the pilot would then release the brakes and continue to hold the yoke back. When the plane lifted off the runway, the pilot was to slowly ease the backward pressure on the yoke, raise the landing gear, and gradually reduce the flaps. (Flaps are controllable sections of the wing, on the lower surface, that can be lowered by the pilot for certain operations. When down, they create more lift, but also induce more drag. They are rarely used for operations other than takeoffs and landings.)

The Army pilots were unconvinced. Miller looked over the flight handbook for the Mitchell, carefully noting the takeoff performance figures. The four fliers walked out to a waiting B-25 and left for a nearby auxiliary field; Miller sat in the copilot's seat, while York and then Jones followed his instructions for a Navy-style takeoff. Greening observed from behind the two pilots. York was airborne when the airspeed indicator showed 50 mph. He and the other Army pilots insisted that the instrument was obviously wrong, but Miller just smiled. Jones took off and held it on the ground a bit longer, but still was flying at an indicated 60 mph. The Mitchell weighed twenty-seven thousand pounds. It simply wasn't possible.[13]

The airspeed indicator was checked. It was correct, as Miller knew it would be. Now the training could begin.

White lines were painted on the pavement at an auxiliary field at Eglin to simulate the flight deck of a Navy carrier, with flag markers on the sidelines every 100 feet. They were impossibly close together, it seemed to the Army pilots. The initial distance for takeoff was set at 800 feet, but within a week almost all of the pilots had been trained by Miller and were routinely taking off at minimum flying speeds, in distances of 350 to 400 feet. Before, none of them would have bet a beer that it could be done. It became a game, of course: pilots who were not flying would line up along the runway, clustered at the painted lines, and cheer or boo when wheels left the ground short of or beyond the mark. And then it became competitive: who could get their bomber off the ground in the shortest distance? Winners crowed, and losers blamed the inconsistent wind that had given the winners a gift of extra lift. Lt. Donald G. Smith took the laurel wreath, lifting his Mitchell from the paved runway in just 287 feet.[14] Even Doolittle, who was not scheduled to fly on the mission, took advantage of Miller's instructional course. He passed, able to take off a Mitchell in 350 feet into a 40 knot wind.[15]

There were some mishaps. One plane, flown by Lt. James P. Bates with Miller aboard, clawed its way into the air, and the gear was quickly retracted. The bomber, however, settled back onto the runway, the propellers grinding up the pavement and throwing up a rooster-tail of hot sparks; the onlooking pilots crouched and ducked, waiting for the fuel to ignite in a fiery explosion, but the Mitchell finally ground to a halt and those aboard scrambled out of the plane unscathed. Eventually, short minimum-speed takeoffs were accomplished by each pilot with fully loaded Mitchells: two thousand pounds of bombs, full fuel, complete crew of five, combat equipment, and full armament. Each pilot qualified, lifting off in distances of 500 to 600 feet with a wind of only 12 mph.[16]

While pilots were training for low-speed takeoffs, navigators were undergoing training in celestial navigation and the fine points of determining a plane's position over the ocean. Classes were first conducted on the ground, and flights out over the open water were made with several navigators equipped with bubble sextants aboard a single aircraft. Speed tests were run over measured courses to calibrate the airspeed indicators on each bomber, since the speed of the aircraft would be a major factor in any navigation computation. When the runs were being made, it was obvious that some aircraft at the same power settings were significantly faster than others; the discrepancy was traced to pitted and worn propellers, so plans were made to install new three-bladed propellers on each bomber. (This was done later, at Sacramento.) In some cases, this caused an increase in calibrated airspeed of more than 55 mph at identical power settings. Additionally, the magnetic compass of each bomber was swung, that is, recalibrated using a precise compass rose painted on the ramp at Eglin. Night navigation flights and navigation under instrument flight conditions were conducted by each crew, on a route from Eglin to Fort Myers to Houston and return. A second Mitchell was damaged on one of the navigation flights when a nose gear collapsed at Houston, leaving just twenty-two bombers to continue the program at Eglin.[17]

Bombardiers were training on low-level bombing runs, and the top-secret Norden bombsight was giving them fits. The B-25s were fast, and coming in low rendered the complicated instrument nearly worthless; it had been designed for high-altitude precision bombing. Its advocates said it could put a bomb in a pickle barrel from twenty thousand feet. But what was needed was a sight that could put a bomb in a factory from a thousand feet from a plane traveling at better than 250 mph.

Ross Greening, who had been an art major at Washington State College, was a bit of a Renaissance man. A gifted pilot as well as an artist, he was also a sometime engineer. He designed a very simple "Mark Twain" bombsight using two small pieces of aluminum. The bombardiers were able to line up a target through a set of open sights similar to those of a rifle; the sights were attached to a calibrated scale resembling a protractor. The device was predicated on simple physics: when a bomb was released from an airplane traveling at 250 mph (or any other speed), the bomb would continue going forward at that same speed for a certain distance before gravity overcame the forward momentum. Bombardiers practiced dropping their bombs at several speeds and varying altitudes, carefully noting the speed of the aircraft, the altitude, and the depression angle of the new bombsight. It proved to be highly accurate, and additional sights were fabricated at the sheet-metal shop at Eglin. Cost to the government: twenty cents apiece.[18]

Gunners and the Mitchell's machine guns were another matter. The B-25B was equipped with rotating turrets on the top and bottom of the fuselage, each with two .50-caliber machine guns to defend against attacks by enemy fighters. It also carried a single flexible .30-caliber machine gun in the nose for the bombardier. One problem was in the turrets: they were electrically operated, for both rotation and elevation of the guns, and they simply didn't work very well. Another problem was the vulnerability of the bomber to an attack from the rear. The B-model had no tail-mounted machine guns.

The issue of an attack from the six o'clock position, dead astern, was solved in a Greening minimalist way: he simply had two broomsticks painted black and mounted in the tail cone of each bomber; perhaps enemy fighter pilots would assume them to be lethal and avoid attacking from behind. All of the Mitchells were then so "armed." The issues with defensive firepower continued, however. The turret guns themselves jammed after a few seconds; the turrets refused to turn. An old-time armorer advised disassembling the guns and smoothing out the parts to remove metal burrs; that corrected most of the jamming problems. But the turrets continued to malfunction, and Greening proposed removing the bottom gun position to save weight; the space could be used for additional fuel. It was done, but all of the modifications had taken time, of which they had very little. Some gunners had been able to fire at small oil slicks on the ocean near Eglin. Slicks were dropped at half-mile intervals, and the pilots flew a weaving course, banking around them as if it were an obstacle course, with a slick on the right side and the next on the left. Gunners had to fire at the slicks from the top turrets while the planes were in a bank, but because of malfunctioning turrets many of the gunners would depart on the mission without ever firing their weapons in the air.[19] The focus of attention on ground-level targets might have given some of the Raiders a hint regarding their destination, but they did not discuss their theories.

The anemic .30-caliber nose gun never proved to be worth its weight. Nonetheless, some bipod mounts were fabricated so that the machine gun could be used on the ground as a defensive weapon. Bombardiers were cross-trained as nose gunners and the engineers as turret gunners.[20]

Flight engineers got a workout on managing fuel consumption, since fuel supply would be critical on the planned mission. No specifics had been given regarding targets, of course, but a minimum distance of nineteen hundred miles was set at the beginning of training. Issues of fuel capacity were still being overcome, but Doolittle had started working on that issue back in January. At his direction, engineers at Wright Field had designed a long-distance fuel system that called for the installation of several additional fuel tanks throughout the airplanes, including over the bomb bays and, now, in the space left by the removal of the bottom gun turrets. A contractor had been found in Minneapolis to fabricate the extra tanks. There were many problems associated with leaking from the tanks and the fuel lines and valves, and they would continue even during the mission, but the issue of additional range had been addressed.

Considerable differences in fuel consumption among the twenty-two remaining Mitchells were noted, so carburetor experts were sent for and the carburetors fine-tuned. In addition, North American Aviation, which manufactured the B-25s, devised a new cruise-control chart. It revealed that maximum range was obtained by using high manifold pressures and low rpm propeller settings. Greening reported that at sea level with a full load, manifold pressures of 30 inches and 1,500 rpm were used; as the load decreased (mainly through use of fuel), the rpm settings could be reduced to 1,275 and a calibrated airspeed of 165 maintained throughout the flight. While the crews were on the night navigation cross-country flights, careful figures had been kept, and fuel consumption of seventy-eight gallons per hour was noted at full loads, decreasing to sixty-five gallons per hour at reduced loads.[21]

For Cole, luck was to play an enormous role in determining his part in the upcoming mission. The airmen still didn't know exactly what it would be—smart money was on a carrier takeoff to some base in the Far East, possibly with a target en route. Even the leaders had not been told the destination. Hilger, York, Jones, and Greening had been briefed on some aspects of the plan in order to effectively convey the need for both thorough training and secrecy. But even they did not yet know the target.

Capt. Vernon Stintzi had been Cole's pilot throughout the training. Then one day, when Cole checked in at operations, York told him: "Stintzi's sick. You'll be flying with the old man today." It stumped the still naive Cole. Old man? Who was that? He didn't want to fly with an old man. Then Doolittle appeared in flying kit. "Ready?" he asked. Cole was to fly that day in the same cockpit with the man he had idolized since his childhood days in Dayton. He remembered the photo in his boyhood scrapbook of a younger Jimmy Doolittle in a leather helmet and goggles. And now he would be sharing flying duties with him. Cole was beyond pleased.[22]

As it turned out, some of his most important training was away from Eglin. In late March, Doolittle needed to fly to Washington. Cole and flight engineer Paul Leonard went along. The skies were overcast, and they flew on instruments the entire flight from Eglin to Bolling Field in Washington. After climbing to their assigned altitude, Doolittle turned to Cole. "Take it." Cole flew the complete distance to DC, and Doolittle took over the controls again only when it came time to descend through the overcast and land. When he had surrendered the controls to Doolittle, Cole became aware that Leonard was just behind him in the doorway of the cockpit. Leonard was a patient man, a master mechanic, and an experienced aircrewman. He grinned at Cole and gave him a thumbs-up gesture. Cole was pleased and a bit embarrassed.[23]

It is possible that this was the trip when Doolittle went to see Hap Arnold and make his case for leading the upcoming mission himself. To date, he had been responsible for planning and organizing the project, for choosing the aircraft and determining what modifications had to be made, for picking the leaders and overseeing the training of the crews, for coordinating the logistics with the Navy. Now, deprived of combat in World War I, he wanted to fly and lead the actual mission.

No, Arnold told him. You're too valuable to me here.

But a determined Doolittle launched into a carefully rehearsed spiel about being the only person who could bring the complicated plan to a successful conclusion. His years dealing with business leaders had conditioned him to overcome initial negativism and press on. Arnold was sympathetic; he, too, had missed combat in the War to End All Wars. Perhaps only to get rid of the insistent lieutenant colonel with the boxer's build, he feigned acquiescence, of a sort. Go see my chief of staff, Gen. Millard "Miff" F. Harmon Jr., he told Doolittle. If he says okay, I'll approve it. In his autobiography, Doolittle says he smelled a rat. When he closed the door to Arnold's office, he sprinted at top speed to Harmon's office and burst through the door. "Hap just told me I could lead the special mission if it's okay with you!" Harmon looked taken aback. "Well, if it's okay with Hap, I don't see how I could object." Doolittle thanked him and left, but heard the phone ringing as he closed the door. "But Hap, I just told him he could go!" he heard Harmon say. It was a classic case of asking Mom when Dad has said no.[24]

Stintzi was still ill with a troublesome stomach ulcer. Time for training was running very short, and they couldn't wait for his convalescence. Doolittle announced that he would be taking Stintzi's crew. By the most improbable of scenarios, Lt. Dick Cole would be flying beside one of the most famous aviators in American history, a man who had never flown a combat mission but would plan and lead the most daring raid in the annals of the Air Corps. In his autobiography, Doolittle said this of the crew he appropriated: "I hadn't known any of these men before, but I liked the way they worked together. Paul [Leonard] was one of the hardest-working, most dedicated mechanics I have ever been associated with; I was satisfied that they all knew their jobs."[25]

Beyond the horizon of the men training at Eglin, things were moving quickly to form up a carrier task force that would carry the Mitchells to within striking distance of Japan. A target date of 1 April was rapidly approaching, and it was time for the fliers of the 17th Bomb Group to begin flights toward the West Coast.

On 23 March, Doolittle assembled the crews. Twenty-two planes and crews would be going to McClellan Army Air Field, near Sacramento, California. The two Mitchells that had been damaged in training would not be making the trip. Cole, Potter, Braemer, and Leonard flew with Doolittle to Biggs Field, in El Paso, Texas, and then on to McClellan, where all the bombers received last-minute checks and adjustments, as well as new propellers. Weeks earlier, the *Hornet* had left Norfolk and sailed through the Panama Canal to Alameda Naval Air Station in San Francisco. There it would load the group's B-25s aboard, sail out with an escort of seven ships, and meet up with Admiral William F. "Bull" Halsey on his flagship, the carrier *Enterprise*, accompanied by an additional seven ships. The sixteen-vessel task force would sail northwest.

As each of the Mitchells landed at Alameda from McClellan, they were met by Doolittle and Ski York. Shouting up to the pilot, Doolittle asked if there were any problems at all, however minor, with their airplane. It was not an idle question. Pilots who reported anything amiss were told to taxi their plane to a parking area on a nearby ramp. Those airplanes would not be taken aboard the *Hornet*. However, all of the crews were to board. For security reasons, no one would be left behind.

Aircraft with no reported problems were directed to a spot by the wharf near the *Hornet*. There, one by one, they were picked up by an enormous crane and lifted to the flight deck of the carrier. Originally, Doolittle thought eighteen of the medium bombers would fit aboard the *Hornet*, but the carrier's skipper, Capt. Marc "Pete" Mitscher, advised him that only fifteen could be safely accommodated. The Mitchells were stored on the flight deck itself, taking up some of the runway portion of the carrier, and Doolittle caught wind that some of the aircrews were apprehensive about the shortened deck now available to them. He asked Mitscher if a sixteenth bomber could be loaded aboard, with plans to launch it when about a hundred miles out to sea to demonstrate to his fliers that there was still plenty of room. Mitscher agreed. Hank Miller, who had accompanied the group to Alameda, would be a passenger aboard that aircraft so that he could return to his duties at Pensacola. Dick Joyce and his crew were slated to fly the additional bomber, but would not participate in the actual mission.

The Army pilots and crews boarded the *Hornet*, mindful of Miller's instructions on naval etiquette. It seemed strange to Cole to salute the national ensign and then the officer of the deck at the top of the ramp. "Lieutenant Cole, reporting for duty." The Navy had some strange ways.

He wandered, a bit awestruck, over the gargantuan deck toward the cluster of B-25s that were the center of activity on the back of the ship. The oversize crane was lowering another one of the bombers toward a group of sailors who were motioning to the crane operator exactly where they wanted it placed. Other deckhands were securing Mitchells already loaded, tying them to rings in the deck by thick ropes. Cole looked at the deck that remained open for takeoffs. He knew, although no one had specifically confirmed it, that they would be taking off in the bombers from this flight deck. Despite the size of the carrier, the deck looked very, very short. He turned away to find his quarters.

On 1 April, he wrote a quick note on a postcard to his mother and put it in an envelope to mail. He was sending her some money—*"just call me J. P. Morgan"*—for her use or to put in the joint account. He hoped she liked the pin he sent: *"I wondered if they were in style or if they still wear them."* No news of what he had been doing, nor any hint of what was to come. But he did underline a request, something he rarely had done before: *"Would rather that you keep the place this is mailed from under your hat."*[26]

# CHAPTER 6

It was April Fool's Day, and Lt. Dick Cole was feeling every bit the fool. There was absolutely nothing intuitive, nothing remotely commonsensical, about a US Navy ship. He wanted to say "boat," but Hank Miller had cautioned against that. It was a ship or a vessel; boats were much smaller. And hallways were passageways, stairs were companionways, right was starboard, left was port, and the floor was a deck. Thank God he would soon be off this . . . this vessel.

As if a whole new lexicon was not enough, the *Hornet* itself was a maze, a rabbit warren as large as a city, a city stacked vertically, street over street, road over alley, track over sidewalk, cabins over more cabins over . . . well, who knew what? How were Army pilots ever supposed to find the dining hall, now renamed the mess deck, or the bathrooms, transmogrified into heads? Rooms were spaces; walls were bulkheads. It was enough to make all of the men of the Doolittle party want to grab some air on the main deck and rethink this whole deal.

If the strangeness of their new surroundings and the renaming of familiar things were not enough, there was also a definite sense that they were interlopers or carpetbaggers.

Cole, carrying his gear and wearing his brown leather jacket with the thunderbird patch on the front, had introduced himself to a couple of Navy ensigns, wearing the equivalent rank of his own gold bar of second lieutenant; they nodded and showed him to a line of cots set up along one side of a companionway. They were decidedly unimpressed with his rank, his wings, or his ability to fly a hot new bomber. Cole thanked them and stowed his gear under the cot, which adjoined that of

61

Lt. William G. Farrow, a classmate of 41-E who would fly plane number sixteen. Cole and the Army fliers were a pain to the Navy, that much was obvious. It was clear that the quicker they could discharge these land-lubbers and their ugly green bombers, the better for everyone. The companionways and cabins would become less crowded, the line in the mess hall would get shorter, and the flight deck could once more be used by the new F4Fs and TBDs that formed the offensive and defensive might of the huge carrier. As it stood, all of the *Hornet*'s own aircraft had to be stored below and would not be available if the carrier was attacked. No, the Navy couldn't get rid of these Army guys quickly enough. Wherever they were to be offloaded by a crane as large as that which had hoisted them aboard, they hoped it was close. Alaska seemed to be the destination on which smart money was laid; Hank Miller was aboard, and several of the junior officers knew he was born in Alaska. There could be no other explanation.[1]

That night Captain Mitscher ordered the *Hornet* to cast off from the wharf at Alameda and make for the middle of San Francisco Bay. It was foggy, and he didn't want to try to navigate the 19,800-ton carrier in the misty darkness with a young and untested crew.[2] Cole and the other Army guys—134 in all—didn't sleep well. There are noises aboard a ship not found at any air base: bells sounded with distressing frequency; there were strange clangings and rattles; rumblings and whirrings came from somewhere deep in the innards of the big vessel. Occasionally, voices, far distant and strangely muffled, could be heard. And in Cole's mind, despite the gargantuan size of the ship, it seemed to rock, endlessly. He thought he could hear the sound of water slapping against the hull but knew that was impossible as well. But for someone spending the night on a ship for the first time, the sounds and sensations were very real.

Cole arose the next morning, 2 April, and wondered about breakfast. He stopped a young sailor in the gray passageway and inquired about the eating arrangements. The young man, in a blue chambray shirt and dungarees, politely directed him, and Cole soon learned that Navy officers eat very well. He found a table and sat with several other Army fliers, all looking as ragged as Cole felt. They were tired and subdued; this sleeping aboard a boat—a ship—was for the birds, or the fish, maybe. Not for humans.

The *Hornet* weighed anchor and began making way shortly after ten, still in fog. The Army men stood on the deck as they glided under the Golden Gate Bridge, looking up at the underside of the famous span. For Ted Lawson, it was his second view, having flown under it on the way to Alameda in his Mitchell.[3] It was a slow, almost stately, exit from the Bay. It seemed strange to Cole to be headed out on a supersecret mission with sixteen Army bombers tied down to the deck of a carrier, in full view of hundreds of thousands of San Franciscans. Or Japanese spies, perhaps. But a story had been planted that the bombers were bound for Hawaii and would be flown off the deck to save valuable time. Cole hoped people would believe that.

Captain Mitscher, well aware of the target for the mission, was beyond gracious in his treatment of Doolittle and the Army fliers. He turned over his own cabin—a suite, really—to Doolittle and moved into a small room off the bridge. The captain's suite contained a large conference room, which Mitscher said he knew would be necessary for private meetings.

On the second day out, a Navy dirigible appeared over the *Hornet* to deliver glass observation domes for the Army navigators. The blisters had arrived too late to install on the bombers before the *Hornet* left Alameda. Cole looked up at the huge floating airship, large as a football field, and gave thanks that he flew the speedy Mitchell. The dirigible looked ripe for accidents; it was a target that no one could miss if they shot at it.

Shortly after the dirigible left, slowly making its way back to Alameda, Captain Mitscher was on the public address system: "Now hear this. Now hear this. This force is bound for Tokyo." The same message was sent by semaphore to the other ships in the task force. The effect was electric. Sailors and airmen alike cheered, some jumping up and down, others slapping each other on the back. Every Navy man aboard, it seemed to Cole, wanted to shake his hand.[4]

That afternoon Doolittle called the Army lads together in the otherwise empty officers' dining hall. There he laid out the plans for the upcoming strike against Japan.

Japan! At last, the reason for the weeks of training, of low-level flying, of short-field, minimum-speed takeoffs, the modifications to their bombers came clearly into focus. Now the obsession with secrecy, the absolute need to push themselves past what they had previously believed were their limits, made sense. Some of the fliers looked a bit smug, telling those closest to them that they had figured it out long ago. A few seemed surprised. None appeared very disturbed. Cole took it all in stride; whatever the target, he would be sitting beside one of the best pilots in the world. It was a good feeling.[5]

Doolittle revealed to the assembled fliers that he, Cole, and his crew-mates would be going in the first bomber off the *Hornet* on or about 19 April. They would launch about four hundred miles east of Japan and fly just above the waves to avoid detection, arriving over Tokyo at dusk. They would fly to their targets in the munitions manufacturing section of the city and drop incendiary bombs, bombs that would start large fires. Flames from the resulting conflagration would serve as a beacon for the remaining bombers, who would take off about three hours after the Doolittle Mitchell, arriving well after sunset. It was hoped that even with Japanese forces on high alert after the solo attack by Doolittle's crew, darkness would aid the Mitchells in avoiding interception by enemy fighters as well as making them difficult targets for antiaircraft guns. More details would be forthcoming.

Other cities to be visited by the Doolittle Raiders—soon, that was their unofficial name to almost everyone—were Yokohama, Osaka, Kobe, and Nagoya. Specific targets would be discussed in the next few days, and to the extent possible individual crews would be free to select their chosen target from the list. The plan called for five flights of three aircraft, with flight leaders already assigned. After bombing their targets, each crew would make its way individually to Chungking, China, where preparations had been made to refuel the bombers; radio homing beacons to guide them in had been delivered to several airfields. Briefings would be held each day they were on the *Hornet*, and information classes would be held on Japanese and Chinese customs, first aid, and other pertinent topics. For now, crews would be responsible for thoroughly inspecting their planes and reporting anything that would enhance the probability of success in the mission.[6]

Once more, Doolittle emphasized that anyone could drop out, no questions asked. No one did. Crewmen from those bombers left back at Alameda offered to swap places with anyone now slated for the mission, but there were no takers.

With Mitscher's announcement, the Army fliers had been suddenly transformed from carpetbaggers to honored guests. The atmosphere, which Greening described as "slightly strained and defensive," now changed completely.[7] Everyone wanted to be their friend.

As the Doolittle crews inspected their bombers, curious and friendly Navy fliers and flight-deck sailors crowded around, eager to see the fliers as well as the Mitchells, full of questions. Tours of the carrier were arranged, and the crew of the hangar deck showed off their own aircraft, planes that could not be brought up to the flight deck because of the

B-25s all tied down there. Cole would later remember the friendly interest of a group of young pilots who flew the TBD Devastator; they were
the flight crews of VT-8, or Torpedo Squadron 8. In just a few months,
at the Battle of Midway, all of them except one—Ens. George H. Gay
Jr.—would be killed in attacks on the Japanese fleet.

As a demonstration to the Army fliers that their Mitchells could actually take off from the carrier, it had been planned that Lt. Dick Joyce
would fly the sixteenth bomber off when they were one hundred miles
out to sea, with Lt. Hank Miller of the Navy riding along, so he could
report back to Pensacola. He had no official orders to be aboard the
*Hornet* and could technically be considered AWOL (absent without
leave). That morning, the winds were calm, and the flight deck seemed
foreshortened with all of the Mitchells tied down on the aft portion.
Doolittle asked Captain Mitscher if it would be feasible to continue with
sixteen bombers instead of fifteen. Mitscher agreed and told a worried
Miller that he would face no discipline for being aboard all the way to
the launch and return to Pearl. Miller was ecstatic; after training the
crews, it seemed a shame for him not to see the result as they lifted off
the carrier.

Each morning and each evening for the next two weeks, the *Hornet*'s
captain sounded battle stations for all hands. Cole and the other Army
fliers ran to their tethered bombers, carefully noting the time it had tak-
en to get to their plane. They were slowly getting used to the ship and
now with experience and a bit of time could find their way to the flight
deck from almost any place they were likely to be on the carrier. When
Mitscher learned that the Army gunners had had little time to practice
while at Eglin, an auxiliary power unit was hooked up to the turrets of
the bombers, and the gunners fired at kites and balloons. Some of the
electric motors powering the turrets on the Mitchells were faulty and
were repaired in the shops of the *Hornet*. Navigators were given additional instruction by the ship's navigators, and the meteorologists and
forecasters worked closely with them as well.[8]

The task force continued to plow through the Pacific, a vast expanse
of gray-green water unbroken to the horizon save for the eight ships
of the Mitscher group. On 9 April, the *Hornet* received a message that
the expected rendezvous with Halsey's task force steaming out of Pearl
Harbor would be delayed by one day. The Mitscher group reversed
course for a short time and reduced speed; it was a complicated task to
turn eight warships around, but the Navy did it efficiently and briskly.

Unseen to Cole and those in the Mitscher fleet were the Halsey ships on a zigzag course to meet them, as well as the submarines *Trout* and *Thresher*, which were cruising in the area of the expected rendezvous to warn of any Japanese surface vessels in the region. On 13 April, the two groups met, with Halsey's carrier, the *Enterprise*, becoming the flagship of the task force. It was comforting to know that the fleet now had air cover, as aircraft from the *Enterprise* set up a continuous air patrol.

The weather began to turn sour. Two tankers had accompanied the fleet of warships and on 16 April refueling of the various ships was tried, but the winds had increased to gale force and the heavy seas made the procedure impossible. The next day, despite the weather, the *Hornet* was refueled in a howling gale, with waves breaking over the deck. A crewman aboard the tanker *Cimarron* was washed overboard but was recovered by a destroyer a short time later.

Belowdecks in the *Hornet*, the Army pilots were all slightly green. Despite the enormous size of the carrier, it rose and fell with a distressing rhythm, the bow of the ship seeming to slam into the ocean at the bottom of each downward motion, and on deck the B-25s were lashed with spray while they strained at the ropes securing them to the deck. The Army fliers worried about saltwater corroding parts of their airplanes or the restraining ropes breaking and the bombers being swept over the side.

For the past week, pilots and bombardiers had studied photographs of the various cities that had been targeted, becoming familiar with identifying landmarks that would mark the position of the target bull's-eyes. Doolittle was adamant: no civilian targets; only those targets that had direct military value were to be bombed. He explained his rationale, and it was not high-mindedness. When the Germans had bombed civilians in London, he was there, he told the fliers, and had seen the resolve of the British harden, morale soar, and the will to continue the fight climb despite high casualties. He did not want that to happen here. Likewise, the emperor's palace, a symbol for the nation, was to be left untouched for the same reasons. Do not give the Japanese a cause for rallying behind the war, he said, as the British had done when Buckingham Palace had been damaged.[9]

The bad weather continued. It was nearing launch day, still scheduled for the nineteenth, when Cole was scheduled to sit beside Doolittle in the first takeoff in the early evening. After refueling on the seventeenth, the *Hornet* and the *Enterprise*, along with four cruisers, kicked up their speed and left the destroyers and tenders in a dash westward toward the home islands of Japan. Winds continued to blow at 36 knots, with waves breaking over the bows of the fast-moving ships in great white plumes that soaked everyone who had to be on deck at the time.

Below, in the officers' dining hall, Doolittle called all of the crews together for a final briefing. It was short and to the point. The men were ready; the planes were ready; everyone knew their job, having already been thoroughly questioned by Doolittle, who had also personally inspected each of the aircraft. Once more, the diminutive former racing pilot with the boxer's build stressed that no one was to strike the Temple of Heaven, the emperor's palace, and no one was to attempt to land in Vladivostok, since the Russians had a nonaggression pact with the Japanese. The Russkies didn't want to fight a two-front war if they could help it, and who could blame them? This would be the final briefing, he said, and once more he made the offer for anyone to ask to be replaced. No one spoke. Finally, one of the fliers asked him what he recommended if they were hit over Japan and had to bail out.

It was deathly quiet. Doolittle looked around at the young faces of the men he was taking on one of the most dangerous missions of the war, a mission that surely was going to result in the death, injury, or capture of many of them. They waited for him to speak.

If his plane was badly hit over Japan and unable to make it to China, he intended to order his crew to bail out, Doolittle said, and paused. The men looked at each other, waiting for the other shoe to drop. Then, he said, he intended to find the best military target available and dive the plane into it. He would not become a prisoner of the Japanese. But he cautioned everyone that each man must make his own decision, and he did not expect others to follow his example.[10]

What none of them knew was that the week previously, the beleaguered American and Filipino troops on the Bataan peninsula of Luzon in the Philippines had surrendered. While the Doolittle team was at sea, the Japanese started a forced march of the prisoners of war that lasted five days. Thousands of prisoners died on the march, to become known as the Bataan Death March; they were beaten and starved, and if they fell along the road they were bayonetted or shot. It was a prelude for the treatment of Allied prisoners for the remainder of the war.

On the afternoon of the seventeenth, Mitscher and Doolittle called the men together for a "ceremony." Frank Knox, secretary of the Navy, had forwarded to Mitscher three Japanese medals that had been sent to him by three former sailors. The men had been crewmen on American warships that had visited Japan in 1908; the medals, presented by the Japanese at the time, commemorated the event. The medal ribbons were red, white, and blue, and the pendant featured the flags of the United States and Japan and a green-leafed tree superimposed on an anchor. After the attack on Pearl Harbor, the former sailors asked Knox to return them in an appropriate manner. Now, Doolittle and Mitscher were going to wire the medals to the fins of the bombs that would be dropped by the crews of the B-25s. When Lt. Stephen Jurika of the Navy learned of the planned return of the medals, he too contributed a Japanese medal he had been awarded while stationed as a liaison officer in Tokyo before the war. A photographer captured the scene, as the Army fliers surrounded Doolittle and Mitscher on the deck of the *Hornet* and the two senior officers affixed the rescinded and spurned medals to a five-hundred-pound bomb. Airmen and sailors alike chalked colorful messages to the emperor on the bombs before the ordnance was loaded aboard the B-25s.

Because they were drawing so close to the point where they might encounter Japanese ships or aircraft, the bombers were relocated to allow maximum distance on the flight deck for takeoffs. The Doolittle bomber, tail number 2344, was stationed first, and Cole overheard Doolittle ask a flight-deck officer the exact distance to the bow from his nosewheel: 467 feet, he was told. The bomber scheduled for the last takeoff, number sixteen, was secured to the deck with its tail hanging over the stern. In addition, two white lines had been painted from the point of takeoff position to the bow, one line for the left main gear, the other for the nosewheel. Keeping both wheels on the lines would mean 6 feet of clearance between the right wingtip and the island—the nerve center including the bridge—of the carrier.[11]

That evening Cole and the others were subdued, many of them writing letters home to be mailed by those not going on the raid when the ships returned to Pearl Harbor. Tomorrow and the next day promised to be long and filled with both eagerness and anxiety as the crews anticipated the takeoff. Apprehension would have been totally understandable, but Cole was sanguine. He had confidence in his crew, and especially in Doolittle. In the end, he was convinced, the raid would go well. Every hour that passed put them closer to Japan.[12]

That night the usual Army-Navy poker game ensued—Mitscher had always turned a blind eye to it—with the Army losing more money to the Navy.[13] Cole, who was not a poker player, went to bed early. He had his flying kit nearby, with his personal gear for the mission: a .45 automatic pistol, a hunting knife, compasses, a canteen, and a first-aid kit.

In addition, he had stuffed a few candy bars in the pockets of his wool flight overalls. He stowed the gear, along with his additional clothing, in his B-4 bag under his cot. In all, it was not much of a survival kit, but each man would also be wearing a Mae West–style life jacket, and a life raft was stowed aboard each bomber as well. No one expected, in any envisioned scenario, that the fliers would need provisions and gear for an extended stay in extreme conditions.[14]

Cole and the other seventy-nine fliers about to depart on the first bombing mission of the Japanese islands might not have been so complacent about their gear had they known of the miscues and antagonism swirling around the project. Lt. Gen. Joseph T. McNarney, deputy chief of staff under George C. Marshall, sent a memo to President Roosevelt on 16 April, advising him that somewhere along the line, Generalissimo Chiang Kai-shek had not been informed of the coming raid prior to 11 April. Gen. Joseph Stilwell had been informed of the strike by Gen. Hap Arnold himself, and it was assumed that Stilwell would pass along the details in person. On 16 April, Clayton Bissell, chief aviation officer for Stilwell, advised that the generalissimo objected to the China portion of the plans. Chiang said that Chuchow, the city at which the Raiders were to land, was not protected by his forces, and he feared loss of the field to the Japanese, as well as retaliation against Chinese civilians. McNarney wrote the president that Bissell had been informed that the plans for the Doolittle Raid were too advanced to cancel and that a second strike, the HALPRO mission, would be under Stilwell's control and would be coordinated with Chiang's desires.

That didn't solve the problem, apparently. Chiang again voiced his opposition to the Doolittle Raid, and a message was sent to Stilwell, directing him to stress the importance of the mission to Chiang and to China and to smooth the ruffled feathers of the generalissimo by stressing that he was not intentionally left out of the planning process but that miscommunications had occurred because of the need for "guarded language for fear of disclosure."[15]

That night, while nearly everyone slept except those on watch, several events occurred that changed the carefully laid plans of Doolittle and company.

The American warships continued through the black water under a low cloud ceiling of one thousand feet; the cloud layer obscured the stars, eliminating them as a source of navigation, but the Navy kept its electronic ears keenly tuned to the airwaves and its eyes constantly on the multiple screens of their radar sets. At 0312, or 3:12 a.m., on 18 April, a radarman aboard the *Enterprise* notified his leader that two unidentified but presumed enemy vessels had been detected at 21,000 yards off the port bow, and a few minutes later a member of the watch spotted a light in the same area. The Navy had been monitoring Japanese radio since the task force departed, and they learned early on that the enemy knew a task force was somewhere in the area; picket boats had been stationed in a semicircle about 650 miles out from the home islands. Presumably, the two unidentified targets were picket boats. No action was initiated; instead, the task force altered course to 350 degrees to avoid contact. General quarters was sounded aboard the *Hornet*; the Army flight crews dressed and waited by their planes. At 3:41 a.m., both contacts left the area of radar coverage, apparently without knowledge of the task force. The all clear was sounded, and most of the Navy crew and the Army fliers aboard the *Hornet* went back to their quarters to attempt to rest.[16] Shortly after 4:00 a.m., the task force turned west once again.

About 5:00 a.m., the *Enterprise* launched a dawn patrol. The closer they drew to Japan, the more important vigilance became, so eight F4F fighters and three SBD Dauntless dive-bombers were sent out to search an area up to 200 miles in front of the American ships. The weather continued to worsen, with winds about 35 knots and seas of 30 feet. It was a miserable time to be on watch or aloft in a cockpit, but each man had his duty and did it without complaint. They were all on a keen knife-edge of anticipation, eager to be a part of the first strike back against Japan.

Just before 6:00 a.m., an SBD pilot spotted one of the picket boats, 42 miles away. He jotted down its position and dropped a note in a sandbagged container to the deck of the *Enterprise*. Halsey ordered the *Big E* to turn left to 220 degrees; the question was on everyone's mind: had the patrol plane or the task force been seen?

The question became moot when at 7:38 another picket boat was spotted by a sailor on lookout aboard the *Hornet*; the boat was just 20,000 yards away, and now it was daylight. The *Hornet's* radioman reported that the picket had sent a message about the time it was sighted; at 7:45 a Navy ensign sighted another boat just 12,000 yards away. Halsey ordered the *Nashville*, a Brooklyn-class light cruiser, to sink the Japanese vessel. It opened up with its six-inch guns, and the boat was destroyed.

At 8:00 a.m., Cole was dressed and on his way to breakfast. Over the loudspeakers, which were situated everywhere, it seemed, came the order: "Army pilots, man your planes! Army pilots, man your planes!" Cole returned to his cot and reached under it for his B-4 bag containing all of his gear, before running to the flight deck. There he met Paul Leonard as both reached their plane at the same time. They removed the canvas covers from the engines and pulled the props through several rotations, a procedure that delivered oil to the cylinders at the top of the round engine. Braemer and Potter soon arrived with their own gear, and the four men entered the Mitchell to complete their separate preflight checks before Doolittle arrived.

All around, men were preflighting the other bombers, orders were shouted over the din, Navy men were running to posts around the flight deck, while all the time waves crashed over the bow and the wind howled under a lowering sky. The entire world, it seemed, was gray, except for the olive green of the sixteen B-25s now being prepared to take off. Cans of gasoline were handed up to the crewmen in back, where they would be stowed and used to fill the first extra tank installed. Orders had been given to hold onto the cans until all were empty, and then the gunner was to cut large holes in each and drop them together. They were not to be discarded immediately when emptied; that would leave a trail back to the task force.

Cole sat in the right seat of the cockpit of plane number one, going over the checklist one more time. He saw Doolittle running toward him, holding onto his hat, the wind plucking at his flight jacket. In less than a minute, Doolittle had settled into the left seat. He looked at Cole, who nodded and gave him a small smile. All set.[17]

# CHAPTER 7

Doolittle had gone to the bridge when the excitement started and was conferring with Mitscher when the word came from Adm. Halsey: LAUNCH PLANES X TO COL DOOLITTLE AND GALLANT COMMAND GOOD LUCK AND GOD BLESS YOU.[1]

As Doolittle left the bridge for his bomber, Mitscher ordered the carrier to turn into the wind, at 320 degrees, and increase speed to 20 knots. The wind was nearly steady at 30 knots, and the crests of the waves were crashing over the bow of the steaming carrier.

The bomber was positioned for takeoff, chocks placed in front of the wheels. Together, Cole and Doolittle went through the complicated procedure for starting the engines, and now the vibrations from the combined twenty-eight cylinders of the two Wright R-2600s could be felt through the airframes and the seats of every crewman, a tingling, primal force that could be felt in the spine of each flier. Cole focused on his job in the cockpit, reverting to his training and all of the drills that had prepared them all for this moment. He felt a controlled excitement that was not on a level with the magnitude of what he was about to do.

The engine oil pressure came up to green; the altimeter was set to zero, and the other instruments all checked. The flaps were lowered. Cole was 100 percent sure that this bomber would fly.

Cole looked out the side window and saw hundreds of sailors everywhere. None, it seemed, wanted to miss this historic event, despite the waves washing across the deck and the slippery surfaces everywhere. Some of them waved; others flashed V for Victory signs. He saw several stand to attention and salute. He touched a finger to his forehead in response, then looked back at Doolittle.

The raid commander was watching the Navy signal officer, Lt. Edgar G. Osborne, who stood on the left side, holding the checkered flag. Crew members all reported by written note that they were ready. There would be no radio check-ins, an effort to prevent any accidental radio transmissions that would betray the mission to the Japanese. The transmitter, which would also allow intercom communication, would be reconnected when they were well past their targets.

Doolittle gave Lieutenant Osborne a thumbs-up. Cole looked ahead; over the glass nose of the Mitchell, the *Hornet*'s flight deck seemed suddenly very short. It had been one thing to take off in the Mitchell with full flaps in a nose-high position and stagger into the air while over the solid terra firma of Eglin Field. It was entirely something else now, with the deck clearly rising and falling as the thirty-foot waves thundered over the bow. While the bow was in the trough of a wave, the horizon could be seen as a blurry dividing line between the darker gray of the ocean and the lighter gray of the sky. When the bow rose, the horizon disappeared below the end of the deck. But at no time did Cole doubt they would make the takeoff.[2] He was, after all, sitting beside one of the most experienced pilots in the world.

The engines were revving up now, the noise rising to a scream while the vibrations continued to be felt in every rivet of the straining bomber and through the spines of each crewman. The signal officer began to turn his flag in circles, increasing in speed, the flag whirling ever faster as Osborne watched the bow of the *Hornet*. He wanted to time the takeoff so that when the bomber reached the end of the flight deck, the bow would be at its highest above the water. The rising ship would help point the heavily loaded Mitchell into the air, the air that was so much thinner than the deck now supporting it.

Hank Miller was on the right side, as planned, with a blackboard on which he would write any information needed by the crews at the last minute. On the left, Osborne motioned for the chocks to be pulled from in front of the wheels, and at the moment that the bow began to rise, he slashed the air with his flag. Go!

Slowly, far too slowly for Cole, the Mitchell began to roll. It picked up speed, but still seemed too turtle-like to become airborne. Cole remembered a time as a boy that he had tried to run through waist-deep water; the feeling now was much the same. Doolittle kept the nosewheel exactly on the right white line; he pulled the nose up as they passed the ship's island. The right wing had plenty of room, which was good, since in the nose-high position they could no longer see anything in front of them. Cole had his hand near the gear lever and kept his eye on Doolittle.

The speed increased. Cole realized that they were no longer on the ship; the bomber was struggling into the air twenty to thirty feet before the end of the deck. The Mitchell was clinging tenuously to flight on the very edge of a stall. Doolittle pushed the nose forward slightly to reduce the steep angle and moved the trim control to lower the nose. In a few seconds, with the plane now in a more comfortable attitude, he jerked his right thumb up and Cole retracted the gear. They wouldn't need it regardless of what happened next, and reducing the drag induced by the hanging wheels and tires might be the margin they needed to continue in the air. Doolittle himself slowly raised the flaps as the bomber gained speed, further reducing the drag.

It was 0820, 8:20 a.m., on 18 April 1942. The first bomber had taken off from a Navy carrier to conduct a bombing mission on Tokyo, just four months and eleven days after the Japanese surprise attack on Pearl Harbor. In the end, they had been overly concerned about the length of the carrier's deck. All the bombers were airborne well before the deck ended; the carrier's speed combined with the wind meant they needed only about 20 to 30 mph of additional speed to be airborne.

Doolittle kept the plane level for a distance to gain more airspeed, then climbed and circled to the left to fly directly down the length of the deck of the *Hornet* to enable navigator Hank Potter to check his drift sight and compare the bomber's magnetic compass with the magnetic heading of the carrier. Two one zero. Two hundred ten degrees to Tokyo.

Cole looked down on the mighty carrier and saw the other Mitchells being prepared to take off. Sailors waved up at the historic first plane off. It was a lonely feeling; they were isolated, traveling through the sky in a small winged box, five men shut off from the rest of the world. "We have just separated ourselves from civilization," he thought. Now, whatever happened, they would have no communication with the ship, or with other aircraft, or with anyone on the ground. But Cole was a master of self-reliance. To shake off any doubts about the outcome of the raid and to put himself in a good frame of mind, he made a conscious effort to focus on the positive side of that coin: "What ever happens to us will be up to Mother Nature, the Good Lord, and any ingenuity that we need to develop as the thing progresses." Years later, he said his thinking was a kind of "self therapy."[3]

The discovery of the task force by the picket boats, and confirmation that a message was sent by one of them to Tokyo, changed the plans for the mission. Now, all of the planes would launch and proceed to their assigned targets, arriving in daylight and probably to an enemy already waiting to blast them from the sky. The early launch had another major downside: they were much farther from Tokyo than planned, 620 miles instead of 400, and fuel, even with the long-range tanks installed, would become a critical factor.

Now listen to the jingle, and the rumble and the roar,
As she dashes through the woodland, and speeds along the shore,
See the mighty rushing engine, hear her merry bell ring out.

The words and music of "The Wabash Cannonball" had been branded into his brain, and Cole could not banish the sound of Roy Acuff's vocals. Since the first week at Eglin, Ted Lawson's record player had blasted the tune nearly nonstop, and now it played on in the ears of Cole's mind. He began tapping his foot, gently at first, then with more animation. His hands began to keep time on the sides of his legs, and soon his entire body was moving to the rhythm of the classic American folk song.

Doolittle turned his head and looked at him as only a lieutenant colonel can look at a second lieutenant. Sheepishly, Cole came back to the presence of the cockpit and left the world of dance music and folk ballads behind.[4]

They were now flying about two hundred feet over the water on economy cruise, keeping the manifold pressure high and the propeller rpm low. Everywhere around them was the gray-green water, with only a thousand feet between the waves and the bottom of the dark-gray clouds. The ceiling was not relevant, though, since the mission had always called for a low-level flight in to avoid enemy radar. Hank Potter was having navigation woes caused by the initially much lower altitude they had been flying. The sight on the drift meter had become blurred with saltwater spray, and he could only estimate the effect of the wind on their course.[5]

Back at the *Hornet*, unseen by the Doolittle crew, the rest of the Raiders had gotten off, but not without mishaps and some tense moments as they initially replicated the takeoffs they had practiced at Eglin Field. Lt. Travis Hoover, piloting the second plane off, duplicated Doolittle's extreme nose-high takeoff attitude and came perilously close to stalling, which would have meant disaster; the aircraft would have come down in the water just in front of the fast-steaming *Hornet*. The big ship would have no way to stop or avoid running over the bomber. Shortly after, Hank Miller wrote on a blackboard for all the pilots to read: "Stabilizer in Neutral." That seemed to help, as the following aircraft held a less extreme attitude.

There were other issues. Ted Lawson, number seven, had retracted his flaps during a pretakeoff check and forgot to lower them before his launch. Without the extra lift produced by the flaps, his plane dipped off the end of the carrier and came within feet of the waves. The plane picked up speed, and he was able to continue without mishap. Lt. Don Smith—the winner at Eglin of the short-field takeoff competition— rammed the tail cone of the bomber ahead of him in the queue and cracked his nose glass. It was deemed flyable, so he took off, his bombardier keeping a close eye on the damaged glass. The most serious incident involved the last plane to take off, that of Lt. Bill Farrow, a 41-E alum who had bunked next to Cole in the companionway throughout the trip. His bomber had been the last in the line, with its tail jutting over the stern. As several Navy handlers pulled his plane forward to complete loading the rear section with fuel cans, a blast from the propellers of the bomber just ahead caused one of the sailors to lose his footing on the slippery deck. He was blown into the whirling propeller of Farrow's Mitchell and suffered a severe gash to his arm. It had to be amputated. For Farrow's crew, it could be seen as an omen for what lay ahead.[6]

About thirty minutes after taking off, Cole looked out to see Hoover's plane flying a mile or so to their right. They would fly together all the way to the coast of Japan.

Doolittle signaled for Cole to take the controls, and for the rest of the mission they alternated the task of guiding the bomber through the air. Potter occasionally passed a written note regarding a slight course correction, and everyone not consumed by other duties continually checked the fuel gauges. The aviation gas was their lifeblood; when it was gone, the flight was over. Inside the bomber, it was quiet except for the roar of the Cyclone engines. To protect their ears, they all had donned their radio headsets, despite knowing the transmitter was not connected. Theirs was now a private world, with very few words spoken. Each man was lost in his own thoughts. Cole occasionally prayed silently; doubtless, the others were doing the same. But fear didn't make an appearance, not even by way of a nagging doubt. It would end well for them, Cole was confident, but he couldn't envision just how it would end. There were too many variables.[7]

Had he known all that had gone wrong on the receiving end of the mission in China, he might well have been worried. Eight thousand gallons of fuel for the Raiders had been delivered over the Himalayas a couple of weeks before, with Col. (later Brig. Gen.) William Donald Old of the Ferrying Command out of India flying the first load in a C-47. It was the first flight of a nascent project that would become known as the Hump airlift. The plan had called for homing beacons to be delivered to a series of airfields—Kweilin, Chuchow, Kian, Yushan, and Lishui—but the plane carrying them had crashed, killing all aboard. Halsey was to have sent a message when the planes launched to alert the Chinese of the approach of the B-25s. They were to light the fields so the bombers could locate the landing areas. But inexplicably—perhaps he was concerned with maintaining radio silence in the face of the Japanese picket boats and the certainty that they had been sighted—the message was never sent.

So the bombers, spread out more than an hour in the gray Pacific sky, continued on their individual courses to Japan. Cole could see Hoover's plane holding position, now a half mile off the right wing. He scanned the sky ahead, going slowly from right to left and back again, starting at the top of the windscreen and continuing down to the horizon. In the nose, Braemer had the best view below and was looking for surface ships. He sent up a note: a camouflaged ship, Japanese, possibly a light cruiser. There was no indication the ship had seen them, and they did not attack. However, Hoover later reported seeing white puffs coming from the cruiser and believed it was shooting at Doolittle's plane.[8] About two hours later, Cole spotted a twin-engine plane flying overhead about three thousand feet in the direction they had come. He pointed it out to Doolittle, who nodded. They watched it until it disappeared behind them, apparently without seeing either of the olive-green bombers below it.

Cole checked the clock on the instrument panel: just past eleven. Still about an hour to go. He thought about his parents. With the time difference, it was the middle of the night in Dayton. He tried to figure the exact time, but his mind was too distracted. In any event, he knew, they would be asleep. What would they say if they knew their boy was in a bomber over the Pacific, sitting beside Jimmy Doolittle, getting ready to bomb Tokyo? His mother, he knew, would be afraid for him. His father would be stoic, but Cole knew he would be proud. Maybe one day he could tell them all the details. What would those details be? They would have to play themselves out before he could tell them. And he would have to survive.

The bomber droned on over the water; a flat horizon encircled them. A cloud layer that was the same color as the sea continued to block the sun. Cole shifted in his seat. He always kidded that he was a member of the NBAA club—"No buns at all"—and sitting for long periods was uncomfortable. He was the only member of the crew who had opted for a seat-pack parachute; the pack served as additional padding in the steel bucket seat of the Mitchell, but after three or four hours he was ready to get up and walk around. It wasn't possible, he knew.[9]

In back, Paul Leonard was scanning the skies in the top turret when he was not switching valves to use the fuel in the long-range tanks. He had long ago added the additional twenty-five gallons that had been stored in back and had punctured the metal cans with his hunting knife, tied them together, and thrown them through the rear hatch when they were well away from the task force. He would be glad when the bladder in the crawl space over the bomb bay was depleted. It was lonely in the back of the Mitchell, with no way to go forward to see the rest of the crew.

Just ahead now, the horizon was slightly different. A hint, no more, of something that was not sea.

After four hours of flying low over the water, they crossed over the coast a bit north of their anticipated landfall, about eighty miles north of Tokyo, on the Chiba peninsula. Cole was surprised at the sudden blaze of color after so much gray. Below, the land was green, bright green in the newness of spring, a patchwork quilt of varying shades of verdure—mint and apple and pine and avocado and teal—a dizzying palette of viridescence. It was the color of life, of peace . . . of irony. Small fields were laid out in perfect harmony, and to Cole it seemed more like a movie set than an enemy landscape. Doolittle descended to just above the treetops, and Cole could clearly see the faces of Japanese as they waved gaily to the American intruders. It puzzled him; later, he learned that an air-raid drill was scheduled for the day, and they had been mistaken for Japanese aircraft. But he had little time to contemplate the greeting of their arrival. His primary task now was to keep a sharp eye open for enemy aircraft and antiaircraft batteries on the ground.[10]

Doolittle decided to turn due south and approach Tokyo from a direction they might not be expecting. If the message had gone out from the picket boat and antiaircraft batteries were awaiting them, they would be looking to the east. The intercom was now connected; Cole kept a careful eye for aircraft, which he reported to Leonard in the top turret. The sky seemed to be filled with planes; Cole counted eighty at one point. But strangely, none seemed especially interested in the twin-tailed Mitchell. Cole noted that many of the Japanese aircraft were biplanes, probably trainers, and would not be armed. At ten miles north of Tokyo, he saw nine fighters, in flights of three, but still they did not pursue the American bomber.

Ahead, they could see the dark blotch that was Tokyo, the straight lines of streets and buildings and the somber color in marked contrast to the irregular shapes and the greens of the countryside. Cole was stunned at its size: as they approached, the city was spread out for what seemed like miles, wrapped around the bay that was now clearly visible. Doolittle used that as a reference to turn right. The weather had improved, though the air was still a bit hazy. Cole could see the imperial palace and downtown Tokyo. He looked to his right and saw that Hoover was about five miles away; he watched as the Mitchell turned toward its target, an electrical plant. He could see the four five-hundred-pound bombs tumble from the bay and saw the explosions as they hit, throwing debris high into the air. Their own target was a bombardier's dream—all of northwest Tokyo—and now Doolittle climbed to fifteen hundred feet in a sudden move that pressed Cole into his seat. Braemer opened the bomb-bay doors. It was 12:15 local time, just shy of four hours since launching from the *Hornet*.[11]

The Japanese at last knew that they were being attacked, and antiaircraft guns began an intense but mostly inaccurate fire at the Mitchell. Northwest Tokyo, with its highly combustible buildings, was just ahead; their speed was 250 mph. There was a slight lift as the incendiary bombs fell from their shackles, and Braemer announced, "Bombs away!" His voice over the intercom was flat and metallic, lacking any indication of excitement. "Bomb-bay doors closing." As large as their target was, they could not endorse the accuracy of Greening's twenty-cent Mark Twain bombsight. Sighting down a broomstick would have been equally effective.

Because Doolittle's plane was supposed to have been the Lamplighter, as Cole called it, they were armed with "banana crates," boxes of small incendiary phosphorous bombs that were intended to start fires; the bombs themselves would burn even in water. The resulting conflagration in the industrial section of the city believed to house many munitions factories would serve as a fiery beacon for the remaining crews that were originally scheduled to arrive over Tokyo and other targets after sunset. They all would then arrive over airfields in China in the morning light.[12]

Dark evil bursts of ack-ack were appearing all around now, as the Japanese gunners tried desperately to knock the Mitchell from the sky. Only one burst was close; it shook the airplane and punched some holes in the tail, but didn't do any serious damage. Doolittle dove the bomber to just above the rooftops and headed west into haze and smoke that gave them some cover.

It was all over in minutes. Later, Ted Lawson would say it was thirty seconds. But for Cole, it had seemed unreal, much more like their practice drills than actual combat over the enemy's capital. And where were the fighters, the iron wall of antiaircraft fire? Why had they been able to slip in, with people waving to them? Was the thought that Americans could bomb the home islands just too fantastic to consider?

The Mitchell flew on alone. Hoover and the others were somewhere— all safe, Cole prayed—but were now entirely on their own. After a short time, Doolittle turned the bomber south so the Japanese couldn't guess their exact destination. They passed over a small aircraft factory, with several planes on the ramp outside, but they did not strafe it. They continued south for about a hundred miles, before turning west to cross the China Sea, banking around the pointed rock of Kagoshima.

For a time, Cole could see Hoover's bomber as it caught up with them after the bombing raid. It stayed with them for a few hours, and then he could see it no more. The Doolittle bomber was alone again in an unfriendly sky.

# CHAPTER 8

Hank Potter sent a note forward from his navigator's cubicle behind the pilots. They would run out of fuel about 180 miles short of the Chinese coast, a result of their early launch. Doolittle ordered everyone into their Mae West life jackets, the yellow horseshoe-shaped bladders that slipped over the head and secured around the waist with straps. When they were inflated, it was easy to see why they had been named for the busty stage queen. Below, they had seen dozens of small ships and could see sharks just below the surface of the China Sea.

If Potter's calculations were correct, and there was no reason to doubt them, it would mean a sodden end to the mission. Forced to leave early after being spotted by the Japanese picket boat added an additional 220 miles to their flight. Fuel was available in China, but it might as well have been in Washington. On 31 March, in a secret memo to Admiral King, Hap Arnold had detailed the fuel that would be at air bases by various cities: Kweilin, fifty-eight thousand gallons; Chuchow, three hundred thousand gallons; Kian, twenty-five thousand gallons; Yushan, twenty-six thousand gallons; and Lishui, thirty thousand gallons. Oil at approximately 10 percent of the fuel figures was also available. These figures noted the aviation fuel currently at Chinese fields, and some of it would be available for Doolittle and his men to top off their tanks and deliver the B-25s to Claire Chennault and his American Volunteer Group, better known as the Flying Tigers. Arnold asked King to forward the information regarding fuel availability to Doolittle.[1] It had to be galling to Doolittle to know that gas was waiting for him but he would never make it.

Ditching the B-25 would be no easy task; it took great skill and a measure of luck to drop an airplane into water moving in waves without immediately becoming a submarine. The pilot's manual stressed the seriousness of such a procedure, while noting that ditching was preferable to bailing out over water, since it would mean the crew would remain together and have access to more survival gear than if they were bobbing around alone in the ocean.[2] Doolittle reviewed the plans: Just before hitting the water, he would advise the crew to prepare for impact; Cole was to slide his seat all the way back and lock it in place, unbuckle his parachute harness, open the overhead escape hatch just prior to impact, and ensure that his seat belt was tight. Potter and Braemer were to sit just behind the cockpit bulkhead, ensure that the lower hatch was locked, and brace for the shock of impact; when they were down, they were to exit through the pilot's overhead escape hatch after handing up any gear that might be useful. Leonard was to throw out any loose gear that might cause injury if propelled by the shock of impact.

The manual also advised the pilot to set the plane down parallel to the waves, with landing gear up and the bomb-bay doors closed, timing it so that the plane would touch at the crest of a swell. If the winds exceeded 30 mph, however, he should land into the wind.[3]

Doolittle, sensing that the crew was apprehensive, tried to turn the mood around. "We agreed that we would try to locate a friendly ship and ditch close by it," Cole said years later. "We would be taken aboard and taken to a friendly port. If we had to ditch by an enemy vessel, we would attempt to take over that vessel and get to a friendly port. I thought about it afterwards. Here we were, five people with five .45s, that was the amount of our armament. I think Doolittle knew it was . . . well . . . but it got everybody in a fighting frame of mind, that we were not going to be taken prisoner."[4]

So Doolittle and his gallant crew vowed not to be plucked from the water like so many fish. They would capture a ship and sail it to the coast, or die like men.

Sometime during the flight, and unknown to Potter, the wind had shifted from a 25 mph headwind to a tailwind of the same velocity. That meant for every hour that passed, they were fifty miles farther than Potter's calculations indicated. They would make the China coast after all; they would not need to ditch, and they could now forget their plans to forcibly take over an enemy ship.

The Doolittle crew had passed just north of Yakushima, where they saw three large Japanese naval vessels but again had not attacked them. It was shortly after that point that Potter had sent his note about running out of fuel before making China. Now, as they neared the friendly coast, Doolittle tried to reach Chuchow, 450 miles inland, calling on 4495 kilocycles as prearranged. The radio crackled with static; there was no answer. Of course, none of the fliers knew that the plane carrying the homing beacon to Chuchow had crashed and no beacons were operating at any of the designated fields. Nor did they know that when their aircraft had been heard by spotters on the ground, the observers believed them to be Japanese bombers coming in to attack. Air-raid warnings were sounded and a blackout enforced.

While the tailwind had proved to be a blessing, it also meant they were entering a high-pressure area, with diminishing visibility and lowering ceilings. A massive storm covered all of eastern China, and the weather forecasts of the day had given them no warning. They went on instrument flight almost immediately after seeing the outline of the coast. Soon, they had to climb to stay above the clouds, and even if lights had been turned on at every landing field in eastern China, they could not have seen them. The cloud base was initially down to 600 feet, lower than the tops of many of the hills, and it continued to sink lower by the minute. Even the canny Doolittle could not fly in those conditions, with imprecise maps and no radio aids to navigation. Light was fading quickly. Doolittle climbed to 6,000 feet and then to 8,000. Below, a storm was raging, with swirling winds and heavy rain.

They had been in the air thirteen hours. Doolittle tapped on the fuel gauges, but there was no tapping more fuel into the nearly depleted tanks. They would have to descend through the clouds and hope to break out in the clear—near-certain suicide—or bail out into the storm and take their chances on making it to the ground. "We're nearly out of fuel," Doolittle told the crew. "We will fly as far as we can, then bail out."[5]

Doolittle asked Leonard to remove the camera that had been installed in the tail, below the twin zero-caliber broomsticks, and put it in his flying suit for safekeeping. It was time, the commander said, to leave the bomber.

They were level at 8,000 feet, airspeed 166. Cole watched as Doolittle set the autopilot, and he then checked his own survival equipment. His extra clothing was in his B-4 bag and would have to be abandoned. He cinched his parachute harness as tight as he could, and when Doolittle signaled, he moved to the lower front escape hatch. Braemer and Potter had already gone through, and Leonard had jumped from the rear hatch. Cole stared at the black hole and for the first time since taking off from the *Hornet* felt real fear.

Army parachute troops since before World War II have gone through an intensive three-week "jump" course at Fort Benning, Georgia, where they learn how to land and thus significantly reduce the potential for injury in the most critical phase of a parachute descent. The first week is known as Ground Week, and the novice paratroopers learn to execute landing falls in the four primary attitudes: forward, rear, left, and right. They practice these by jumping, and jumping and jumping again, from a six-foot platform into sand. Learning how to fall in the various attitudes is critical to preventing injuries, as the direction and velocity of the wind will affect their canopies and how the troops strike the ground. The second week, Tower Week, begins with a hoist up a 34-foot tower and a mock-up of an aircraft cabin. Here, they learn to jettison equipment before graduating to a 250-foot tower, three of which were secured from the 1939 World's Fair. Instructors, known as Black Hats, repeat each item of instruction for each trainee, and then the would-be paratroopers are strapped into a harness and hoisted to the top of the arm; a loose canopy is deployed, and the airborne soldier descends under control to the earth. Only during the third week do the airborne troops actually jump from airplanes, at altitudes of 800 to 1,000 feet. The rate of descent is about 22 feet per second, but winds add a lateral coefficient and the actual rate might be much faster. The secret to preventing injury, the soldiers are taught, is to keep their elbows locked tightly to their bodies, their feet and knees together, keeping their knees slightly bent and toes pointed toward the ground. And in the final seconds before landing, it is critical to firmly press their chin into their chest. Failure to do so might well mean a broken neck.[6]

But for fliers in World War II, the training was somewhat less, although they might reasonably have expected to have to descend to earth by way of a parachute. Instead of weeks of training, they were shown a film, and the pilot's manual had a page devoted to bailing out. Of the five men in Doolittle's crew, and probably every other man in the sixteen bombers, only Doolittle had ever jumped from an airplane before.

As Lt. Dick Cole stood staring through the escape hatch at the blackness below, the uncertainty of what lay ahead forced many questions that would be answered only by jumping. What was below? How would the storm affect his descent? And what would the landing be like? "That was the scariest time of the whole thing. You're in an airplane, staring down into a black hole that's going to exit you into . . . you don't know what. The other part was the big thunderstorm, having to jump into it."[7]

But there were no other options. It was dive through the hole, count one thousand, two thousand, three thousand, and pull the rip cord, or ride the airplane down. Holding his crook-neck GI-issue flashlight in one hand and finding the rip cord with the other, Cole dove headfirst through the hatch.

It was like jumping into a bottomless mine pit. He left the solid confines of the Mitchell and entered a new world of seeming weightlessness, a world without dimensions, without visual clues, without sound. Almost instantly, the thunderous roar of the bomber was gone and all was silent. Cole skipped the first two numbers and said "Three thousand!" as soon as he cleared the hatch. He jerked the red-painted D ring and felt a shock as the twenty-four-foot silk canopy popped open and brought his short free fall to a jarring halt, or so it felt. The straps going between his legs dug in, and he nearly lost his grip on the flashlight. His face hurt; he had pulled the rip cord so hard that he had punched himself. His eye was blackened, he would learn later. Cole looked up, but it was too dark and the air too cloudy even to see his parachute canopy. In the swirling air, he had no sense of downward speed, no feeling of descent, no clues at all as to his attitude or position. He might have been upside down and his chute below him or sideways or totally gone for all he could tell after the initial jolt.

Cole wondered what the landing would be like and if he would break anything: an ankle or leg would be catastrophic, of that much he was certain. What was he going to hit? He hoped he would emerge from the clouds in time to prepare for landing, but there was no certainty of that, since many of the hilltops had been in the clouds when they began to climb. What was it they said to do? Keep your parachute, it will make a good tent or sleeping bag, and you can use the cords for a variety of survival needs. The canopy itself might be useful for bartering. He continued to float downward in a world without sensory clues for what seemed like many minutes. At the rate of twenty-two feet per second, from eight thousand feet it might well have been four to six minutes, depending on the elevation of the earth at that point.

Something was happening. Cole sensed that his descent had been arrested; something had brushed his legs, and the harness straps were again digging into his groin. But he had not touched the ground; there had been no bone-jarring slamming into the earth. He turned on his flashlight, the yellow beam carving a hole in the night. Above, he could see that his chute had draped itself over the top of a pine tree, and he had just experienced the softest landing in the history of parachuting, so far as he knew. In his right hand, he still gripped the red-painted D ring and rip cord, which he then stuffed into his jacket pocket.

He was still alive and, except for a sore eye, unhurt. He found footing on branches, released his harness, and climbed up to free his chute from the top of the thirty-foot pine. With the folds of the canopy over one arm, Cole worked his way down and looked around. He was on top of a steep, rocky mountain. It was late, it was dark, it was still raining; he might as well make a hammock and stay in the tree. After settling in, he shined his flashlight once more at the ground around the tree. Staring up at him was a small rabbit. It hopped away.[8]

Cole felt very alone and vulnerable before he remembered something. He unzipped his flight suit and pulled out a red wool hunting cap, the sort with earflaps that tie up or fasten under the chin. He pulled it on, glad for its warmth but equally for its connection to home and a happier time.

Cole couldn't sleep. He was cold, wet, and scared. He relived the mission, the scenes playing out in his head like a movie. It seemed incredible that he had survived, but the game wasn't over. Japanese troops would be looking for him, that he knew for certain. After hours of cold, sodden darkness, the sky transitioned to gray and then grew lighter still; at last, the young pilot climbed down from the pine and repacked his chute. He stared down the steep slope, nearly a vertical cliff, over which the pine stood sentinel. Had he tried to walk in the darkness, Cole easily could have fallen and tumbled hundreds of feet. He took a deep breath and surveyed the countryside. It was mountainous and heavily forested; some of the mountains were fantastically shaped, like upside-down ice cream cones. The scene was very much an alien landscape to the boy from Dayton, and it looked like it had no end. As far as he could see were jagged ridges and towering, majestic trees. The hills and low mountains were steep and craggy, and a mist swirled around the tops of the highest peaks. The indefinite sky was lowering even as he watched.

The raid over Tokyo had been brief and exciting. It was obvious that this next adventure was going to take considerably longer and require more physical effort on his part. And there was no guarantee that he would survive.

# CHAPTER 9

The bombing raid in the heart of Tokyo stunned Japanese civilians, who had repeatedly been told that the Allies would never touch the home islands. Disbelief turned to rage within the emperor's military, where face was life itself and had been lost, badly and very publicly. The American mobsters who had humiliated them would pay dearly if captured, and across China a massive manhunt was under way to find the Doolittle fliers.

Entire villages were burned. It will probably never be known how many Chinese were slaughtered in the manic search, but some estimates put the figure as high as a quarter million.[1] As the crews tried to get to Chungking, and thence out of China, Japanese troops were often just hours behind. Vehicles were stopped and searched, boats were halted on rivers and scoured for hidden Americans, homes were ransacked and burned to the ground. It was an operation on a scale in inverse proportion to the actual damage inflicted by the Raiders, but the Japanese understood the true meaning: no place was safe from American air attack. Sixteen planes, carrying four bombs each, could produce little actual damage on a city the size of Tokyo; subsequent years of the war would see hundreds of mighty B-29s dropping tons of explosive and incendiary bombs on Japanese cities that laid waste to hundreds of square miles. But the goal of the Doolittle mission from the onset had been to induce fear and uncertainty in the Japanese, while boosting optimism and creating hope in the American public. By that measure, it was a huge success. The Doolittle Raid was psychological warfare gone kinetic.

The Tianmushan Mountains, fifty miles east of Hangchow today, are a UNESCO Biosphere Reserve; a view of the mountain ridges shows them marching to the horizon, looking like jagged strips of colored paper laid one behind another, each one a paler shade of blue. The area is home to giant Japanese cedars, ginkgo trees, ancient pines, towering golden larch, and groves of bamboo. Waterfalls tumble over fantastic rock formations, and streams fill the sharp, deep valleys. One mountain in particular lends its name to the entire range: Tianmu Shan, or Heavenly Eyes Mountain, for its pair of ponds atop the apex, has two peaks, one at 4,941 feet, the second at 4,860 feet. These and other peaks in the range are shrouded by low-hanging clouds much of the time. The region today is a tourist destination and a paradise for hikers. Its beauty is breathtaking.

But the most scenic places on the planet are frequently the absolute worst for humans to traverse.

As much as twenty-six-year-old Army pilot Lt. Dick Cole had loved the outdoors all his life, he was not in a state of mind to appreciate the natural beauty that surrounded him on that mountaintop on 19 April 1942. He was cold, wet, tired, and numb. He was alone in a country occupied by Japanese soldiers who desperately wanted to capture or kill him. He was hungry. And his eye hurt.

So where to go? When the crew bailed out, the bomber was nearly out of fuel and on a course of 260 degrees, almost due west. Each crew member would have landed in a line below the plane's flight path. Doolittle, the last man out, would be somewhere to the west, closest to where the plane would have crashed. Potter was somewhere east, with Braemer just a bit farther toward the coast, and Leonard probably would have been the first out and somewhere along the same line. Doolittle's plan for grouping up after bailing out was simple: head for the crash site. The plan was not detailed or elaborate, for they had counted on landing wheels down at an airfield, not on jumping from the Mitchell.

Cole took stock of his earthly possessions: he still had his .45 with two extra magazines, for a total of twenty-one rounds of ball ammunition. It might work to scare an enemy, he thought. He couldn't hit anything with it, and the kick was terrible. Still, it gave him a sense of security. If he had to, he could use it as a club. His trusty hunting knife was still on the web belt, and he smiled as he touched the smooth stacked-leather handle. It was a Marble, made in Gladstone in Michigan's Upper Peninsula; a four-inch blade with a wide fuller, or groove, gave it a businesslike appearance. The edge was razor sharp. He had owned the knife since he was a boy, hunting the fields around Dayton; it had cost him $2.50 in 1929.[2] Now he hoped it would serve him as well in China. He checked his one-quart canteen to see that it was full and felt the pouch of his first-aid kit to ensure that the contents had not been lost in the jump. Both the canteen and the first-aid kit were attached by hooks to his web belt, along with the holster for his .45. In a pocket of his flight jacket he had a Bakelite match safe with a small compass in the lid and his D-4 flight computer, a circular slide rule for figuring time-speed-distance problems. It was the one he had been issued in flight school. It wouldn't do him much good now. A calendar would be a better measure of his speed, he thought. He had the crook-neck flashlight, which he clipped to his belt. Two chocolate bars were in his pocket, and Cole took one out now and ate it, slowly.

From his right pants pocket he pulled out the smooth silver-colored Wittnauer compass that looked like a pocket watch, with a cover stamped "U.S." He pressed the button that opened the top and watched the blue arrow-shaped needle swing around the silver face. When the cover was closed, an arm locked the needle in place to prevent its being jarred off its red-jeweled pivot. Even without a map, it gave him a sense of security simply knowing directions. He felt around his neck for the turtle amulet that was also a compass—a gift years earlier from his brother Fred—and checked his left pocket for his spare open-faced compass. He was well equipped to tell which way was north. And more important, which way was west. Cole looked in the direction he would have to walk—opposite the rising sun—and took a deep breath. Ridge after ridge, covered in mist-draped trees, as far as he could see. He stuffed his parachute into its pack and started walking down the mountain, staying on the crest of ridges as much as possible. This had two advantages: he could walk evenly, and he could go down either side should he spot danger.[3] He might be in China, but the area was occupied by Japanese imperial troops.

Fog or mist continued to hang heavily over the forested ridges, and the ground beneath his boots was damp and spongy from a thick layer of needles and old vegetation. Everything was draped in diaphanous folds of white; tree trunks were ethereal poles rising to unseen heights, the branches overhead lost in a gauzy cloud. It was as dreamlike as his descent through the storm, a magical world of natural beauty that Cole might have appreciated in other times. The dampness and mist reduced visual clues, but also wrapped an auditory cloak around all sound; it was eerily silent as he trudged along, feeling as much a stranger in a strange land as any figure from Exodus.[4] He remembered his basic instrument flight training at Randolph Field. Trust your instruments! He checked his compass every few minutes.

Despite the chill of the morning, after a couple of hours of hard walking Cole could feel the heat building in his body. He was wearing his khaki shirt and trousers, sturdy ankle boots, a wool coverall, and his leather A-2 flight jacket. He unzipped his coveralls to his waist to cool. The parachute was not heavy, but it was awkward to carry even tied up neatly in a small bundle. He tucked it under his left arm, so he could reach his pistol with his right hand. Cole was a child of the Depression; the parachute was still perfectly good, and it would have been wasteful to leave it behind.[5]

It was tough going. Seeking to avoid heavily traveled trails, he was often forced to stoop below branches for what seemed like miles; he could feel the strain in his back from the awkward duck-walk position. Cole stopped about noon and ate his remaining chocolate bar, swigging it down with a mouthful of water. Someone prior to taking off had cautioned against dehydration, so he took a long swallow and then another, knowing he could refill the canteen from the many small streams that splashed down every ravine. His legs were tired. He sat down and leaned against the trunk of a towering golden larch; the bright green of the lacy, delicate needles reminded him of the vivid splashes of verdure that had greeted him when the bomber crossed over the coast north of Tokyo. How long ago was that? It seemed impossible that it was just yesterday.

Early in the afternoon, he saw humans. He stopped, his heart pounding, and watched them, unsure whether they had seen him. They were Chinese, apparently, and were gathering wood in the forest. They paid him no attention at all, so after several minutes he continued walking. He looked back, but they were all bent to their task. No one looked up at him. Later he saw several farmers, with the same result. It was as if Cole were invisible.

Would the farmers around Dayton react the same way to a stranger, an Oriental perhaps, wearing a uniform and with a pistol around his waist who suddenly appeared at the edge of their fields? No, Cole decided. But perhaps these people had seen wars come and go, and all they wanted was to be left in peace. Or maybe they had learned it was best to ignore intruders and carry on with the really important things in life, like feeding your family or keeping them warm with plenty of firewood. But Cole had his own duty, and that was to continue until he found Doolittle and the rest of the crew, or learned of their fate.

Late in the evening, after walking perhaps ten or fifteen miles—it was difficult to judge, since most of it was up and down—Cole came to a heavily traveled path, virtually a highway in those parts. The wide track circled around one of the taller mountain peaks, and there seemed no way to avoid walking openly along it. Soon, he met an elderly man who seemed very curious, the first sign of interest from any of the Chinese he had met during the day. Cole was not pleased with the man's presence, but despite his emphatic gestures—shooing and pointing—the man would not leave. Finally, Cole drew his .45 and waved it menacingly, and the traveler withdrew a safe distance while continuing to follow the American. After a time, Cole could no longer see him.

A short while later, he saw below him on a lower hilltop a small cluster of buildings, the first he had chanced on since heading out that morning. It might be time, he decided, to learn whether the local villagers were friendly. Farmers and wood gatherers had totally ignored him, but at some point he was going to need help in finding the rest of his crew. He started down the side of the mountain and approached the settlement, where to his relief he saw the Nationalist Chinese flag flying over one of the buildings.

A small boy ran out, shouting something that Cole couldn't understand, and a Chinese soldier appeared in the doorway of one of the buildings. When he saw Cole, in his flying togs and still carrying his parachute, he motioned for him to come inside. Should he go? It might have been a trap, but Cole didn't think so. The soldier seemed excited and pleased to see him, and the American, admittedly naive in some of the ways of the world, responded accordingly. His instincts proved correct. Inside, the man in uniform was animated and smiling. The soldier showed him a drawing of a twin-tailed airplane with five parachutes descending from it. Cole pointed to chute four, indicating it was his.

Other soldiers clustered around, pointing to the drawing and speaking very rapidly. It took some doing, but Cole was finally able to communicate that he wanted to be taken to the man who had drawn the picture. Two soldiers escorted Cole to another small outpost, where he was ushered into a building on the edge of the compound. Inside was a damp and odoriferous James Doolittle.

"Boy, am I glad to see you!" were Cole's heartfelt first words to his commander.

Doolittle had been the last man out of the Mitchell, following Cole through the hatch by a minute or less. As he drifted down under his canopy, the old man was worried about his ankles. He had broken them in a plane crash many years earlier and knew he would be in a bad way if he would break either or both again in a rough or awkward landing. As things work out sometimes, he needn't have been concerned. Instead of a hard landing on rocks, he hit softly in a very wet, very muddy field that had been fertilized with human waste. Doolittle fell backward and sat down in the foul-smelling slime; he was immediately disgusted at the stench. He spied a house nearby with a light on and headed for it.

"Lushu hoo megwa fugi," he shouted, a phrase that Lieutenant Jurika on the *Hornet* had taught them meant "I am an American."[6] It didn't help. The light inside the house went out, and he could hear a door bolt slide into locked position. He found a water mill and spent a cold and wet night out of the rain but extremely miserable. The next morning he found a Chinese man who led him to an army headquarters, where eventually he was able to convince an officer that he was an American airman who had parachuted from a plane that must have crashed in the vicinity. Doubt was clearly written on the faces of the Chinese troops; suspicious of possible spies, they accompanied Doolittle back to the site where the American said he had landed in his parachute, but the farmer denied any knowledge of the event. The Chinese officer then demanded Doolittle's gun and ordered his men to seize the flier when he refused. However, Chinese soldiers searching the house of the farmer came out with a parachute, and immediately Doolittle was treated as a hero. Search parties were sent out to find the rest of the crew, but Cole was the first one to be reunited.

Later that night, the other three crewmen were brought in to join them. They had had some harrowing experiences. Tianmushan's rugged landscape proved ideal for guerrilla bands operating against the occupying Japanese forces, but it also proved to be a haven for outlaws as well.

Leonard, who had jumped first, was disappointed that the in-flight camera he had stuffed into his flight coveralls was lost when he pulled his rip cord. He landed without injury and spent a chilly night wrapped in his chute. The next day, after walking six hours without finding anyone from his crew, he retraced his steps and was accosted by four armed Chinese men, who pointed their rifles at him. The feisty flight engineer-gunner pulled out his .45, ready to fight. One of the four took aim and fired, so Leonard shot as well. No one on either side was hit, but the Chinese fled. Leonard climbed to the top of the mountain and hid, watching as more armed men gathered below him. He resolved to hide out the rest of the day and strike out in a westerly direction that night. About an hour and a half later, he saw more armed men and, in their midst, Sergeant Braemer and Lieutenant Potter. Thinking they were prisoners, Leonard let out a war cry and bounded down the slope, .45 in hand, hoping to scare off the Chinese. It turned out that they had indeed been captured by renegade guerrillas, who took their weapons and gear, tied them up, and herded them into a small village. A young boy who spoke English realized they were Americans and ran to get the guerrilla chief, who arrived and ordered the men released and their weapons and gear returned. When Leonard spotted them from his perch on the mountaintop, they were all out searching for him.[7]

Doolittle was glad to have found all of his crew, with the only injury a sprained ankle suffered by Potter when he landed hard. But what had happened to the other fifteen crews and their bombers? Cole saw that the hard-nosed former boxer and daredevil air racer was worried to the point of depression. The mission, so far as they knew, was a complete failure, and perhaps all of the bombers suffered the same fate as their own, with many of the crew dead, injured, or captured. The next day, the Chinese military leader reported that they had found the wreckage of Doolittle's B-25, not very far away, and he and Leonard went to the site, accompanied by a squad of Chinese troops. There was little to be salvaged, and the bomber was only a sad pile of aluminum and iron. Pillagers had reached it first; even the brass buttons off Doolittle's dress uniform, which he found in the wreckage, had been cut off.[8]

When he returned, the Chinese officer informed him that four additional crews had been found, and there was word that some of the Raiders had been captured, but he did not know whether by Japanese troops or renegade Chinese guerrillas. It was a relief to hear that some crews were safe for the moment, but hearing no specific news about the remaining eleven crews was nerve-racking and worrisome. The Chinese began making plans for the Doolittle crew to be taken to Chuchow and then on to Chungking. It was a demanding and dangerous trip, one that would take ten days by boat, horseback, and foot. For Cole, it was a blur of strange locations, constant threat of the Japanese patrols, and joyous Chinese officials and ordinary people who wanted to see, to touch, to honor the men who had dropped the first bombs on Japan.

At one point on the long journey, Doolittle was walking behind one of the small pony-size horses that the Chinese were using both as riding mounts and as pack animals. Cole was a few feet behind Doolittle when the horse suddenly kicked the raid commander squarely in the solar plexus, knocking the wind out of him and planting him on his posterior, gasping for air. The former flyweight had taken many punches, but this one had caught him totally unprepared. No one laughed as he struggled to his feet, holding his stomach. Then, as the column started to move forward, Doolittle quickly stepped ahead of the fractious horse. Their guide, who spoke English, looked alarmed.

"He bites, too," he warned Doolittle. Now, they were all able to laugh.[9]

Unknown to Cole and to each of the other seventy-nine men who launched from the *Hornet* was the massive search for them then under way that lasted for weeks across China, both by friendly Chinese and by imperial Japanese troops. A flurry of cables flowed from Stilwell's office in Chungking, and they revealed the uncertainty, the misinformation, and the widespread concern regarding the fates of the Doolittle Raiders. On 24 April, six days after the raid, Stilwell informed the staff at AMMISCA—the American Military Mission to China—that the Chinese Air Force reported twenty-five men were safe and uninjured at Chuchow, but that the whereabouts of Doolittle himself was unknown. The same cable stated that the CAF was reporting three crewmen had been killed, but that the information needed further verification, and that a plane had crashed at Chungan, in Fukien Province. The cable listed the names of Lt. Harry C. McCool, Sgt. Robert J. Stephens, and Cpl. Bert M. Jordan, but did not state their condition or fate.

The next day, 25 April, one week after the raid, a cable from Stilwell to AMMISCA reported the Chinese Air Force had accounted for a total of fifty-four crewmen, including twenty-eight uninjured and currently at Chuchow. The message also reported that Lieutenant (Dr.) White had requested from Linhai (longitude 121 degrees 6 minutes, latitude 28 degrees 53 minutes) a "transfusion set, surgical dressings and sulphur drugs be dropped by parachute." The CAF, AAF, and National Health Bureau were coordinating efforts to deliver the needed medical supplies, which were for the badly injured Ted Lawson. The same cable indicated that Doolittle, now safely located, had requested transmission to Arnold the following message: "Bombing mission to Tokyo carried out as planned. Owing to bad weather conditions in China, it is suspected all planes have probably been destroyed or damaged. So far 5 pilots are definitely known to be safe."

The 25 April cable notes that the Doolittle message was sent 20 April through the office of the Chekiang provincial government. On 28 April, Stilwell cabled AMMISCA that additional crewmen were safely at Chungking.[10]

As a B-25 Mitchell flies, it was about four hundred miles to Chuchow from their camp in Tianmushan. It was much farther by horseback and boat. After a day of traveling by horse, that night they boarded a small riverboat and were ushered belowdecks. Doolittle, Cole, Potter, Leonard, and Braemer kept their .45s close by. The elderly Chinese man who had first encountered Cole on the road served as their guide for the next week, but they were often in parties of Chinese of whom none spoke English. Shortly after boarding the riverboat, there was a knock at the cabin door.

Cole and the others froze with their hands on their pistols. No one dared breathe, and Cole could feel his heart pounding. Earlier, they had seen Japanese patrol boats on the river, their searchlights sweeping the banks and any boats under way. Doolittle looked at his men and made a signal to keep silent. The knock sounded again, and a voice asked: "Are there any Americans in there?"

Paul Leonard snorted. "Hell, no Japanese can talk like that!" The sergeant opened the door to a tall, haggard-looking man who appeared delighted to see them. He introduced himself as Rev. John Birch, a missionary who had fled Hangchow when the Japanese were rounding up all Caucasians. Birch offered to help them and wanted very little in return: just a recommendation to American authorities for a commission so he could serve officially, perhaps as a chaplain, or in any other capacity to defeat the Japanese. He accompanied them as far as Lanchi, serving as translator. (John Birch was later commissioned a first lieutenant by Gen. Claire Chennault as an intelligence officer; he was killed by Chinese Communists just days after the war ended.)[11]

Despite the ever-present patrols of Japanese, the Doolittle crew managed to make it up the river to Hengyang, where they were then flown by C-47 to Chungking, the wartime capital of the Nationalist Chinese, arriving on 28 April as part of a group of twenty that included several other crews as well. Doolittle, Cole, Potter, Leonard, and Braemer were listed by name in a cable from Stilwell to AMMISCA. Over the next couple of weeks, other groups of Raiders arrived from Hengyang: a group of twenty-one on 3 May, and eighteen arrived on 14 May. A final group of five survivors landed in Kunming from Kweilin on 4 June; they included a badly injured Lt. Ted Lawson.[12] All the crewmen were debriefed by Col. Merian C. Cooper at the American consulate.

For Cole and the rest of the Doolittle crew, the next day after their arrival in Chungking brought an invitation to the palace of Generalissimo and Madame Chiang Kai-shek. There, they and men from other crews were decorated with the white, blue, and red ribbon and colorful enameled pendant of the Chinese Army, Navy, and Air Corps Medal, Class A, which was pinned to their shirts or leather jackets. Doolittle was given another, higher-ranking, medal on a ribbon that was draped around his neck. Cole was decidedly uncomfortable. He was acutely aware that the American fliers were wearing dirty, unkempt uniforms, the same clothing they had on when they jumped from their bombers twelve days earlier. But the patrician Chinese couple were gracious and welcoming and appeared not to notice the lack of clean clothing on the tired bomber crewmen. They also displayed no trace of the anger Chiang had reportedly expressed when he first learned of the mission.

Reports of the scattered crews arriving at various points around China continued to be sent to American personnel, with copies sent to a variety of offices, including Arnold's. Most ominous was one dated 4 May, from Stilwell, in which he advised AMMISCA: "Chinese report 3 crewmen captured and 2 crewmen dead of following: Lieuts W. G. Farrow, R. L. Hite and G. Barr. Corporal J. Deshazer [*sic*] and C. Spatz. These crewmen reported in custody of local Japanese puppet government. Negotiations for their release by purchase initiated by Doolittle thru General Koo Chow Tung of Chinese Army."[13] Reports continued to be circulated as additional information about the scattered crews came in to Stilwell's office in Chungking.

The raid, brief and small as it was, turned out to have a huge impact on the war, far beyond its limited destructive impact on targets in Tokyo and other cities. Morale in the United States soared; Ted Lawson's book *Thirty Seconds over Tokyo* was a best seller when it was released in 1943, and a 1944 movie based on the book starring Van Johnson and Spencer Tracy was a huge box-office success. It had the opposite effect, of course, in Japan, where the unbroken string of early easy victories by the forces of the Rising Sun came to a halt. The Battle of Midway in June 1942 was largely the result of the embarrassment caused to the Japanese military machine by the Raiders; Adm. Isoroku Yamamoto was determined to draw out and destroy the American carriers that had made the raid possible. But the Americans by then had broken the Japanese communication code and were waiting for them off Midway. In the ensuing battle that involved the flight crews of the *Hornet* as well as the *Yorktown* and *Enterprise*, the Japanese carrier task force was destroyed. Four irreplaceable Japanese carriers were sunk, and hundreds of Japanese planes, with nowhere to land, ended up splashing down in the Pacific. It was the beginning of the end game for the Pacific war. And it was put in motion by a random thought: could Army bombers take off from a Navy carrier?

They could, and they did. As the United States awoke to the news of the raid on Japan, the details were kept under wraps so as not to imperil any crews still trying to escape the dragnet of the Japanese army in China. When President Roosevelt was asked from where the planes had launched, he coyly replied, "Shangri-La!" Not all were as lucky as Cole and the rest of the Doolittle crew; some paid a very high price. Two crews were captured. Lt. Dean Hallmark's crew ditched their plane near the beach at the China shoreline, Cpl. William Dieter and Sgt. Donald E. Fitzmaurice drowned, and Hallmark, copilot Lt. Robert Meder, and navigator Lt. Chase J. Nielsen were captured after evading for several days. Meder had gone to flight school with Cole. Meder and Nielsen, afraid they would die in prison and no one would know their fate, carved into the wooden floor of their cell the following: "Lt. Robt. J. Meder, Lt. C. Jay Nielsen, U.S. Army Air Corp, Bombed Tokio April 18 1942, crashed in Yellow Sea same day, was captured April 24 1942. Sentenced to life imprisonment on Oct 15 1942." On another board they carved five names: C. J. Nielsen, R. J. Meder, Geo. Barr, R. L. Hite, and J. D. Deshazer [*sic*]. They took the floorboards with them when the war was over.[14] Lt. William G. Farrow, Cole's next-bunk neighbor aboard the *Hornet*, bailed out along with his crew near the occupied city of Nanchang. They were quickly captured: copilot Lt. Robert L. Hite, navigator Lt. George Barr, bombardier Cpl. Jacob DeShazer, and engineer-gunner Sgt. Harold A. Spatz. The Farrow crew was the last plane off, and it was their plane that was involved in the accident in which a sailor was blown into their propeller and lost an arm.

The Japanese tried their eight prisoners in a show trial in Japan; and in Shanghai, Farrow, Hallmark, and Spatz were led to a cemetery, tied to crosses, and shot by firing squad on 15 October 1942. Word of the executions was slow getting to the Allies. On 21 April 1943, more than a year after the raid, General of the Army Air Forces H. H. Arnold wrote a memo to all personnel of the AAF:

> In violation of every rule of military procedure and of every concept of human decency, the Japanese have executed several of your brave comrades who took part in the first Tokyo Raid. These men died as heroes. We must not rest—we must re-double our efforts—until the inhuman warlords who committed this crime have been utterly destroyed.
>
> Remember these comrades when you get a Zero in your sights—have their sacrifice before you when you line up your bombsights on a Japanese base.[15]

When Lt. Robert M. Gray's crew bailed out over China, Cpl. Leland D. Faktor was killed, either by striking the tail of the airplane or by the failure of his parachute to open. In the Lawson crew, the pilot himself was badly injured when they ditched their bomber rather than bailing out. Lawson eventually had his leg amputated by (Dr.) Lt. T. R. White, who had volunteered as a gunner on Lt. Donald Smith's plane. Lawson's copilot, Lt. Dean Davenport; navigator Lt. Charles L. McClure; and bombardier Lt. Robert Clever were also badly injured. Sgt. David J. Thatcher was able to help all of them to shore and give them first aid. Thatcher and Doc White were later awarded Silver Star medals for their heroism.

All of the bombers except one that had taken off from the *Hornet* were destroyed when the crews were forced to crash land or bail out over China. The Mitchell flown by Ski York, desperately short of fuel because of malfunctioning engines, landed near Vladivostok in Russia. The plane was impounded and the crew interned until they managed to escape to Persia (Iran) after a year.

From Chungking, the Raiders were flown in groups of about twenty to Calcutta. At the airfield in China, Cole and the others in his group—they included the rest of his crew except for Doolittle, who had been flown out separately—lined up for a photograph in front of a C-47, the "Fujiama Foo Foo," an obvious take on "Chattanooga Choo Choo." They wore their flight suits, leather jackets, sidearms, and a variety of military headgear. Cole still wore his red hunting cap.

One of the pilots to fly them out was Lt. Paul F. Conroy, who later that month would earn the Silver Star for his heroic flights into Burma to evacuate Allied troops and refugees when the Japanese conquered the northern regions of that country. Conroy would eventually fly the Hump with Cole; they would become lifelong friends.

In Calcutta Cole and his fellow Raiders were fitted for new uniforms and had time to tour the city. The first strike against Japan was over for them, but the war was not. For Cole and most of his flying buddies, it was just beginning.

# PART II
# THE HUMP

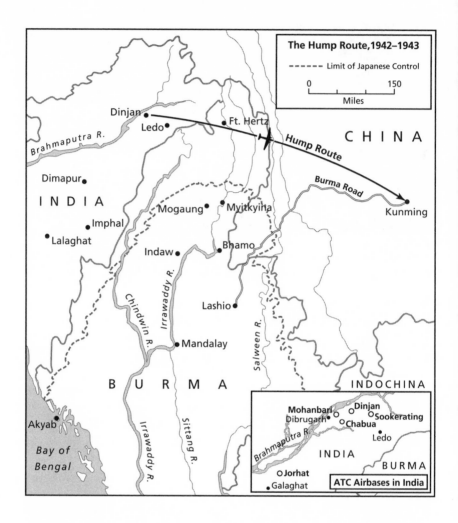

The Hump routes from Assam in northeastern India over the Himalayas to Kunming, China. The airlift was the first of its kind; American pilots flew the hazardous route to provide China with supplies to keep that nation in the war against Japan. Cole was among the earliest of the Hump pilots following the raid on Tokyo. (Map by Chris Robinson)

HOUSE of Snow. Those who live close to the world's highest mountain chain have named it appropriately; the highest peaks in the Himalayas are perpetually crowned with snow, a white topping that delights the eye and seems very much to be the work of the Winter Gods. But the Himalayas are among the most inhospitable places on the planet.

The mountain chain is a monument to violence, a titanic clash between shifting tectonic plates millions of years in the making as the plains of what is now India met the plateau of Tibet. Neither would give, and the resulting upheaval drove the rock surface skyward to form a continuous chain more than fifteen hundred miles long, from the peak called Nanga Parbat in the Kashmir region of the northwest to Namjagbarwa in Tibet to the southeast. Four distinct and parallel belts of mountains form what is collectively called the Himalayas, covering nearly a quarter of a million square miles of the earth's surface. It is the spine of the planet, easily visible from outer space; 110 peaks in the range soar into the sky more than twenty-four thousand feet.

Movement by land through this area is extremely difficult and in many places simply impossible. Thus, for centuries, the mountain range formed an impassable barrier between India and China. Four decades into the twentieth century, humans were regularly traversing the globe in airplanes, easily sidestepping traditional geologic impediments to travel. But, as if foreseeing this new technology, the Himalayas gave rise to the world's worst flying weather. One-hundred-mile-an-hour winds are common, and when those winds hit the upslope side of the mountain chain, they rise in updrafts that lift aircraft at five thousand feet per minute, only to turn into downdrafts on the other side that hurl them earthward at the same terrifying rate. The moisture-laden air turns to ice above fifteen thousand feet, where it quickly builds on wings and renders them useless, and monsoon rains lash the air as well as the ground from May through October.

It was over this that American fliers sought to deliver supplies—gasoline, arms, food—to China in an effort to keep that country in the war against the military machine of Japan, in aircraft that would not fly high enough to clear the peaks. The American military fliers had largely learned to fly in Texas, where the weather was reasonably good for flying and the land flat. Their training did not correspond to the conditions in India and China, to put it mildly. Lt. Dick Cole, who stayed in the China-Burma-India theater following the raid on Tokyo, had experience in mountain flying in the Northwest, but he was the exception.

But in the way of Americans, they played down the challenges posed by the formidable ridges of granite. The mighty Himalayas were home to the highest peaks in the world, including Mount Everest at more than twenty-nine thousand feet. But to the young aircrews assigned to fly over it, the mountain range was simply the Hump.

# CHAPTER 10

Over the next several weeks following their transport out of China to India, a majority of the Doolittle Raiders returned to the States, some to hospitals to recover from their injuries, others to be reassigned to combat units in Europe and North Africa. For twenty-eight of them, however, including Lt. Dick Cole, orders to return to the United States did not arrive, and their time in the China-Burma-India theater would be confusing, frustrating, and occasionally exciting. For several, it would prove deadly.

They had been debriefed on the Tokyo Raid by Col. Merian C. Cooper on 1 May 1942 in Chungking, where they stayed at the American Mission for a week. Cooper himself was a colorful character. A US Air Service pilot in World War I, he had been shot down and captured by Germans. From 1919 to 1921, he volunteered with the Polish Air Force in a war against Russia and was again shot down and this time imprisoned by the Russians. Later, he was a founder of Pan American Airways and in the 1930s was a film director in Hollywood. Cooper's biggest film before the war was *King Kong*. Shortly after debriefing the Raiders, Cooper would be assigned to Dinjan, in Assam, the northeast corner of India, as part of Ferrying Command. Later, he would become an aide to Gen. Claire Chennault of the Flying Tigers and 14th Army Air Force. Over the next year, Cole's path in the CBI would frequently cross that of Cooper.

On 4 May, shortly after leaving China, Cole wrote his parents a one-page letter that must have been confounding as well as comforting to them.

Delivery of mail from India and China was a long and laborious process. It would be nearly two months before they read the note from their son, his first since the raid on Tokyo:

*I haven't the slightest idea when you will get this letter, but hope it will be soon. I realize you are probably both worried and wondering as to my whereabouts and safety. The long silence on my part was imperative and someday you will know why. I cannot say where we are, but can tell you that I am and have been well and happy and hope you are the same.*

*It is pretty hard to write a letter without writing about your activities, but I guess it's o.k. to tell you that I have had my first taste of combat and find it not too bad. "Lady Luck" is still riding on my shoulders and I hope she stays there in the future.*[1]

Cole and nineteen others left Hengyang by C-47 on 3 May 1942 in the second group of Raiders to depart. They flew as far as Yunnan-yi, about fifty miles from Kunming, the westernmost airfield on the Chinese side of the Hump. There they remained overnight and met several pilots and ground crew of the American Volunteer Group (AVG)—the Flying Tigers—who had just left Burma ahead of the advancing Japanese. Leaving Yunnan-yi early the next morning, the Raiders got their first view of the Hump. They stared down silently at the Rockpile, awed by its primordial rawness and its siren beauty. The C-47 refueled in Dinjan and then took off for Calcutta, landing at Dum Dum airport, north of the city.

Wooden-sided station wagons with Indian drivers carted the Raiders to the Great Eastern Hotel, the Jewel of the East, a magnificent four-story edifice with a colonnaded exterior and some of the finest rooms in India. Built in the 1840s, it had hosted numerous titled and distinguished travelers in the preceding century. The tired, unshaven, and dirty American fliers trooped into the hotel, ignoring the stares of the staff and other guests.[2]

Lt. Lucian N. Youngblood, copilot of crew 4; Lt. Ross R. Wilder, copilot of crew 5; and Lt. Robert M. Gray and Lt. Jacob E. "Shorty" Manch, pilot and copilot of crew 3, roomed together after leaving China with the first group. After cleaning up using the hotel's soap and towels, they ordered two bottles of scotch, ice, and soda. After a round or two, the four headed downstairs to dinner in a formal air-conditioned dining room that was the equivalent of any to be found in the States. White tablecloths covered each table, and each place was set with crystal glasses, fine silver, and bespoke china. A waiter stood by each table, ready to take their orders. The Americans would remember this splendor later, when their own living conditions were wretched beyond description while still far better than those of most Indians.

The next morning after breakfast—once more an elegant experience—the Raiders headed out to the quartermaster for an issue of new clothing and to purchase personal items and shaving gear. American uniforms were still in critically short supply in India, so British khaki shirts and baggy shorts with kneesocks became their new unofficial uniforms.

When Cole arrived four days later, he and his comrades also trooped down to the quartermaster depot for new clothes. He liked the bush jacket, but was less impressed with the shorts: *"You should see us in shorts. The English have acquired a 'short poise.' You can tell a Yankee in shorts a mile away—awkward and droopy."*[3]

Cole and the Raiders stayed in Calcutta eleven days, largely acting as tourists since they had no further orders. Calcutta was a city full of stores with bargains for shoppers—jewelry, silks, clothing—but they quickly learned the meaning of caveat emptor. At one point, Manch purchased a large, flawless emerald in a white-gold setting, a pinnacle of the jeweler's art, which he proudly displayed to his buddies that night. He set it on a white linen cloth covering the top of a small table, and during the evening the young fliers began drinking scotch, American style with ice. Some of them set their drinks on the cloth, which soon became damp from the condensation on the glasses. Eventually, one of the airmen noticed that the cloth was turning green in a stain spreading from the "emerald."

The next morning, Manch; Lt. Richard A. Knobloch, copilot of crew 13; Lt. William Fitzhugh, copilot of crew 2; and Cole went to the jewelry shop in Calcutta where Manch had purchased his bargain ring. Manch, who was called Shorty because he stood nearly six foot six, had strapped on his .45 automatic. The four fliers marched into the store and walked up to the counter, where the shopkeeper smiled broadly. His face froze when Manch pulled out his .45 and laid it on the counter. The towering American then plunked the bleeding faux emerald beside it and leaned down to place his elbows on the display case. "I want my money back," he said gently, with a smile. The wide-eyed Indian did not say a word.

He opened a cash box and handed the giant American a wad of bills.[4]

A couple of nights after Doolittle arrived in Calcutta wearing his new star as a brigadier general, the Raiders hosted a party for him, a rather tame affair in all. Doolittle departed for the United States shortly after, and, as promised, he wrote a personal letter to the families of each of the seventy-nine men who had accompanied him on the raid. Cole's mother received hers in late May:

> I am pleased to report that Dick is well and happy, although a bit homesick. I left him in Chungking, in China, a couple of weeks ago. He had recently completed a very hazardous, extremely important and most interesting flight—the air raid on Japan. He comported himself with conspicuous bravery and distinction. He was awarded the Distinguished Flying Cross (DFC) for gallantry in action, and also was decorated by the Chinese Government.
>
> Transportation and communication facilities are extremely bad in the Far East and so it may be some time before you hear again from Dick directly. I assure you, however, that everything is going smoothly with him and although plans for the future are uncertain he will probably be returning home sometime in the not too distant future.
>
> I am proud to have served with Dick, who was my copilot on the flight, and hope that I may have the opportunity to serve with him again.[5]

But Doolittle was far off target on how soon Cole would return home.

After several days in Calcutta, Cole and his Raider friends were sent to New Delhi for four days and finally on to Karachi in far western India (now Pakistan). Karachi was to be the entry point for American troops into the China-Burma-India theater. There, time dragged for the young aerial warriors, who felt themselves stranded in limbo. They had no orders, no duties, no tickets home. Worst of all was no mail. Delivery of correspondence from home would not improve during Cole's entire tour of duty in India.

Near the end of May, Cole wrote his parents again, sending it by way of another friend who was headed back to the States. He was confident that word of the Doolittle Raid was now out: "*I guess you know by now that I was in on the raid pulled by Gen. Doolittle. Wish I could tell you the whole story from beginning to end, but it will have to wait awhile yet.*" He did reveal that he had to parachute from his bomber: "*Lady Luck* *is still with me. As the result of having to 'bail out' at 8500' I am charter member prospect for the 'Catipiller Club' [sic].* Got the Distinguished Flying Cross—for taking part in the raid—and have been promoted to 1st Lt. Better knock on wood I guess."* The lack in India of so many things that he had taken for granted in the States prompted a poignant note: *"Will be expecting a big letter from you with all the dope in it. Put the baseball standings in it too please. . . . How about a cow? Have had no milk since left U.S. and boy! Do I miss it."* Cole was also aware that perhaps he had said too much about the raid. In the margin of the second page, he wrote a postscript: *"Some things in this letter would have been censored so see that it doesn't get out of your hands."*[6]

All of the Doolittle Raiders except Doolittle were awarded Distinguished Flying Crosses; Doolittle himself received the Medal of Honor from President Roosevelt. The Raiders left in the CBI had the medals pinned on their shirts in India, but the citations that accompany such decorations were given them when they returned to the States a year later. Cole's citation read: "For extraordinary achievement while participating in a highly destructive raid on the Japanese mainland on April 18, 1942. Captain Cole volunteered for this mission knowing full well that the chances of survival were extremely remote, and executed his part in it with great skill and daring. This achievement reflects high credit on Captain Cole and the military services."

On 6 June Cole wrote his parents again and described his impressions of India: *"The orient is just as one imagines it, exciting, mysterious, and picturesque. From our tent, we can see great long camel caravans loaded with supplies coming to and leaving the docks. In town you see magicians, snake charmers, fortune tellers and native women carrying big jugs of water balanced on their heads. You can buy many kinds of stones, jewelry and trinkets. Course they sell a lot of junk too."* Cole did not mention the Manch episode, and baseball was never far from his mind. He added a postscript to his father: *"Watch the 'Reds' Pop!"*[7]

It didn't take very long for the Americans in India to see colonialism in action. Keenly aware that the United States had begun life as a British colony, they looked around at the extremes in unimaginable wealth and abject poverty. "It was very evident. It didn't take very long to understand that what England was doing was taking all the raw material, sending it to England, making it into various products, and then selling it back to them at inflated prices," he said many years later.[8] The other obvious difference at work in India, and unrelated to colonialism, was the rigid caste system. It was nearly obscene to the young Americans to see lower-caste Indians crawl up to those above them in status, beseeching an anna or two.

Cole and several other Raiders visited Agra, in Uttar Pradesh, to see the Taj Mahal. It was an impressive sight, even with the main dome securely swathed in bamboo scaffolding to protect it against possible war damage. It was one of the few places where India looked like a nation at war. With the exception of large numbers of uniformed men, and despite its proximity to Japanese advances, India was not obviously fighting for survival. There was little evidence of bombing attacks, and there were no antiaircraft batteries situated in parks and school yards, no blackouts at night, no sandbagged positions for machine-gun crews. During the day crowds strolled the streets of major cities in gaily colored clothing. It was difficult to reconcile the seeming normalcy of everyday life with the notion that a powerful, nearly invincible enemy was knocking on the door in the East.

But all was not tranquil. Many Indians were outraged at British rule of their country, and in the summer of 1942 the situation reached a boiling point. The Indian National Congress adopted resolutions supporting Mohandas Gandhi's "Quit India" movement, and the British responded by jailing the movement's leaders, including Gandhi. Disturbances and riots erupted in Bengal and Bihar in August. Cole was focused on the war against the Japanese, and everything else seemed like a distraction.

In a letter to his sister Jo, he wrote: "*The natives are still bust'n each other's heads and sometimes kill each other but that is the extent of their riots.*"[9] News of Britain's political problems would not be widely dispensed among the American troops stationed in India. Cole, like most Yanks stationed there, would see only disconnected events that were not easily understood or seen in any wider perspective.

# CHAPTER 11

Expecting each day to receive written orders sending them back to the States, the Raiders were disappointed to learn in Karachi that they had been assigned to the 11th Bomb Squadron, 7th Bomb Group, flying B-25s. When Maj. Gen. Louis Brereton assumed command of the 10th AAF and began operations against the Japanese, his total aerial force consisted of nine B-17s. He quickly realized that medium bombers, such as the B-25 or B-26, would be more practical. No fighter escorts for the heavy bombers were available, so the faster, more maneuverable twin-engine bombers would be more effective. Eventually, enough mediums for two squadrons arrived, and there were experienced crews from the Doolittle Raid still in theater. They would remain in India. The source for that decision remains unclear, but Cole and other Raiders believe that Brereton, recognizing their value as combat crewmen, issued a stop order and prevented their return to the States.[1]

Dick was as let down as any, but he was philosophical about it. There was a war on, after all, and he was a combat pilot. Not much use for those in Dayton, Ohio. In a letter to his family 28 June, he was resigned:

*I guess you know that some of the Tokyo crews are back in the States and there are still about twenty of us still over here. Don't know whether they sent the best home and kept the worst here or vice versa. I would like to come home, but chances are we would get sent on something worse. So I am very well satisfied to stay here. Sgt. Leonard left for U.S. last Sat. Said he would drop you a line as to my health, wealth, happiness and whereabouts.[2]*

Cole could not have been more prescient regarding reassignment to something worse. Paul Leonard, the faithful, fatherly crew chief who asked to remain with Doolittle and who mailed Cole's letter, was killed in North Africa on 5 January 1943 in an attack by German aircraft on his air base. Other Raiders would be killed or captured in the coming years of the war.[3]

The 11th Bomb Squadron was sent to Allahabad, an ancient city at the confluence of the muddy-brown Ganges and the greenish water of the Yamuna River. One hundred and twenty miles southeast of the city of Lucknow in the state of Uttar Pradesh in north-central India, Allahabad boasts magnificent architecture and a rich cultural history. A huge fort, built by the emperor Akbar in 1583, dominates the river-banks; an ancient thirty-foot polished sandstone pillar, topped by a sitting lion, commemorates the ascension of Emperor Jahangir in 232 BC; Allahabad University displays a unique blend of Victorian and Islamic architecture; and the public library, with its massive domed roof and four colonnaded and bell-shaped corner towers, has lured the literate of the city since 1864.

Most of this splendor and history was lost on the American fliers who were camped in tents on the city's outskirts. What they were most conscious of were the heat and the rain. Plenty of both battered the American fliers across India.

In a 28 June letter to his parents, Cole wrote of temperatures nearly unfathomable to the Americans. *"Boy! I thought I had seen it rain but you 'ain't seen nothin' 'till you get a load of the Indian monsoon. Was at Allahabad when it came. Temp. went up to 142⁰ F and the rains broke it dropped down to 100⁰—nice and cool—137 people died in one week from heat stroke and exhaustion."* Cole might have exaggerated the temperature, or perhaps the thermometer was faulty, but there was no doubt that the weather in India was far different from that to which Americans were accustomed. In another letter, dated 15 July: *"Well the famous 'rains have come.' It rained about 6 inches in less than 48 hours. The ground is so hard and the water doesn't soak in, it just runs in all directions washing out roads, tents, and everything else in the way."*[4] In October 1941, a cyclone coming in from the Bay of Bengal killed more than sixty thousand people.

One afternoon after a particularly sweltering day, Cole and Dick Knobloch watched as Hindu pilgrims bathed in the Ganges. "Want to try it?" one asked the other. "Sure, why not." So the two young American fliers stripped to their GI shorts and plunged into the muddy waters, only vaguely aware that the mighty river was used as a sewer by cities up and down its banks. Despite the dangers of a smorgasbord of deadly diseases, both survived without apparent ill effects.

At the end of June, after nearly two months in India, Cole sent home a package containing his prized possessions, and in this letter he carefully lists the contents:

> *The package will contain the following things. 1 parachute rip-cord, 1 Calcutta newspaper, 2 buttons all that was left of my uniform, 1 letter from the famed Madame Chiang Kai-shek, pair of 2nd Lt. bars, 3 group pictures taken in China—get a load of that advertising in no. 2—how about that—huh!—a small packet which contains my watch and a Chinese Medal of Honor presented by the Generalissimo and the Madame Chiang Kai-shek in person,—watch is broke has to be fixed before any more running. Five pictures of our wrecked airplane, 1 parachute inspection and packing card, it is customary when one makes a chute jump to give the packer a box of cigars so you can see I owe D. C. Gray Parachute Dept. Sacramento Calif Air Depot a box of cigars. Don't know when I can do it but won't forget it. 1 silk shirt presented by Chinese Aeronautical Society. Some pictures here and there in China and India.*

Baseball still was never far from his mind. He teased his father again, an avid Cardinals fan. "*Hey Pop! What's happened to the Cards? The Reds are going to pass 'em right up pretty soon. Brooklyn must be pretty tough this season huh! Yankees too.*"[5]

As time dragged on for Cole in the CBI, he eventually forgot about parachute packer D. C. Gray and did not send the customary box of cigars, a commodity that would have been extremely difficult to obtain in India.

Earlier that month, on 2 June, just a few days after the arrival of the Raider veterans, the 11th Bomb Squadron flew its first bombing mission with a new commander. It was a disaster. Maj. Gordon Leland had arrived a couple of days earlier with several new B-25s and crews. A plan to send six B-25s for a two-week stint in Kunming, China, was approved, and despite his unfamiliarity with the theater, Leland scheduled himself to lead the flight. The route was over the Hump, with a side trip to bomb Japanese positions in Lashio, the southern terminus of the Burma Road. Weather forecasts were dire; it was the start of the monsoon season, and heavy rain, dense clouds, and extremely poor visibility were expected. Pilots familiar with the region, including Col. Caleb Haynes with Ferry Command, advised against the mission, particularly since none of the pilots scheduled for the raid had ever flown in the theater. Leland disregarded their warnings.

At 0600 on 2 June, six B-25s, each with a full bomb load and carrying one extra crewman, lifted off from Dinjan for temporary assignment in Kunming, which eventually would become the permanent base for the 11th. "Leland didn't know anything about the area or the weather," Cole recalled many years later. "But he insisted on going ahead."[6]

Of the six bombers, only two arrived. Forty-five minutes after take-off, the weather worsened as forecast, but the flight did not turn back. They arrived over the airfield at Lashio and dropped their bombs on the runways, inflicting some damage, but one B-25 became separated from the others. Two Japanese fighters immediately attacked it, their machine guns killing the radio operator who was manning the bomber's gun turret. The pilot, desperate to escape, dove low and initiated a series of violent maneuvers just over the jungle treetops, finally managing to evade the pursuing fighters. Full of holes and with tanks nearly empty, the bomber eventually managed to land at Kunming. Others were not so lucky.

The remaining five Mitchells continued through the solid clouds at ten thousand feet, the pilots flying on instruments. They were too low; pilots more experienced in the region would have been at a minimum of sixteen thousand feet. With devastating swiftness, the leading three bombers smashed into a mountaintop; the flashes of the explosions allowed the two following bombers to take evasive action and avoid a similar fate "by only a fraction." The crews reported seeing "grass and trees through the heavy cloud" just below their wings as they turned. One of the two landed safely at Kunming, but the second ran out of fuel fifty miles north of Kunming and the crew bailed out. It took the men two weeks to walk to the base. In what to Cole was unbearable irony, three men who had survived the raid on Tokyo and the subsequent bailout over China had been taken along as extra crewmen in the event they were needed during the two-week assignment in China. Lt. E. F. Mc-Gurl, navigator on crew 5; Sgt. M. J. Gardner, engineer-gunner on Ross

Greening's crew number 11 (aboard the "Hari Kari-er"); and S/Sgt. O. A. Duquette, engineer-gunner on the Bower crew (number 12 in the "Fickle Finger of Fate"), had all remained in India and were taken on the mission as extra crewmen. All three were killed.[7]

The horrific mission left the 11th with just four B-25s and more than thirty pilots, an imbalance that meant no one would get much flying time. Meanwhile, the Ferrying Command was crying for more experienced pilots to take transport aircraft over the Hump, and someone had contacted Brick Holstrom, the acting commander for the bomb squadron following the death of Gordon Leland. Holstrom, another Doolittle Raider who had sunk a Japanese submarine while the 17th Bomb Group was patrolling the northwest coast, announced that he was going to place the names of all the pilots in a hat and draw to determine who would be transferring to the Ferrying Command. Cole and two other former Raiders, E. E. McElroy and Shorty Manch, said, "Don't put our names in. We're volunteering now for the Ferrying Command."[8] They expected to get more flight time there than in the underequipped and overmanned bombing squadrons.

So that was how Cole became a Hump pilot. Shortly after transferring, Manch transferred back into the 11th Bomb Squadron when that unit began to acquire more aircraft; after flying a few ten-hour Hump round-trips, McElroy transferred to the 491st Bomb Squadron, striking targets in Burma. He had injured his back bailing out of his bomber after the raid on Tokyo and found he could not tolerate the long round-trips to Kunming and back. The shorter bombing missions against Japanese targets were easier on his back, he decided.

That left Cole as the only Raider to fly a tour as a Hump pilot, with an occasional day-off bombing raid thrown in for good measure.

# CHAPTER 12

The war situation in India, China, and Burma at the time of the raid and up through mid-1943 was perilous, confusing, and frequently contentious. Americans there at the time said it took a crystal ball and a copy of *Alice in Wonderland* to begin to understand it.[1] Envision the array of problems facing US planners in the CBI as a series of overhead transparencies, each depicting its own unique set of challenges: alone, the issues seem thorny but solvable, but as each transparent chart is laid over the others the total becomes an enormous, seemingly intractable vexation, a tangle of lines of authority and competing goals. China was in grave danger of falling under total domination of the Japanese, which would have been a disaster for the Allies; the China-Burma-India theater was quite literally the end of the pipeline for supplies; the Chinese were suspicious of the British, and many Indians were pressing for independence regardless of the state of the war; the region itself was geographically and climatically a terrible place to fight a war; and the US Army Air Forces in the region was racked by a lack of personnel and equipment, frequent changes of command and organization, and competing demands and jealousies. This last was perhaps most troubling, because it should have been something easily controlled by the Allies, yet it continued to be problematic throughout the war.

The rapid and frequent changes in command structures and the seeming lack of supervision at the ground level meant for Cole and other American troops a confusing and often frustrating tour of duty in the CBI.

In early February 1942, Lt. Gen. Joseph Stilwell was appointed commander of all US Army forces in the newly created CBI as well as chief of staff for Chiang Kai-shek. His appointment boded well for actively engaging the enemy, less so for smooth diplomatic relations with the British, or the Chinese for that matter. On 25 February, Maj. Gen. Louis Brereton arrived in India to assume command of the 10th Army Air Force, which was to be the primary American combat unit in the theater. In fact, the United States never committed more than a few thousand ground combat troops to the CBI, concentrating instead on an aerial force to keep the Japanese from invading India or southwestern China. Brereton was charged with preparing the region for offensive operations against the Japanese while keeping the air lanes to China open.[2] But in the beginning, he quite literally was commander of an organization that was an air force in name only. He arrived with just nine B-17s and acquired ten P-40 fighters from Australia weeks later. A few more aircraft and crews were scrounged from Australia and the Philippines, but the rest of the 10th AAF was still at Patterson Field, Ohio, preparing for deployment to India.[3] The already existing air arm in China, the American Volunteer Group, or Flying Tigers, was not assigned to him. That omission was a source of irritation to the new commander, but the Flying Tigers would not be absorbed into the US military until July and would remain under the command of Claire Chennault.

Brereton might have been a curious choice to head a nascent air force. He had had a roller-coaster career, one that had seen him decorated with the Distinguished Service Cross as a pilot in World War I only to struggle with personal issues and alcohol in the 1920s. A 1912 graduate of the Naval Academy who had transferred to the Army, Brereton gained a reputation as a bon vivant while stationed in Paris. As World War II began for the United States, he was in the Philippines as commander of the Far East Air Force (FEAF) when the Japanese destroyed most of the aircraft on the ground. He did not get along with Air Marshal Sir Richard Peirse of the Royal Air Force (RAF), among others, and requested a transfer.[4]

The fifty-two-year-old Brereton was short and stocky; he wore steel-rimmed glasses that lent him the appearance of a mild-mannered accountant. But he was combative and by war's end had served continuously in combat theaters across the globe and throughout the duration of hostilities. When he landed in New Delhi to head up the 10th, he set up a series of meetings with American and British senior officers to determine how best to proceed. His orders were to give top priority to keeping open the air routes to China while also organizing combat missions against the Japanese. The two missions were intended to be co-ordinated and complementary, but proved instead to be a source of contradictory goals and divided loyalties. As he saw it, he had been tasked to head a combat unit with a tactical mission of attacking the enemy. The idea of an aerial supply line was a totally new concept at the time, and although it was strategic in nature, Brereton did not appreciate it fully. But it was of utmost importance.

Despite two years of war across Europe, and with Japan on the march across Asia since 1937, lawmakers in Washington had not materially built up the armed forces of the United States prior to the attack on Pearl Harbor. A few programs had been enacted, such as the Civilian Pilot Training Program—eventually it produced 435,165 pilots, including Dick Cole—but by and large the American military machine was not ready for war in 1942. And while the first blow against Americans had been struck by the Japanese in the Pacific, the war planners had decided that the main thrust of the Allies—including Great Britain, Canada, Australia, and New Zealand—would be in Europe. Only when the Germans had been beaten would attention shift to defeating the Japanese. For the Asiatic-Pacific theater, which included India and China, the efforts would be to prevent further defeats.

China's involvement was seen as critical by these planners—the combined chiefs of staff of Allied armies, navies, and air forces. So long as China remained in the war, up to two million Japanese soldiers were committed there, which meant they could not be thrown into the fight against American troops in the island campaigns. Additionally, in the long-range strategy of the Allies, China was seen as the staging area for an anticipated bombing campaign of the Japanese home islands, a campaign seen as necessary for the total surrender of the emperor and his forces.

But plans have a way of coming up against hard reality, and regarding China this meant that there were few good options available for providing arms and supplies to keep it in the war. Prior to March 1942, when Rangoon fell to Japanese forces, matériel had been shipped to Rangoon, then placed on railcars and transported to Lashio, where the Burma Road began. The famed roadway, in places hardly wider than a single lane, runs more than seven hundred miles from Lashio to Kunming, in Yunnan Province; much of it is through the mountainous eastern end of the Himalayas in a series of switchbacks so sharp that often trucks had to stop, back up, and go forward again multiple times to negotiate the turns.

Airlifting supplies over the Hump was not the original plan and was possible only at that moment in history when aviation came into its own. After the fall of Rangoon, the idea—it seems improbable today, but options were few at the time—was to ship the needed supplies to Calcutta and then send them a thousand miles by train across India on a series of tracks that were a variety of gauges (necessitating unloading and reloading boxcars many times); at Sadiya, in far eastern India, they would be airlifted about two hundred miles over the Naga Hills to Myitkyina (pronounced "Mitch-i-naw"—most fliers referred to it as Mitch), where they would be floated down the Irrawaddy River to Bhamo, Burma, and thence on to the remaining portion of the Burma Road. That complicated plan was dashed when the Japanese captured Bhamo, Myitkyina, and Lashio.

That left the totally untried method of an airlift for the entire route. Every gallon of gasoline, every bullet, every canned meal, every uniform, every bandage: all would be loaded aboard aircraft in Assam and flown over the mountains and jungles of northern Burma. It was a daunting task. In an interesting bit of irony, the first Hump flight was flown by Lt. Col. William D. Old on 8 April 1942; he carried eight thousand gallons of aviation fuel intended for the Doolittle Raiders. But, of course, they never got it.

Added to the competing missions in the CBI was the logistical nightmare of sending supplies to the "end of the pipeline." The shortest route from the United States to India was thirteen thousand miles, and by ship around Africa the trip took more than two months. Added to the daunting figures of distance and time was the reality that other theaters—mainly North Africa and Europe—had higher priority in the Allied plans to win the two-front war.[5]

Personnel, equipment, and airplanes continued to dribble into India in the first half of 1942. In April two combat commanders arrived, Cols. Caleb Haynes and Robert L. Scott, with additional bombers and transports.[6] (Scott would become well known as the author of *God Is My Co-Pilot* and as a Flying Tiger ace.) Haynes and Scott were there initially as part of the coordinated multipronged plan to attack Japan directly, having flown from the United States to South America, across the Atlantic, over North Africa, and finally into India. They had led twelve B-17s and a B-24 as part of a planned bombing attack on Tokyo from bases in China. With the successful Doolittle Raid, that plan was scrapped. Even as Brereton's resources slowly increased, communications with Washington compounded a bad situation. Planners there consistently overestimated the force Brereton had in theater. Often, those in DC counted all aircraft that were dispatched to India, while in fact they might have crashed, been down for major repairs somewhere in Africa or the Middle East, or arrived so badly worn out that they required major overhauls despite the severe lack of parts. An example is the ten P-40s that arrived in April. They were part of a group of eighty fighters sent by ship from Australia; one of the ships was sunk, another was badly damaged, and only one in eight fighter planes actually made it to India.

One problem regarding communication was the distance involved, of course, but the main bottlenecks were the antiquated telegraph and telephone systems in India and throughout most of the region. Adding to delays of written orders and communiqués was the confusing and rudimentary transportation system. Because each railroad had its own gauge for tracks, it necessitated loading and unloading supplies multiple times in trips across India. A railroad trip for personnel took three weeks from Karachi, in what was then western India, to Assam, in the Northeast; the same trip took about six weeks for equipment.[7]

Adding to this misery was the climate itself—often described as "too hot, too cold, too dry, and too wet"—that took an enormous toll on men and machines. In the rainy season, roads were frequently impassable, and during the dry months dust was a major problem for anything mechanical, as it clogged filters and seeped into machinery, where it ground down metal parts.[8] Men succumbed to a variety of illnesses endemic to the area: malaria, typhus, cholera, dysentery, and venereal diseases depleted available manpower.

As if the deck was not already stacked against Brereton and the goals of the 10th AAF, organization and command difficulties were thrown into the mix. His chief of staff, Brig. Gen. Earl Naiden, was charged by Washington with the administration and command of the air route to China, with that as his sole duty, a charge to which Brereton objected most strenuously.[9] He was a combat pilot and a combat commander, and he argued that airdromes and other facilities were needed in common by the cargo planes and bombers and that to split them was to reduce the effectiveness of the unit. A theater commander needed the flexibility to use aircrews and aircraft as tactically needed, and a split command made that impossible, he argued. Other commanders, including the head of the Ferrying Command, saw the seemingly mundane mission to airlift supplies to China as a strategic one, a mission that could at times trump tactical concerns.

Adding to the confusion were the multiple layers of military—and occasionally civilian—administration and operations either already in the region or that would be created after Brereton's assignment to the CBI. In July 1941, the American Military Mission to China had been established to facilitate Lend-Lease to China, under the command of Brig. Gen. John Magruder. China's military, despite the occupation by Japanese troops of much of eastern China, seemed to be at least as focused on the political battle within the country as on engaging the Japanese. Nationalist troops under Chiang Kai-shek and Communist soldiers led by Mao Tse-tung had, at best, an uneasy truce and an overarching distrust of each other. Magruder dealt with Chiang, but things were never smooth. AMMISCA was still in operation when Brereton arrived in India and continued for several months until absorbed by the new military commands in India. Among the earliest Hump fliers were AMMISCA pilots, including 2nd Lt. James Segel, who left the States on 13 May 1942, bound for Karachi and ultimately Assam. Another was Lt. Jacob Sartz, who would be awarded a Silver Star for his heroic flights into Myitkyina, Burma, to evacuate British troops and civilians when the Japanese took that city in May 1942. Both Segel and Sartz would fly with Dick Cole out of Assam on the Hump route.

Still another entity compounding the complexity of the organization table in the CBI was the expansion of Ferry Command, which started out as a means of delivering completed aircraft to bases in the United States as well as Lend-Lease fighters and bombers to Great Britain. In May 1941, Brig. Gen. Robert Olds had been assigned to command a new entity, Ferrying Command, and he was given authority to procure pilots from any military unit to fill his needs. After Pearl Harbor, the military pilots were ordered to report immediately to their original units, and Ferrying Command, now short of airplane drivers, looked to the airlines for experienced pilots. This meant that theoretically, competent high-time pilots would be making the long ocean crossings and transcontinental flights required. It also meant that often these men were not terribly concerned with the niceties and nuances of military deportment and expectations.

And sometimes the airlines were cagey. Lt. Jim Segel left Florida in the right seat of a C-47 that had been fitted with additional fuel tanks and packed with all the gear and goods the four-man crew could stuff into it. Sitting in the left seat was a former airline copilot, Curtis Caton. According to Segel, when the military advised the airlines that they needed seventy-five seasoned captains for the AMMISCA mission, some of the airlines had hurriedly promoted copilots to captaincies and placed them on the "available" list so as to not lose valuable, experienced senior flight crews.[10]

For Brereton in India the next year, the Ferrying Command was one of several command and organizational challenges that doubtless left him confused and frustrated. As the Japanese navy and army appeared poised to attack India, the alarmed British called for American aerial forces to be used in support of underequipped and overextended RAF units. In early April, Brereton had ordered—and led one flight himself—a bombing attack by B-17s on Port Blair in the Andaman Islands, just off the Indian coast. The raid damaged two Japanese ships in the harbor there. But Brereton had not cleared the raid with Stilwell, who cabled the Air Force theater commander that all future such actions must go through him in order to coordinate with any planned ground actions.[11] On 15 April, General Marshall sent Stilwell a somewhat vague directive: "In the Bay of Bengal and Indian Ocean area from Ceylon northward, Brereton's Air Force will be used in conformity with the British."[12] Brereton saw the RAF request for American aid as further dilution of his control and of the capabilities of his airpower. He cabled Washington for clarification and was told to cooperate with the British as requested.[13] Stilwell, never a fan of the British, protested that he had had no say in the matter and that such actions would cause friction with the Chinese, who were considered necessary allies in the war against Japan and who saw the British as getting preferential treatment.

On 3 May, Brereton cabled Washington again: "It is imperative that command and final decision relative to use of AAF not be passed to the British but remain with me."[14] The War Department confirmed to Stilwell that he was still in command of all US forces in the CBI, and Stilwell said he would instruct Brereton to remind the British that the 10th AAF was still under American command.[15] Shortly after Brereton's bombing raid, the Japanese withdrew many of their forces from the Indian Ocean and Bay of Bengal, thus alleviating the immediate threat of a major invasion of India. One of the competing organizational and command conditions was thus mitigated.

But other issues were not resolved, and would not be. The China National Aviation Corporation (CNAC) was a civilian-government airline jointly owned by Pan American Airways and the Chinese government. Many of its pilots were Americans. When Hong Kong fell to the Japanese on 8 December 1941, CNAC DC-3s and other commercial aircraft flew into the airport there to evacuate their personnel despite the dangers of attacks by Japanese warplanes. Later, CNAC helped evacuate people from Myitkyina and other towns in Burma when the Japanese advanced northward through that country. With the close of the Burma Road, it was CNAC that pioneered air routes from Assam to Kunming, China. The airline continued to operate throughout the war, carrying supplies into the beleaguered country. While their contributions were laudable, often done at great risk (and many CNAC flight crews died in the process), it was an auxiliary supply line over which Brereton or the Allied military had no control but which had to be considered in the overall operational picture.[16]

Brereton was still feeling the sting of being rebuffed in his efforts to acquire the Flying Tigers and on 10 April received another message from General Marshall that surely made him grind his teeth. In response to Brereton's request that ferrying personnel and equipment in India be assigned to the 10th AAF, Marshall further confused the already convoluted chain of command: "Policies relating to the movement and supply of planes will be administered throughout by the ferry system operated by central office in Washington. Control of ferry operations insofar as they are affected by military operations in India will be exercised by you. The air freight route from Sadiya to China will be for the 1st Air Ferrying Group and General Stilwell will control these operations."[17]

But Stilwell was headquartered in Chungking, and communications between there and New Delhi were by way of Washington. It was obvious that Stilwell could not personally direct the ferry operation, so Brereton insisted that the duty be delegated to him. Gen. Hap Arnold got involved after Brereton notified Washington that Pan American and Ferrying Command aircraft were flying all over India without direct control by anyone in the country. Arnold cabled Stilwell that he would have direct control of all ferry aircraft intended to supply China and that Brereton would have direct control of aircraft operating solely within India. It was an unclear clarification, as it turned out.

The 1st Ferrying Group began arriving in March, with Brig. Gen. Clinton W. Russell in command. Russell soon fell ill, and the responsibility again fell to Brigadier General Naiden, Brereton's chief of staff. Two commands were established—the Trans India, which would fly from Karachi to Dinjan in northeastern Assam, and the Assam-Burma-China command, which would operate out of Assam, across Burma, and into Kunming, China—with the ABC command receiving priority. Col. Caleb Haynes was tapped to lead the latter, with Col. William D. Old (not to be confused with Brig. Gen. Robert Olds) as his executive officer. Ten Pan American DC-3s had been made available; they were sent to India from Africa, but one was damaged en route to Dinjan and therefore unavailable.

Just five days after the Doolittle Raid, Colonels Haynes, Scott, and Merian Cooper—who had debriefed the Raiders in Chungking—arrived in Dinjan, where they found the facilities inadequate. It proved to be nearly impossible to neatly separate the two commands—Trans India and ABC—so Haynes frequently ignored the ordered distinction and sent planes that arrived in Dinjan from Karachi and other Indian cities on to China rather than unload them and reload the cargo onto a plane officially designated to fly to Kunming. Time passed and few additional personnel or aircraft were forthcoming, and the dual command was quietly dropped. Trans India became India-China Ferry, while the route from Assam into China kept its name for several more months.[18]

It was into this that Dick Cole and other Raiders entered the war in the CBI. Most stayed on as bomber pilots and crewmen; Cole alone flew an entire tour as a Hump pilot. The route over the Himalayas held its own challenges and dangers, in many ways as perilous as bombing missions.

# CHAPTER 13

In the tradition of soldiers in combat zones, Cole's letters never revealed to his parents any threat of personal danger to himself or his buddies. But of course there were very real dangers in flying the Hump: the world's worst flying weather, horrific terrain with inaccurate maps, inadequate airplanes that couldn't fly high enough, lack of navigation aids, and the Japanese air force itself. Part of the route would become known as the Aluminum Trail, littered with the broken pieces of hundreds of cargo planes that hit violent weather or were blown off course in low visibility, possibly hit by enemy planes, or that, in some cases, simply blew up as a result of serious aircraft design flaws and inadequate maintenance.

## WEATHER

The monsoon season in India, beginning in May but rising to its full drenching potential in June, is the economic lifeblood of India. The word itself is from the Arabic *mawsim*, meaning "season," and in meteorological terms refers to the seasonal winds that flow first from the southwest, carrying moisture off the Indian Ocean, and then reverse in the fall, blowing from the northeast. Much of India by 1942 was still a region dominated by agriculture, whether by small, indigenous farms or colonial estates; the southwest monsoon winds brought moisture to the region that turned the landscape from a sere brown to a lush green. It had been thus for centuries, probably longer, and while it might bring flooding and misery, its appearance was cause for celebration in India.

But while the Indians cheered the arrival of the monsoon season, pilots flying the Hump cursed the relentless, pounding rains and the gale-force winds. For the men who flew from Assam to Kunming and back, the summer season and the accompanying southwest monsoon winds brought unremitting misery, often accompanied by terror and, all too frequently, violent and lonely death. The heat was oppressive, the humidity was choking, and flight conditions over the Himalayas were, as the British might say, bloody awful.

Weather en route from the airfields in Assam to Kunming, in Yunnan Province, China, wore a variety of masks depending on the time of year and location. It could be deceiving: the weather on the ground was no indicator of what flight crews would encounter at fifteen thousand feet or higher. Crews on the ground in summer khakis sweltering in midsummer heat would find their feet were numb with cold as they climbed through the air and watch in horror as ice built up on wings as they droned on through the clouds that seemed perpetually to await them. And just to keep things interesting, the weather at the China end of the flight was frequently vastly different from that in India, five hundred miles away. Some of that was due to the differences in altitude: Assam was a few hundred feet above sea level; Kunming was more than six thousand feet.

Pilots no doubt sometimes thought that weather along the routes between Assam and Kunming was capricious and personal, targeting them specifically, waiting to ambush them in some inexplicable feud between the forces of nature and men who dared approach their lairs. The real problem was luck, or lack of it. The Assam–Kunming route just happened to be in the center ring of a mighty clash among three Eurasian air masses that were stirred and conflated by the presence of the Himalayas themselves. Moist, warm air from the Indian Ocean to the south produced high pressure that swept north, while cold, dry air from Siberia moved south. These lows and highs were extreme, producing violent winds in excess of one hundred miles an hour, and when those winds hit the immovable mass that was the world's tallest mountain range, they shot upward at startling speeds until they cooled and then rushed downward in terrifying drafts that hurled airplanes and their fragile human occupants earthward at stupefying rates of descent, sometimes more than five thousand feet per minute. Turbulence inside the cloud mass was severe; pilots reported being flipped upside down by violent wind gusts, while many others were unable to report anything because they went missing. Hail, sleet, and torrential rains could lash the aircraft so loudly that it often sounded like demons with hammers pounding the thin aluminum skin.

For Cole, such turbulence and terrifying up- and downdrafts were just part of the routine. He didn't fight the elements and tried merely to keep the plane in a level attitude. "I knew the updrafts would wear themselves out, and the downdrafts would take you down but they would let you go before you hit the ground. Or at least, that was the hope."[1]

Spring was the worst time for flying weather. Thunderstorms built suddenly, explosively, sending boiling cumulus clouds to more than thirty thousand feet in what seemed like minutes. Flight crews watched as the blue sky in front of them suddenly turned into a white, boiling cauldron shooting upward at dizzying speed, and they knew it was not going to be a good day. Too high to fly over, it meant they must penetrate a swirling, opaque world that not only meant no visibility but also frequently meant icing. A buildup of ice meant the airplanes would lose altitude, and in the mountains that often meant disaster. The peaks of the Hump were waiting; pilots called them cumulo-granite or hard clouds.

By May the nightmare weather began to recede, but that is a relative term. Now, the winds began to shift from primarily southwestern—that is, blowing out of the southwest—to variable. A new wind, called Bordoichila, arrived from the northwest, and its extreme gusts could be destructive. Clouds began building by early morning in individual masses, and by noon they formed a solid wall reaching far higher than the cargo planes could fly; it meant flight by instruments for most of the route. Severe turbulence and icing could be expected between the first ridge and the primary chain of the mountain range. Monsoons were now beginning and from May through August drenched the region in torrents of rain that seemed to fall by the bucketful, soaking everything and everyone equally in a miasmic, soul-drowning deluge. In the cockpits, pilots gave up trying to see out the windscreens as rain slammed against the Perspex in unremitting waves; even as they concentrated on the instruments to keep flying on course and at a safe altitude, water dripped on them as it forced its way through small openings in the windscreen frames or through joints in the aircraft's skin itself where turbulence had stressed and twisted the individual sheets of aluminum.

In the fall, following the monsoons, the weather for airmen in India was generally good, with clear skies and relatively smooth air. When they cleared the Hump for China on the final leg, however, they invariably seemed to hit rain and foul weather. Finally, in winter until late January, the winds once more began to pick up, and the cycle began over again.[2]

Turbulence and rain were frightening and uncomfortable, but ice could kill pilots and probably accounted for many aircraft gone missing. Sartz and Segel experienced some frightening flights when ice formed on their wings, and doubtless every pilot who flew the Hump had stories about ice. For Cole, it was just part of doing his job; he remained cheerful and optimistic throughout his tour and didn't talk about the dangers of ice or weather.

He was just as sanguine about flying through the weather in his letters home. In a 12 September 1942 letter to his sister Jo, near the start of his Hump tour, he addressed the issue: "*It is still hot and there is so much humidity that our clothes never dry out. This Ferry Command is O.K. Have been logging a lot of first pilot time plus getting a lot good instrument and weather flying.*"[3]

## TERRAIN

The most obvious geologic feature in the area was the range of towering peaks that formed the main chain of the Himalayas. When weather in the form of clouds and storms obscured them, they formed an impenetrable wall that took a heavy toll on aircraft and the young men who flew them.

But the mountains were only part of the story. Much of the route to Kunming and back was over northern Burma, which was covered in jungle, thick and impenetrable, scored with deep gorges, rimmed by steep hills, and framed by wide, swiftly flowing rivers. Roads were nonexistent; trails were primitive and impassable during the wet season, when mud turned them into a sticky, slippery gumbo. Few villages existed, and virtually no cities, and often the few inhabitants were unfriendly. One tribe, the Naga, was reputed to be headhunters, but others might equally mistreat downed fliers or turn them over to the Japanese for a reward. More than forty species of highly venomous snakes existed in the Burmese jungle, and pythons, which could grow to more than twenty feet in length, waited in trees to drop down on unsuspecting prey. Though not poisonous, pythons squeezed large mammals to death and swallowed their victims whole.

If an aircraft struck one of the mountains of the Himalayas, its crew seldom faced traversing the inhospitable high ground: they were nearly always killed on impact. And although a variety of survival manuals recommended staying with the aircraft and crash-landing in preference to bailing out, there were few places to safely put an aircraft down in the jungles of northern Burma.

In 1944 Lt. Gen. William H. Tunner headed the Air Transport Command, successor to the Ferry Command. He flew the route once in daylight, in good weather, to better understand what his pilots were going through. His impressions of the jungle portion of the Hump route are recorded in an official Air Force publication, *Over the Hump*:

Beneath the upper crust of lush, dense foliage was the perpetual shade and gloom of the jungle floor. We had lost planes all through this area, and had never again heard from many of the crews and passengers. Perhaps they had perished in the crash. If they had parachuted out, they may have been caught in the treetops, or injured, and starved to death. They could have wandered aimlessly in the dense undergrowth until they dropped with exhaustion. They could have been found by native tribes, and been mistreated, murdered, or turned over to the Japanese. On this bright, sunshiny day, from our altitude of over fifteen thousand feet, the green carpet below did not seem so forbidding. But flying over it at night, or in the monsoon season, with the clouds billowing in from the Indian Ocean, or in the spring, with thunderheads towering high over the highest mountains, with buffeting winds and severe vertical currents, with ice getting thicker and thicker on the wings, its weight pulling you down—then thoughts of the unseen jungle below could easily build up to produce panic.[4]

Tunner was a no-nonsense career officer, not one given to exaggeration or wild tales. In his account of the Hump, he related the story of a young sergeant, a radio operator on a C-46. The crew was forced to bail out over the Hukawng Valley in northern Burma; the pilot and copilot were able to find each other and hike out in seven days. But the unfortunate radioman's parachute was hung up in trees, and in struggling to free himself from his chute harness, he had fallen partway out. His foot was caught in the sturdy webbing of his harness, and he was held tight, upside down, with his head and hands touching the floor of the jungle. Despite a violent struggle, he was unable to free himself. Then, as a search party later reconstructed it, he had pulled out his .45 pistol and tried shooting the harness that held him prisoner. Before the white web straps could be severed, red ants had found him and began a steady, unrelenting campaign to eat him alive. The young sergeant, doubtless driven to near madness, saved the last bullet for himself. He shot himself in the head.[5]

## INADEQUATE AIRCRAFT

More than ten thousand C-47s were procured by the armed forces during World War II, and hundreds were still in use seventy-five years later. It surely was one of the most successful aircraft designs of all time. It was used in every theater of the war, from remote islands in the Pacific to the invasion of Europe, and was still in the Air Force stable as late as 1975. But the Gooney Bird was not a perfect airplane. The earliest models had a service ceiling of about twelve thousand feet, according to Cole—service ceiling is the altitude at which an aircraft can no longer climb at a minimum rate of one hundred feet per minute—so it was not a great choice to haul tons of supplies over the highest mountain range in the world, in the planet's worst weather. Its greatest attraction in 1942 was that it was available at the time transport aircraft were needed, so it was drafted for the job.

Some of those first C-47s were in fact DC-3s, which had been flying for American-owned airlines in South America. They had only a single small door in the rear left fuselage instead of the double-wide door of the military version, and they lacked the strengthened deck throughout the cabin. Most disconcerting to Lt. Dick Cole, however, was that all of the placards with instructions for flyers were in Portuguese.

Like most aircraft of the era, the C-47/DC-3 was not pressurized, and its Pratt and Whitney R-1830 engines were not turbocharged. Oxygen was provided through masks from tanks strapped at various points in the cabin; fliers had to periodically crush the flexible tubing to knock out ice that built up from their exhalations. Cockpit heat was virtually nonexistent, and any form of crew comfort was evidently not in the plans when the military adopted it from the ranks of civilian airliners.

Officially nicknamed Skytrain by the USAAF and Dakota by the Royal Air Force, the C-47 was universally called Gooney Bird by the irreverent men who flew it. Individually, the flyers christened their own aircraft, frequently painting risqué images of young women or comic-strip characters on the nose. The nose art added a colorful and poignant note to the otherwise dull, olive-drab paint scheme decreed by the military brass.

The Gooney Bird design was barely thirty years removed from that kitelike first-powered flying machine of the Wright brothers that stayed aloft on Kill Devil Hill for all of twelve seconds. But it was light-years more advanced than that flimsy contraption. The C-47 weighed in at more than eighteen thousand pounds when empty, and its maximum weight for takeoff was thirty-one thousand pounds. Its cockpit to young fliers could be a bewildering place jammed with switches, gauges, buttons, levers, dials, fuses, handles, and warning placards in the front instrument panel, overhead, between the seats for pilot and copilot, on the sides, in every conceivable location except the small windscreen itself. The famous French aviator and writer Antoine de Saint-Exupéry recounts in his wartime memoir, *Flight to Arras* (*Pilote de Guerre* in the French version), that on a long reconnaissance flight in 1940, he counted the number of instruments and switches in his twin-engine Bloch 174: 103, counting the trigger and safety for his machine guns.[6] Certainly, the Gooney Bird had at least that many, and probably more, as additional instruments were fitted in after it left the factory.

That the C-47 was rugged, no one could dispute. The military version added strengthening to the floor and a wider cargo door on the left side. Fitted with a tail wheel, the Gooney could be dropped in without damage by unskilled pilots who flared too high on landing. The tail-wheel configuration also allowed for landings on rough airstrips, on fields that would have collapsed or stripped off a nose-mounted gear. And it could take a punch, evidenced by the many C-47s that arrived safely with gaping holes in the wings or missing large sections of tail surface or so perforated with holes that they resembled colanders.

No, the C-47 was a great airplane by all accounts. It would prove its worth to the world on D-day when Gooneys delivered paratroops and gliders to the combat zone in France. The issue in Hump flying was that it was frequently overloaded before trips into China, and the same at Kunming returning to Assam, making it difficult to climb high enough to clear the peaks of the Himalayas. The gaping double-wide cargo doors invited ground crews to load anything that would fit, regardless of weight, and the thick, tapered wings would nearly always lift the 47 from a runway. The elevation at Chabua airfield was 367 feet (mean sea level), so the air was heavy at takeoff. As they climbed, the air grew thinner, and so did its ability to support the wings of a heavily laden aircraft.

But Cole and the other early Hump pilots didn't fuss when given a 47 and told to fly over those mountains and land in China. As its shortcomings became apparent, however, they dreamed of bigger, more reliable airplanes, aircraft that could fly higher, be less prone to icing, haul more cargo. But throughout Cole's stint in the Hump airlift, the old reliable Gooney Bird continued to be the workhorse of the China run.

The limitations of the C-47 were well known, and throughout the war commanders continued to search for the ideal Hump aircraft: one that could carry heavy loads, fly high enough to avoid the peaks of the Himalayas, and perform in the high winds, ice, and instrument flying conditions along the route of the airlift. They thought they found it in the Curtiss C-46 Commando. The first of these new cargo haulers began to show up in the CBI in 1943, near the end of Cole's Hump tour.

From a distance, the Commando bears a passing resemblance to the C-47: a low-wing, twin-engine aircraft with a tail wheel. But up close, any similarities are quickly forgotten. The Commando is a huge airplane, one of the largest two-engine aircraft ever built. It was more than 76 feet long, with a wingspan of 108 feet. Two powerful Pratt and Whitney (R-2800) engines were affixed to the wings; each produced 2,000 horsepower. Enormous cargo doors allowed large items such as artillery pieces to be loaded easily. It could carry more than fifteen thousand pounds of cargo and frequently was loaded far past that. Later models were pressurized. It could fly comfortably at twenty-four thousand feet, with a cruising speed of 173 mph; the Commando had a range of more than three thousand miles with full tanks. On paper, it was the perfect airplane for the Hump operation.[7]

But the Commando had been rushed into production, and when the first ones arrived in India, they were accompanied by technical orders that listed more than fifty modifications that had to be made in the field before it could be safely flown operationally. It continued to be plagued with mechanical glitches—the mechanics called them gremlins— throughout its military career, and by November 1943 more than seven hundred modifications had been made to the transport. Pilots called it the "Whale" or "Dumbo" and, more ominously, the "Flying Coffin."

When Gen. William Tunner landed for the first time at Chabua, in August 1944, it was a sobering experience: "I could hardly fail to see the huge black blotches at the end of the runway. I knew too well what they were. Each was a lasting memorial to a group of American airmen, the crew of the plane that had crashed and burned at that spot."[8]

The most critical time for airplanes is the takeoff. It is then that an engine, under maximum power, is most stressed and most likely to fail. In a single-engine airplane, the procedure is simple: if you are less than five hundred feet above the terrain, land straight ahead. Failure of one engine in a twin-engine plane (other than straight-line thrust aircraft such as the Cessna 337) is rather more complicated. Because the thrust of the good engine is offset from the centerline of the plane, and the propellers of the dead engine are now creating drag instead of providing propulsion, the aircraft begins to roll toward the dead engine. If the plane is turning and the inside engine quits, it becomes almost impossible to control the aircraft. The result, almost invariably, is a crash.

Add to that scenario the additional factors of overloaded aircraft, dusty and hot conditions on the airfield, lack of spare parts, and pressure to keep 'em flying, and the danger to those young and largely inexperienced aircrews was extreme. On top of all of those negative ingredients was a truly cursed airplane. In the first five months of operation over the Hump, 20 percent of the Commando fleet was lost.

There were major problems with the control systems—it used a hydraulic assist instead of the more conventional wire-and-pulley setup—and with the carburetor icing controls that were to prevent the engines' carburetors from clogging with ice. Most unsettling were the many midair explosions reported. The mysterious fires and explosions on Commandos as they flew the Hump route became the stuff of legend and were unsettling, to understate the case, to the flight crews scheduled to fly them. The Air Force reported at least thirty-one known instances of explosions or fires in midair involving the C-46 and assumed that others that simply went missing had experienced a similar fate. The problem was eventually traced to the unvented fuel system that allowed aviation gasoline leaking from lines in the wings to pool at the wing root; there, a small spark from an electrical component would turn the transport into an exploding bomb.

Near the end of his tour as a Hump pilot, Cole flew one round-trip from Chabua to Kunming in a C-46, one of the first consignment of Commandos to the theater. The flight was without incident.[9]

The search for the perfect high-altitude cargo hauler continued. Cole made several—perhaps three or four—flights in a C-87, the cargo version of the four-engine Consolidated B-24 bomber. In December 1942, Richard Kite led a flight of three C-87s into Chabua. Kite had been the pilot who flew Wendell Willkie around the world in a C-87. Cole and Jake Sartz were selected to be checked out in the new aircraft, and the next day they took off for a familiarization flight. They did two or three daylight landings at Chabua and one at night. The following morning they were both on the schedule to fly as first pilots in C-87s to Kunming.

The C-87 could fly high—Cole flew it at thirty thousand feet—and clearing the highest peaks of the Himalayas was no problem. It was not a particularly good replacement for the C-47, however. It could fly higher, but it was slow to climb after takeoff when heavily loaded, and it had a reputation for being unable to handle icing conditions. The word was that it would stall and enter an uncontrollable spin if the wings began to ice, and apparently it did not take much for that to happen. Ernest K. Gann, the famed author and pilot, flew with Air Transport Command during the war. In his book *Fate Is the Hunter*, he avows that the C-87 "could not carry enough ice to chill a highball." Furthermore, the C-87, as a converted bomber, was "an evil bastard contraption, nothing like the relatively efficient B-24 except in appearance."[10]

On Cole's first flight in the C-87, they had to shut down the number-three engine and feather the propeller (inboard on the right wing) when the engine developed an oil leak on the return trip to Chabua. They landed at Yunnan-yi, in China, where their crew chief repaired the leak. Cole was able to continue the flight, but he lost confidence in the airplane.[11]

In time, six C-87s were assigned to the ferry squadron at Chabua. Within six months, all six had crashed or gone missing. One of them was flown by Cole's friend Bobby Cook.

## LACK OF NAVIGATION AIDS

Added to the abysmal weather, the horrors of the jungle itself, and aircraft not sufficient to the task were the inaccurate maps of the region and an absence of radio aids to navigation. Fliers were provided with heavy paper aviation maps of the area, but they bore notations that users should not trust elevation figures, or even the position of villages depicted, particularly in Burma. Silk survival maps, usually called walkout maps, were given to Hump fliers, but they were at least as useful as bandages or slings than as representations of actual details on the ground.

Cole and the other early Hump fliers used sectional maps, that is, maps not much different from travelers' road maps but with special indications of value to pilots such as elevations of mountaintops, location of airports and emergency fields, and terrain types. He carefully drew in pencil the route to Kunming from Chabua and marked it in fifty-mile segments; it was five hundred miles to the base in China on a course of 110 degrees; return course was 290. It was of little value for determining position by looking down and noting recognizable features, then matching them with the corresponding depiction on the map, a form of navigation known as pilotage. For most flights over the route, the cargo planes were flying in IMC, or instrument meteorological conditions. The ground was nowhere to be seen. Still, the maps served a function for navigation known as dead reckoning (from "deduced reckoning"). If a plane flies on a known course at a known speed, theoretically a pilot should know his position based on time, or how long he has been flying at that speed on that course. This was tremendously helpful in situations where the aircraft was in distress, such as overloaded with ice, and the pilots needed to know if it was safe to descend through the clouds.[12]

Later, in the final year or so of the Hump airlift, radio navigation aids were installed at points along the route, and charts or maps were printed showing only the instrument flight routes and the necessary radio beacons and their frequencies or call letters. No details of the terrain below were shown, and pilots referred to the maps much as a subway rider might scan the underground rail routes to determine at what station to exit.

Almost as soon as the first airplanes flew, men began working on ways to help with navigating these ships of the sky. Obviously, when flying in daylight hours in good weather, maps no more detailed or sophisticated than an automobile road map were more than adequate. However, in the 1920s, when the US Postal Service saw the potential of aviation to deliver the mail, they became involved in the development of aids that would help pilots find their way across the country. The first aids were rotating beacons, mounted on fifty-one-foot towers, placed every ten miles on major routes between cities to assist pilots in staying on course at night. This early attempt at aiding aerial navigation had obvious drawbacks, however. It was not useful in foul weather or diminished visibility, for example.

Radio was a rather new invention in the 1920s. It might be called a slow-motion invention, because it evolved rather than springing forth full-bloomed. For a century, theorists and inventors had worked around the phenomenon of electromagnetic force fields, and by 1899 Guglielmo Marconi had successfully broadcast the results of the America's Cup race from a ship at sea using Morse code. From that early broadcast, improvements came rapidly, and radio stations appeared around the country and became an everyday staple in American life in the 1920s. So when the Postal Service determined to use airplanes to deliver the mail, radio signals as a means to navigate in reduced visibility were a natural successor to those early lighted towers.

For aircraft, radio waves involved equipment on the ground and in the plane for both receiving and sending signals. At first, communication was by Morse code in a series of short and long audible signals that required the addition of a radioman to the flight crew. Aviation stations were set up around the country that transmitted identifying signals; a receiver in the aircraft was tuned to a specific frequency, and a dial pointed to the direction of the broadcasting station.[13]

In India, Burma, and China, there were very few radio beacons for aircraft navigation. As airfields were built, radio transmitters that sent out identifying signals were set up on the fields as well. For Kunming, the identifier was CL7; Chabua was NR0. But there were five hundred miles between those two termini, and the sudden, often violent, storms that seemed to be a daily misery to those flying the Hump meant they could easily be blown miles off course, shrouded in clouds, and unaware of the dangers of peaks higher than their altitude.

Carl Frey Constein, a Hump pilot in the later phase of the airlift, wrote of one flight in January 1945. Flying through a violent storm, with ice building on the wings and hurled in chunks off the propellers, Constein and his flight crew were able to tune in a couple of beacons en route. They learned to their horror that they had been blown more than forty miles north by an unseen and undetected wind that screamed in from the Bay of Bengal at more than one hundred miles per hour. Had they not had radio beacons, they would have been pushed into the hidden peaks of the Himalayas.[14] Before the beacons were installed, there were doubtless many crews who perished when they were blown off course and into the unseen mountain chains of the high Himalayas.

## JAPANESE AIR FORCE

When the Japanese rolled north through Burma after conquering Rangoon in March 1942, Allied high command took some comfort in the thought that the distances to the northern regions as well as the daunting terrain, paucity of roads, and dismal weather would prevent the loss of the upper half of the country. They were wrong. Japanese forces launched attacks to the north, and the Burma Road was soon imperiled.

The Allies, recognizing that the air route into Kunming was the only path still open for the vital supplies that would keep China in the war, immediately saw that Japanese warplanes based at Myitkyina, in northern Burma, would prove disastrous to the unarmed cargo haulers operating out of bases in upper Assam. Moreover, they were within easy striking distance of Dinjan, at the time the only ferrying base in operation. The British had agreed to build airdromes for the Americans flying the Hump, but a lack of materials and heavy construction equipment had made that job seem more like a wish list than a realizable goal.

No antiaircraft guns were at Dinjan; aircraft had no dispersal areas, so they were clustered together, making them easy targets; and although an RAF fighter squadron was based on the field, they had no early warning system.[15]

So when the former ferry base at Myitkyina fell to the Japanese on 8 May 1942, commanders of the 10th AAF determined that the best defense of Dinjan would be an attack on Japanese forces at Myitkyina. Despite very limited numbers of bombers and ordnance in theater at the time, a raid was ordered for 12 May, when four B-17s of 9 Squadron took off from Dum Dum airport, near Calcutta, in daylight. They struck at the runways in an effort to render them useless and reported that several aircraft were also damaged or destroyed on the ground. The B-17s suffered no losses. Two days later, they struck again, dropping their bombs on runways and buildings, again with no losses to the bombers. Two more air strikes against the airfield at Myitkyina within the next few days were carried out before the scarce and valuable heavy bombers were directed against Japanese targets around Rangoon. But on 29 and 30 May, the small force of B-17s again released their bombs on the Myitkyina airfield and reported no sign of activity there.[16]

This did not mean the end of the threat of Japanese airpower, however. Enemy fighters equipped with long-range fuel tanks that could be dropped for aerial combat were often spotted by Ferry Command crews. During operations by Ferry pilots and crews to evacuate men from doomed cities in northern Burma, no cargo planes were lost to enemy fighters. On one flight that contained an all-star crew, however, the Japanese would have scored a real victory had they been able to shoot it down. Col. Caleb Haynes was flying in the left seat, Col. William "Don" Old the right, and Col. Merian Cooper was flying as observer. They had taken a load of ammunition and fuel to the AVG contingent at Lashio, Burma, before it fell and were jumped by a Japanese fighter, which they identified as a Zero but was more likely a Hayabusa Ki-43. Haynes left Old to fly the plane, while he and Cooper went to the rear cabin door and fired magazine after magazine at the fighter with Thompson submachine guns. It wasn't much of an aerial gun, but it was all they had; Old went down to treetop level to prevent the Japanese fighter from coming up from below them, and eventually the enemy pilot turned away.[17] The flight crews from then on frequently carried Thompson submachine guns, although they were more for morale than an actual threat against a Japanese fighter.

With the Japanese in control of nearly all of Burma by mid-1942, Dinjan, Chabua, and the other Hump bases were in range of enemy bombers. Raids were infrequent, but they did occur, and because radar was essentially nonexistent in the region they were usually low-level surprise attacks. In late October 1942, the bases were hit three times. The first, on 25 October, was a well-planned and -coordinated attack by more than one hundred enemy aircraft that struck at Dinjan, Chabua, Mohanbari, and Sookerating simultaneously, with Dinjan and Chabua as the primary targets. The Japanese bombers released their ordnance from eight to twelve thousand feet, then dove to strafe the runways from one hundred feet. Five transports and five P-40 and two P-43 fighters were badly damaged, and the runways were cratered. Warning of the attack came just four minutes prior to the bursting of the bombs. The attack was followed the next day by another strafing attack by thirty-two to fifty aircraft and again on the twenty-eighth.[18]

During one of these raids, Cole had just landed his C-47 and was taxiing to the ramp to unload his cargo. To his horror, explosions suddenly erupted just ahead of his plane. He jammed on the brakes and pulled the mixture controls back to idle cutoff as his crew was already headed to the cargo door. The Gooney Bird was still rolling slightly when Cole lifted himself from his bucket seat and made for the rear door as well. He hit the ground already running and soon was in the tea bushes that grew right up to the runways and taxiways at Dinjan. There, he could see five or six twin-engine bombers—probably Bettys, by their configuration— some coming in low from the east, a couple of others climbing out after dropping their bombs. Gunners in the Japanese bombers were spraying the field with bullets, and he ducked his head.

An explosion that seemed just feet away shook the ground, and Cole could hear the strange sound of insects buzzing through the trees and bushes around him. Then something hot dropped on his head, causing him to flinch, and he grabbed for his cap. A three-inch piece of shrapnel fell in front of him. Iron insects! The bombing and machine-gun fire continued for a couple of minutes longer, and then the enemy bombers were gone as swiftly as they had appeared. Cole picked up the souvenir shrapnel and put it in his pocket.[19]

Capt. Joe Walker had been coming in to land behind Cole, and when the Japanese attacked he had just set up his final approach. He retracted his flaps and landing gear, gave it full throttle, and made a hard left turn, then jinked and jived like a fighter pilot. The C-47 was no fighter, however, and his maneuvers probably made him an inviting target, for one of the enemy bombers broke away from its attack position and began firing on him. Walker stayed just above the treetops and skidded and swerved over upper Assam for about ten minutes until his flight engineer reported that the Betty was nowhere to be seen.

The tower at Dinjan announced that it was "safe to come home," and Walker headed back to the airfield. Upon landing, he declared that thenceforth he would have a machine gun mounted in his C-47. There were none available, of course.[20]

True to form, Cole never wrote his family about such matters. When he mentioned Japanese fighters, their presence was treated as a joke. In January 1943, after several months of flying the Hump, he wrote about wild fowl in China: "*Boy! You should see the ducks and geese over there. Several times now we've passed 'em flying above us and we are just about always flying around 15,000 ft. They scare us sometimes with their good formations cause from a distance they resemble a flight of 'Slant Eyes' till you see their wings flapping.*"[21]

Cole was surely not the only Allied flier to have been fooled. Bar-headed geese (so-called for the two dark stripes on the backs of their white heads) are the world's highest-flying birds, with formations reported flying at altitudes of twenty-seven thousand feet.

# CHAPTER 14

For Cole, the transition from bombing missions to hauling freight over the Hump was informal and nearly unregulated. In a 28 June letter to his parents, he notified them that he had been transferred, with a few others, to the Trans India Ferry Command, "*which is a pretty good job. Flying cargo and transporting personnel. The ships are the same as airliners.*" Evidently, he then let slip something the censors didn't like, for a small section has been snipped from the letter. "*I hate to leave my ole B-25, but flying transport is good training for a job after this brawl is over. So begins another chapter.*"[1]

Despite the transfer, actual flying still seemed to elude him and others. He continued to fly an occasional bombing mission with his old friends among the Raiders. Dick Knobloch was now with the 491st Bomb Squadron—they became known as the Burma Bridge Busters—based in India, and Cole spent part of his time with them as well. The 11th and 22nd Bomb Squadrons had been part of the 7th Bomb Group, but a reorganization had moved them to the 341st Group, along with two newly formed squadrons, the 490th and 491st.

Most of the former Raiders who had stayed in the CBI were assigned to those four squadrons. William Fitzhugh, Douglas Radney, Jacob Manch, Brick Holstrom, Lucian Youngblood, Richard Joyce, Eugene McGurl, Horace Crouch, George Larkin, Edwin Horton, Omer Duquette, Clayton Campbell, and Adam Williams went to the 11th. Fred Braemer, the engineer-gunner on Cole's B-25, went to the 22nd Bomb Squadron, along with Carl Wildner, Robert Gray, David Jones, Harry McCool, Robert Stephens, Bert Jordan, Frank Kappeler, Thadd Blanton, Edgar McElroy, Richard Knobloch, and Robert Bourgeois. When the 490th and 491st Squadrons were formed, several were transferred to the new units: Jones, Knobloch, and Jordan to the 490th and Braemer, Wildner, Blanton, McElroy, and Bourgeois to the 491st. Royden Stork remained with the 7th Bomb Group in Allahabad.

One day while Cole was in Kunming after a rare Hump flight, his buddy Elmer Tarbox asked him if he wanted to fly as copilot in a B-25 raid on Hong Kong. Tarbox was an old friend from the 17th Bomb Group from the Pendleton, Oregon, days, but did not go on the Tokyo raid.[2]

"Sure!" So, without being attached to the unit, Cole flew another bombing mission, a long flight to an occupied and heavily defended city. In some ways, it was a repeat of the Tokyo mission, without the carrier takeoff. At dawn on 25 October 1942, twelve B-25s from the 11th and 22nd Bomb Squadrons left Kunming for Kweilin, which was about 450 miles closer to Hong Kong. The bombers were led by Col. Caleb Haynes, who had been supervising the ABC Ferry Command after the Aquilla mission was scrubbed. The Mitchells were escorted by a dozen P-40s, led by Col. Robert Scott, who had been the executive officer under Haynes for the ABC Ferry Command. After refueling and a briefing by Chennault, the strike force headed for the Kowloon docks in Victoria Harbor at Hong Kong, lifting off from Kweilin just before noon. The bombers were loaded with 500-pounders.

A three-hour flight to Hong Kong gave Cole more B-25 stick time, as he and Tarbox shared flying duties. The weather was clear; they were flying at seventeen thousand feet. The flight passed over Macau and then turned to their bomb run off the tip of the Kowloon Peninsula. Below, Hong Kong and Kowloon were spread out around the harbor. Lt. Col. Harold "Butch" Morgan, the lead bombardier for the 11th Squadron, used a Norden bombsight to target the docks; the other bombardiers dropped their bombs when they saw his fall. Around them, as at Tokyo, black puffs of flak began to appear, and they could feel surges and jolts as the antiaircraft fire began to explode around them. It was light, however, and inaccurate; Cole never felt fear or even a sense of danger from the barrage. The raid had caught the defenders largely unaware, and as he watched the bombs tumble from the bays of the bombers ahead he felt a slight lift as their own bombs were released to explode on the shipping docks below. In all, the American bombers dropped thirty thousand pounds of high-explosive bombs and about two thousand pounds of fragmentation bombs.

Haynes turned the flight across Victoria Harbor and then set a course for Kweilin. They would not escape unscathed, however. Japanese fighters from an airstrip on Sanchau Island had scrambled, and about twenty engaged both Scott's P-40s and the B-25s. The bombers put up a hail of defensive fire, and the enemy fighters were unable to penetrate their formation, but one B-25 had been hit over the target and lagged behind, where it was attacked by a half-dozen Ki-43s. The plane eventually belly-landed in a rice paddy, and four of the crew were captured while two escaped. The Americans claimed six Japanese fighters shot down, with another seven claimed as probable. Cole's and the other ten Mitchells returned to Kweilin and eventually to Kunming.[3]

Combat operations in the CBI were indeed informal. "Things were real loose at that time. We didn't have to report to anybody in the mornings, or anything like that. I went on three or four more bombing missions while I was over there."[4]

# CHAPTER 15

In mid-July 1942, Cole wrote his parents again to give them two addresses: Lt. Richard E. Cole O-421602, 1st Ferry Grp 6th Ferry Sqd, APO #886, c/o Post Master, New York, New York. In the event of an emergency, he advised, they should telegraph Lt. Richard E. Cole, c/o American Consul, Karachi, India. (This was before the formation of Pakistan.) Cole's assignment in the CBI was now official, and he abandoned his early hope of returning home soon.

He had transferred into the Ferry Command because he was getting very little flight time in the bomb squadron. Too many pilots, not enough airplanes. Now, as a ferry pilot, he faced the same issue, and he was despondent. In the same 15 July letter to his parents, he listed three reasons that he was feeling low: the lack of mail (he still had not received any letters from home), not being sent back to the States after the bombing raid on Tokyo, and the lack of flying opportunities. "*The third reason would relieve the pressure of the others if we were keeping busy, cause idle time really hangs heavy on your hands in this country.*"[1]

But all that was about to change. In August Cole and others in the Trans India Ferry Command were first sent to Dinjan, a Royal Air Force base in far northeastern Assam that had been hurriedly constructed on a tea plantation using native labor. There was no paymaster for the Americans at Dinjan and few facilities, and pilots were housed in the plantation manager's large house, which he had rented to the Allies.

For the expanding transmontane airlift that would become known as the Hump, the Allies were hurriedly turning northeastern Assam into an almost contiguous series of runways laid atop existing tea plantations. Separated by only a few miles, Ferry Command initially operated from four bases: Chabua, Jorhat, Mohanbari, and Sookerating. Dinjan was a temporary base while Cole was there, but would be one of three more that would be built or expanded in 1943, along with Tezpur and Misamari.[2]

While at Dinjan, Cole met Col. Robert Scott, the famed P-40 pilot who wrote *God Is My Co-Pilot*. At the base, a Chinese American officer named Yi was in charge of housing transient crews. On his first flight into Dinjan, Scott inexplicably wore a flight suit with a lieutenant's bar affixed to the shoulders. He asked Yi about where he would be quartered, and Yi was noncommittal. "Beats the hell out of me, Lieutenant." As a colonel, he was quickly afforded housing.[3]

Dinjan was primarily a base for transports, but Scott flew lone-wolf missions against the Japanese at every opportunity. At the age of thirty-four, Scott had volunteered for the Haynes mission to bomb Japan from China, the Aquilla project. Eager for a chance at combat against the Japanese, he had lied when asked if he had ever flown a B-17; figuring that he might as well be in for a dollar as for a dime, he said he had eleven hundred hours in the four-engine bomber. In fact, he had none. Scott had been an instructor pilot before the war, with several thousand hours in trainers and single-engine fighters. When the Haynes mission was canceled and both Haynes and Scott were sent to direct the ABC ferry operation, he was devastated. On a trip into Kunming, he asked Claire Chennault for use of one of the P-40s being used by the American Volunteer Group, to provide defense for the unarmed cargo planes flying the Hump. Chennault, never one for a strict observance of the rules, loaned him one of the famed fighter planes. Back in Assam, Scott had the fearsome snarling tiger mouth painted on the nose of the Curtiss fighter and immediately set out on solo missions of opportunity against Japanese targets in Burma.[4] On 4 July, the American Volunteer Group was formally disbanded and some of its members inducted into the Army Air Forces. The AVG was transformed into the China Air Task Force (CATF), under now-General Chennault, and would operate fighters and bombers. The fighters were organized into the 74th, 75th, 76th, and 16th Squadrons and the 11th Bomb Squadron. Haynes led the bombers, and Scott wound up leading the CATF fighters. Their stint with the Ferry Command had been short.

The fighters of CATF, which would change again to become the 14th AAF in March 1943, racked up a notable score of victories over Japanese aircraft, including at least thirteen by Scott. Unfortunately, the first

American bomber lost was shot down by an American fighter pilot, an incident that underscored the confusion abundant in the region. On 16 July, after a raid on Japanese positions at Hankow, Haynes's B-25s were flying to a dispersal base at Lingling when "a terrific burst of machine gun bullets poured through and around" one of the Mitchells. In a few seconds, another burst knocked out one of the bomber's engines and slightly wounded a crewman. As the plane lost altitude, the crew bailed out, and they eventually were able to return to their base. There they learned that their attacker, unaccustomed to seeing B-25s in China, had misidentified them as a Japanese bomber. In the tangled set of possible responses to this incident of "friendly fire," it was noted that the crew felt a certain amount of pride in learning that it had taken two passes by the fighter pilot to knock them from the sky.[5]

While the CATF and 10th AAF squadrons were beginning initial forays into combat, Cole was learning about the C-47, the airliner turned transport that would play such an important role in the Hump. At Dinjan the operations officer assigned Cole to a check ride with Capt. Johnny Payne, a former Eastern Airlines pilot who had been drafted into the Ferry Command and came over with the first AMMISCA group. It was a flight to remember. The two pilots took off from Dinjan early in the morning and flew west to Cooch Behar, following the Brahmaputra to where the provincial governor had a private airstrip. They landed, and Payne discussed procedures for start-up, takeoff, landing, and emergencies such as losing an engine. "Let's go." Cole referred to the printed checklist for starting and taxied without incident to the end of the runway. After taking off, they performed a few near stalls and recoveries, talked through single-engine operation, and then returned to the field for landings.

The first was a bit fast, Payne said. Cole had set up the approach as if he was still flying a B-25. They shot four or five more landings, until Payne was satisfied that the former bomber driver could take off and land the Douglas. They departed Cooch Behar.

Turning to Cole, flying in the left seat, Payne asked, "Have you ever looped a C-47?"

"How could I? This is my first flight in one. I never thought it was possible."

"Want to?" Payne grinned at the younger flier. The response was predicable in those devil-may-care days of young men and flying machines far from official eyes.

"Sure!"

Payne carefully set up the controls for an inside loop and then pushed forward on the yoke to gain airspeed. The airliner-in-uniform nosed downward, and the wind noise past the cockpit increased to a high-pitched shriek. When the airspeed indicator approached the red line, Payne pulled back hard on the yoke, and the snub-nosed cargo plane began to climb, the horizon dropping below the windscreen that now was filled with blue sky and a few clouds. Soon the horizon was visible again, this time on the top half of the windscreen, and then the earth below filled the entire front view out of the cockpit. Cole had done loops many times during training in Texas, but always in small, light aircraft designed for the stresses of aerobatic flight, never in a twin-engine machine clearly not intended for inverted flying.

The C-47 came out of the loop and settled back into straight and level flight. Cole grinned at Payne, who smiled back. "Want to try one?"

So now Cole was at the controls, as the pilots repeated the maneuver in the skies above Assam. There might be a war on, but these men had been given the gift of wings and the space and opportunity to enjoy them. They were not about to waste the chance. The next day, Cole was on the schedule to fly the Hump as first pilot.[6]

Payne, a husky, brown-haired native of Paducah, Kentucky, later flew the first night trip to Kunming and back, a daring act that soon became routine and doubled the time available for cargo to be hauled into China.[7]

Scott also wrote about Payne, whom he called "Long Johnny." The situation in Burma at that time was confused, and Payne was credited with the saying: "If at first you don't succeed, give up, for no one in this country gives a damn anyway." That was hardly the spirit with which he flew, however. At Fort Hertz, in northern Burma, with Scott as his copilot, Payne nonchalantly plunked his C-47 down on a nine-hundred-foot strip hacked out of the jungle. He then supervised the loading of forty sick and wounded Ghurka troops, the tough little fighters from Nepal, and took off again. The mantra for such heroics everywhere in the CBI quickly became "All in a day's work."[8]

In August, Cole learned the fate of some of his friends from the raid on Tokyo. *"Jo will remember Bill Farrow,"* he wrote his parents. *"The big tall thin fellow. She met he and Ferguson up at Pendleton. Anyway, Bill was captured by the Japs in China. They also got Bob Meder a good friend of mine who was from Cleveland and went to Parks and Randolph."*[9]

While the Doolittle Raid on Tokyo was linear, with a clear sense of progress toward a final goal of bombing the enemy's capital, the work of the Hump pilots was recursive, cyclical, and far less climactic. When the airlift finally began in earnest, the pilots rose before the sun, took off in predawn darkness, flew over some of the most inhospitable terrain on the planet, through some of the world's worst flying weather, landed and unloaded their cargo, reloaded, and reversed their route. Then they did the same thing again, and then again, each day's requirements largely the same. The Japanese had fighters out seeking the unarmed transports, but the real enemies were the weather and fatigue. Added to this mix were largely inexperienced crews, aircraft that by necessity were often poorly maintained, unsanitary living conditions, lousy food, intolerable heat, monsoon rains, and a lack of preparations to recover crews that went down along the way. It was grunt work, soul-killing labor, lacking glamour or the satisfaction of knowing that the risks they incurred resulted in tangible destruction of the enemy's ability to fight. Hump fliers were carrying cargo—vital cargo such as gasoline, arms, raw materials, clothing, mail—but still cargo. Stuff. Things that they knew often ended up on the black market after being paid for in blood, the lives of the crews. The work sapped the morale of men, wore out machinery at an astonishing rate, and resulted in the deaths of more than nine hundred American fliers.

Cole was among the first of the Hump fliers, during a time characterized by some writers as the "cowboy" or "barnstorming" period.[10] It was loosely organized, badly underequipped, with not enough planes and ever-increasing demands for more tonnage, more cargo to be hauled over the Himalayas. When Cole started in the theater, no system of rotation for aircrews had been established. It was unknown just how long and at what physical and emotional cost to themselves pilots could fly in the stressful conditions they encountered over the Hump.

Although Cole never hinted in his letters that he and his fellow fliers were ever in any danger, the hazards were many and very real.

Sundays were never a day of rest for the Hump crews, and 18 October was no exception. Its promise at dawn was a clear day. The monsoon rains had finally ended, and the air was fresh and pellucid, with only the tiniest chill. It felt good, after the months of intolerable heat and the daily drenching of gear and spirit. Cole was awakened early for the flight over the mountains and went through his usual routine of breakfast and preflight inspection of the C-47 he was to fly that day. When he arrived at the hardstand, he heard the growl of twin R-2600 engines, the familiar full-power, guttural roar of a B-25 taking off, one of two stationed at Dinjan as a detachment of the 11th, most of which was now flying out of Kunming. Pilots are constitutionally unable to look away while a plane is rolling down a runway, and Cole turned to view the twin-tailed Mitchell lift from the strip at Dinjan and immediately raise its landing gear. It was obviously heavily loaded, meaning a full bay of bombs. He watched it for a few more seconds as it climbed to the east, doubtless on a mission to a target in Burma.

Cole completed his walk-around, and the flight crew boarded and went through their pretakeoff checks. A quick call to the tower and they were cleared for takeoff. The cabin was filled with drums of aviation gasoline, the usual cargo, and the acrid fumes filled the cockpit. The nasty oxygen masks would be a welcome respite from the odoriferous air emanating from the cabin, and the crew opted for oxygen long before reaching ten thousand feet.

As the transport crossed into Burma, a plume of black smoke could be seen just to the right of their flight path. It rose in a thin column, dense and oily, and began to thin and scatter at their altitude of seven thousand feet. Cole had seen enough to know it was either a plane crash or a bomb strike on a fuel depot. As they drew closer, he could see that the smoke rose from a heavily overgrown area of jungle, with no roads, river, or railroad anywhere in the area. That effectively ruled out a fuel dump as a source for the thick smoke.

The copilot was now watching the smoke plume with interest. He turned to Cole and gave him a knowing look. Cole nodded once and turned the plane slightly to bring it closer to the source of the smoke. They looked down, certain now. A large swath of trees was down, and a blackened hole in the green canopy of the jungle was evidence of what they already knew: a plane had gone in, coming to a violent end as it met the earth for a last time. From the visual evidence, there could be no survivors if the crew had stayed with the plane. Even at this altitude, Cole could smell smoke as the C-47 flew through the funeral pyre. Cole told the crew to look for signs of parachutes. They saw nothing. Cole radioed Dinjan to report the crash.

Cole flew on to Kunming, where the gasoline was unloaded and several boxes of heavy tungsten ore were loaded aboard, along with a dozen Chinese soldiers. They were poorly dressed, and all looked very young.

A check with the operations officer, a quick weather briefing; they departed Kunming and picked up a heading of 290 degrees to bring them back to Dinjan.

After landing, he heard the news. The wreckage was that of the B-25 he had watched take off that morning. Flying it was Robert M. Gray, who had been pilot of the third bomber—"Whisky Pete"—to take off from the *Hornet*. He was considered an excellent pilot, one whom Cole had known well. Gray had survived the carrier takeoff, the bailout at night over China, and several bombing missions over Burma. Also among the five men killed in the crash was Sgt. G. E. Larkin Jr., engineer-gunner on the Richard Joyce crew, tenth off the *Hornet*. The Joyce aircraft had been hit over Tokyo, suffering an eight-inch hole in the fuselage, but had continued on to China, where the crew bailed out. The entire crew had remained in India following the raid.

The cause of the crash was never learned. Many of the pilots suspected sabotage. Cole himself had flown the Mitchell the previous day, making a bombing run into Burma on his day off from flying the Hump, and found nothing wrong with the airplane.

Five of the twenty-eight Raiders who had remained in India and China following the mission to Tokyo were dead within six months. Cole had known them all, and their losses were like kicks to his stomach.[11]

*(Above)* Aviation cadet Richard E. Cole as a member of Class 41-E at Kelly Field, Texas. (Courtesy of R. E. Cole)

*(Top right)* "The lids off." Lieutenant Cole's letter to his mother on the evening of 7 December 1941. Cole would be involved in several key actions during the war. (Courtesy of Richard E. Cole Collection, Alden Library, Ohio University)

*(Bottom right)* Lt. Hank Potter (left), navigator of the Doolittle crew, and Lt. Dick Cole in March 1942. They are in front of Cole's house in Dayton, Ohio, while on a trip with Lt. Col. James Doolittle to Wright Field during training for the Tokyo mission. (Courtesy of R. E. Cole)

MARCH FIELD
DEC. 7, 1941

DEAR MOM:

Well! THAT 20 DAY LEAVE
WAS A GOOD IDEA ANYWAY, BUT
TAIN'T NO MORE, THE LIDS OFF.

WE HAVE BEEN AWAITING
ORDERS SINCE NOON WERE SUPPOSED
TO GO TO SACRAMENTO AT 6 P.M. TONITE
BUT IT HAS BEEN CHANGED AND WE
ARE TAKING OFF TOMORROW AT 5:30 AM
FOR PENDLETON TO GET OUR EQUIPMENT.

THATS ABOUT ALL I CAN TELL
YOU AT THE PRESENT CONCERNING
OUR MOVEMENTS. No CAUSE FOR EXCITEMENT
THOUGH I WOULD LIKE TO SEND MY
CAR HOME, BUT DON'T KNOW HOW TO
DO IT. IF YOU HAVE ANY IDEAS I WOULD
LIKE TO HAVE THEM. AS FOR CHRISTMAS
PRESENTS — HMMM — GUESS YOU
MIGHT AS WELL PUT THE MONEY IN
YOUR POCKET CAUSE I HAVEN'T THE
SLIGHTEST IDEA OF WHERE TO SEND
THEM. THERE IS A RUMOR THAT WE
WILL BE ON COAST PATROL AND
WORK OUT OF HERE. SOUNDS GOOD
TO ME, BUT IT IS STILL A RUMOR.

*(Top left)* The first crew to launch from the USS *Hornet* to attack Japan on 18 April 1942. From left: Lt. Henry "Hank" Potter, navigator; Lt. Col. James H. Doolittle, aircraft commander and raid leader; S/Sgt. Fred Braemer, bombardier; Lt. Richard E. Cole, copilot; S/Sgt. Paul Leonard, engineer-gunner. Each crew was similarly photographed before the historic mission. (US Air Force photo)

*(Bottom left)* B-25Bs on the deck of the USS *Hornet* before the raid. The Army bombers made it impossible for the *Hornet*'s own aircraft to be lifted to the flight deck. (US Navy photo)

*(Above)* The Doolittle crew in China after bailing out of their bomber, 19 April 1942, Tianmushan, China. From left: S/Sgt. Fred Braemer, S/Sgt. Paul Leonard, Chou Foo Kai, Lt. Richard Cole, Lt. Col. James Doolittle, Henry Shen, Lt. Henry Potter, and Gissing Chang. (Courtesy of Richard E. Cole Collection, Alden Library, Ohio University)

*May 4, 1942.*

DEAR FOLKS:

I HAVEN'T THE SLIGHTEST IDEA WHEN YOU WILL GET THIS LETTER, BUT HOPE IT WILL BE SOON. I REALIZE YOU ARE PROBABLY BOTH WORRIED AN WONDERING AS TO MY WHEREABOUTS AND SAFTEY. THE LONG SILENCE ON MY PART WAS IMPARATIVE AND SOMEDAY YOU WILL KNOW WHY. I CANNOT SAY WHERE WE ARE, BUT CAN TELL YOU THAT I AM AND HAVE BEEN WELL AND HAPPY AND HOPE YOU ARE THE SAME.

IT IS PRETTY HARD TO WRITE A LETTER WITHOUT WRITING ABOUT YOUR ACTIVITIES, BUT I GUESS IT'S O.K. TO TELL YOU THAT I HAVE HAD MY FIRST TASTE OF COMBAT AND FIND IT NOT TOO BAD. "LADY LUCK" IS STILL RIDING ON MY SHOULDER AN I HOPE SHE STAYS THERE IN THE FUTURE.

I HAVE NO PRESENT ADDRESS SO YOU CANNOT WRITE ME AND WILL HAVE TO BE CONTENT WITH MY LETTERS WHEN I GET A CHANCE TO SEND THEM. REMEMBER, I THINK ABOUT YOU AS MUCH AS YOU THINK ABOUT ME AND SILENCE ON MY PART DOES NOT MEAN OTHERWISE. ARE THERE A LOT OF STRAWBERRIES THIS YEAR? BOY! WOULD I LIKE TO HAVE SOME. I SUPPOSE THE "REDS ARE BEATING THE ☒ CARDS" AS USUAL THIS YEAR — HEY POP! THE LAST FOUR WEEKS HAVE VINDICATED MY LIFE-LONG OPINION — THAT THERE IS NO PLACE AS GOOD AS THE UNITED STATES — NO PLACE —
MY REGARDS TO EVERYONE AND ALL MY LOVE TO YOU
DICK

(*Above*) "Well and happy." Lieutenant Cole's first letter to his parents following the raid on Tokyo. Unable to communicate for several weeks, Cole was still restricted from revealing details about his activities or location. (Courtesy of Richard E. Cole Collection, Alden Library, Ohio University)

May 20, 1942

Mrs. Fred Cole
747 Faulkner Avenue
Dayton, Ohio

Dear Mrs. Cole:

 I am pleased to report that Dick is well and happy although a bit homesick. I left him in Chungking, in China, a couple of weeks ago. He had recently completed a very hazardous, extremely important and most interesting flight — the air raid on Japan. He comported himself with conspicuous bravery and distinction. He was awarded the Distinguished Flying Cross for gal- · lantry in action, and also was decorated by the Chinese Government.

 Transportation and communication facilities are extremely bad in the Far East and so it may be sometime before you hear again from Dick directly. I assure you, however, that everything is going smoothly with him and although plans for the future are uncertain he will probably be returning home sometime in the not too distant future.

 I am proud to have served with Dick, who was my co-pilot on the flight, and hope that I may have an opportunity to serve with him again.

    Very sincerely yours,

    J. H. Doolittle
    Brigadier General, U.S.A.

*(Above)* "Proud to have served with Dick." Doolittle, who received the Medal of Honor and promotion to brigadier general following the successful raid on Tokyo, wrote to the families of each of the seventy-nine men he led on the mission. (Courtesy of R. E. Cole)

*(Top left)* A Curtiss C-46 Commando over the rugged Himalayas. Hump fliers had to contend with the extreme geography as well as terrible weather, inadequate navigation aids, poor maps, and the threat of Japanese aircraft as they flew supplies from India to China. (US Air Force photo)

*(Bottom left)* Chinese soldiers were frequently carried by Hump aircraft as they returned from Kunming to airfields in Assam in northeastern India. The soldiers were then transported to British bases for special training. (US Air Force photo)

*(Above)* A blood chit or safe-passage flag. These were issued to Hump pilots and flight crews operating in China. They were sometimes sewn onto flight jackets but more frequently carried in a pocket. The message reads: "This foreign person has come to China to help in the war effort. Soldiers and civilians, one and all, should rescue and protect him." This chit was carried by S/Sgt. Lynn Johnston, the author's father-in-law, who flew Hump missions in 1944. (Photo by author)

*(Top left)* Chinese soldiers read the blood chit on the flight jacket of a Hump pilot. (National Archives photo)

*(Bottom left)* Happy pilots, just returned to the United States from a hazardous tour flying the Hump. From left: Capt. Jake Sartz, Capt. Jim Segel, Capt. Dick Cole, and Lt. Paul Conroy. (Courtesy of R. E. Cole)

*(Above)* Capt. Dick Cole in the summer of 1943 as acceptance officer and test pilot, Tulsa, Oklahoma. Cole was in the States after the Tokyo Raid and a tour flying the Hump before leaving again for the invasion of Burma. (Courtesy of R. E. Cole)

*(Top left)* Miss Lucia Marta Harrell as a student pilot in 1943 in Tulsa, Oklahoma. (Courtesy of R. E. Cole)

*(Bottom left)* Capt. and Mrs. Richard E. Cole, October 1943. The couple was married just before Dick reported to the 1st Air Commando Group; he shipped out for India and Burma later that year. (Courtesy of R. E. Cole)

*(Above)* Flight crew of Cole's C-47 "Hairless Joe," of the 1st Air Commando and the aerial invasion of Burma. Cole is kneeling, left. Lt. Ralph Bordley, copilot, is standing left, wearing the special-issue airborne jumpsuit. Maurice Ray Roberts, assistant flight engineer, is kneeling right. (US Air Force photo)

*(Top left)* Tropical chic. Glider pilots James "Mickey" Bartlett (left) and Lt. Vincent Rose, deputy commander of the glider section of the 1st Air Commandos, are informally dressed for the heat and humidity of India and Burma in 1944. Note the sidearms and knives for both; Bartlett is wearing "mosquito boots," popular among pilots during the war. (Courtesy of John Bartlett)

*(Bottom left)* A Waco CG-4A glider. These large cargo aircraft were towed, often two at a time, behind "tugs" such as Cole's C-47; the tugs were specially equipped with machinery that allowed them to fly low and snatch gliders from fields too small or rough for conventional aircraft to land. (US Air Force photo)

*(Above)* Cole's C-47, number 2100446, tows a glider over rugged hills in India just prior to the invasion of Burma in March 1944. The question mark was the unofficial insignia of the transport section of the 1st Air Commandos. (US Air Force photo)

*(Top left)* Maj. Gen. Orde Wingate of Britain, here boarding an Air Commando C-47, was the unorthodox leader of the Special Force that invaded Burma by glider. The sun helmet, beard, and rifle were hallmarks that were easily identified during his frequent visits to the forward bases of the Allies. (US Air Force photo)

*(Bottom left)* Col. Johnny Alison (left), cocommander of the 1st Air Commandos; Lt. Col. Walter P. Scott, recipient of the Distinguished Service Order and Military Cross, of Britain; and Maj. William H. Taylor Jr., head of the glider section of the 1st Air Commandos, at the clearing code-named Broadway in March 1944. (US Air Force photo)

*(Above)* Col. Philip Cochran (third from left) briefs C-47 pilots before the start of Operation Thursday on the evening of 5 March 1944. Cole's C-47 "Hairless Joe" was the third aircraft to take off from the Air Commando base at Lalaghat, India, for the daring mission. (US Air Force photo)

(*Above*) Special vintage. Lt. Col. Richard E. Cole opens the bottle of 1896 Hennessy cognac for the final toast of the Doolittle Raiders on 9 November 2013 at the National Museum of the US Air Force, near Dayton, Ohio. Visible at right is Lt. Col. Edward Saylor, who died in January 2015. (US Air Force photo)

(*Below*) The last two surviving Doolittle Tokyo Raiders, Staff Sergeant David J. Thatcher (left) and Lieutenant Colonel Richard E. Cole, with the Congressional Gold Medal awarded the Raiders in April 2015. The medal, one of only 158 awarded since the first to George Washington in 1776, was given to the National Museum of the U.S. Air Force at Wright-Patterson Air Force Base on 18 April 2015, the seventy-third anniversary of the famed mission. Thatcher was engineer/gunner on aircraft 7, and Cole was copilot to then Lieutenant Colonel James H. "Jimmy" Doolittle in the first B-25 to fly off the deck of the USS *Hornet*. (U.S. Air Force photo by Niki Jahns)

# CHAPTER 16

A few months after he began flying Hump missions out of Dinjan, Cole and many other transport pilots were transferred to Chabua, about twenty miles away, which was to become the headquarters for the airlift. Chabua had been built by the British using Indian labor, mainly women, since here as elsewhere around the world so many men were in uniform. Rocks were broken by hand or in primitive rock crushers and carried in baskets on the heads of workers. By mid-1942 it was still a very primitive field, with a single runway (05-23 to correspond with the prevailing monsoon winds) and a few hardstands—hard-surfaced parking areas—for the three squadrons of C-47s of the 1st Ferry Group. The control tower was a shack built in a tree on the edge of the field. Accommodations for personnel, including the flight crews, were spartan. Shacks made of bamboo, with thatched roofs and no plumbing, constituted most of the buildings at Chabua, including housing. Beds were of the charpoy variety—wooden frames with a spiderweb of rope for springs. A few wrecked planes were scattered around the base; more would be added in the next couple of years. Primitive it might have been, but it was busy continuously as a stopover and refueling base for aircraft on the Karachi to Kunming run. A bomb squadron of B-24s and a fighter squadron of P-40s were also stationed at the base, in addition to the Ferry Command cargo planes.

Cole described living conditions at Chabua in a letter to his sister in September 1942. He had turned twenty-seven on 7 September, and the letter was written five days later. *"We are way up on the 'North-eastern' frontier, right in the middle of 'monkeyland.' About fifty miles to the north lie the great Himalaya range. Seeing the famed Mt. Everest is quite a thrill.*

*It's one of the few places left on earth that has never been explored by man. Our airports have been hacked out of the jungle and we are living in barracks made of wood, bamboo, mud cement and a typical thatch roof.*"

The monkeys apparently were quite pesky: "*We are having a battle all our own with the monkeys, they jabber and scold us all day long. Dick Bechtel and I had a little one for a pet, but had to get rid of him cause he was too much trouble. We took him for a ride and he passed out at 8,000 ft. from the lack of oxygen I guess—sure was a cute little fellow though.*"[1]

Shortly after he moved into his new basha at Chabua, Cole met Lt. Jacob Sartz, who walked through the door of the newly constructed hut and breezily stuck out his hand. "Jake Sartz. I'm your new roommate." Sartz would become one of Cole's closest friends. He was a big man, six foot one, with the build of a football player. A graduate of the University of Pennsylvania, he had been married and divorced, was not easily cowed, and was already famed as the daring pilot who had possibly set a world's record for the number of passengers he had been able to cram into a C-47 and take off.[2]

Sartz had arrived, along with Jim Segel, with the first group of AM-MISCA pilots, the American Military Mission to China, in May. Things had quickly turned sour for the Allies, as the Japanese launched an attack on Burma and easily overran Rangoon. Soon the northern half of the country was under attack, and as the Chinese and British troops there, along with the AVG, had begun to withdraw, it quickly turned into a rout. Gen. Joseph Stilwell was among the troops caught in Burma, and while many were flown out he declined the offer of a flight and opted to hike out with his men. Meanwhile, the American C-47 pilots had been pressed into service to bring out wounded and key personnel from Myitkyina before it was overrun by the Japanese. The pilots routinely carried far more people than the twenty-four passengers that the engineers said the C-47 was designed for. On one flight, with increasingly desperate people clamoring to board, Sartz had taken off with seventy-three passengers. When he landed at Dinjan, 190 miles away, the British Customs officials counted seventy-four. A woman had given birth en route.[3] For his daring flights into Myitkyina, in the face of an advancing Japanese army, Sartz had been awarded the Silver Star.

Cole and Sartz were a good balance, the kind of same yet different personality types that seemed to click, the kind that allow friendship to last a lifetime. In flight school, Cole had been the conformer, the cadet eager to avoid any gigs or demerits, a bit fearful of not making it, of washing out. Sartz was rather more brazen, seemingly without fear of upperclassmen. On one occasion, Cole learned, Sartz had been accosted by one of the dreaded senior cadets who called him to attention and demanded to know what he had done in civilian life before the Army had so obviously lowered its standards and allowed him into the flight training program.

"Sir! I made one-half toilet seats, Sir!" The tall, curly-haired Sartz looked straight ahead, his chin tucked, his arms firmly at his side. The upperclassman looked confused.

"Half toilet seats, Mister? Why half?"

"Sir! For half-assed upperclassmen like you, Sir!"

Whether the story was apocryphal or true, it illustrated to Cole the almost complete lack of fear in Sartz.[4]

While flying the Hump into China at the very outset of the airlift, Sartz had frequently flown with Colonel Scott, and some of those flights were recounted later in Scott's *God Is My Co-Pilot*. On one, the legendary fighter pilot said he still had nightmares as he recalled a particularly gut-wrenching flight in monsoon weather. After discharging their cargo of aviation gas in Kunming, Scott and Sartz had opted to carry back to Dinjan a 6,000-pound load of tin ingots, based on weather forecasts of clear air in Assam and not so good over Burma. The load of tin was 50 percent more than they would normally carry, but they intended to fly south into Burma to burn up gasoline and then be able to climb high enough to clear the lower Himalayas. As they crossed into Burma, two Japanese fighters intercepted them, and the American pilots ducked into a cloud to avoid them.

The clouds turned out to be a massive monsoon storm. They were now on instruments, unable to climb above thirteen thousand feet; they needed a minimum of fifteen thousand to clear the peaks. So Sartz and Scott agreed to fly north and south, the direction of the valleys and chains of peaks, until they burned enough fuel to climb. But they soon hit turbulence, and Scott left Sartz alone in the cockpit to fly while he went back to the cabin to try to throw out the heavy load of tin. Each ingot weighed 112 pounds, and the air rushing outside prevented his opening the cargo door, so Scott eventually abandoned his plan. For the next hour, the pair flew on instruments up and down what they hoped was a valley below them, burning off fuel, rocking and bouncing in the violent turbulence, doing their best to hold their heading and altitude. They were able to struggle to eighteen thousand feet, but without any radio fixes or homing beacons they were uncertain whether they had been blown far north, where the peaks were twenty to twenty-five thousand feet. If they had been and headed west to Dinjan, they would meet a quick and violent end as they flew into a granite mountaintop.

They had been in the air for four and a half hours, with a long way to go, and now fuel was becoming an issue not of weight but of enough to get them there. They talked, agreed to chance it, and turned west, waiting in agony for the split-second screech of tearing metal that would tell them they had just hit a cloud-shrouded mountaintop and were a millisecond from death. Outside, the storm was black, with zero visibility. Finally, they spotted a light patch in the clouds and ducked down into it; through the mist, Sartz spied the Brahmaputra, the miles-wide meandering river just west of their base. But it wasn't over. A dark column of intense rain was directly over Dinjan, obscuring all visual contact with the ground while dumping buckets of water over the base. Neither flier could see the runway, despite two approaches from the island in the river that was the final approach point for arriving aircraft. On the third attempt to land, Sartz spotted the runway under a foot of water, turned the C-47 sharply to the right and set it down on what appeared to be a lake. It had been a nightmarish flight for Scott, but for the Hump pilots in the months and years ahead it would turn out to be a typical flight, hardly worth mentioning.[5]

For the duration of Cole's deployment to the Hump, Sartz would be his roommate, and on several trips they flew as pilot and copilot on food-drop missions to resupply Office of Strategic Services outposts deep in northern Burma. On one flight, they carried an agent who parachuted into a small clearing in the jungle. Such missions beyond hauling freight over the Hump were fairly common, and the pilots looked forward to the breaks in routine. Sartz was steady and unflappable, with a grand sense of humor that fitted well with Cole's quiet demeanor. Early in their Hump career, they had each obtained a bottle of scotch. With a demanding flight schedule, and already enervated by lack of rest, poor food, and the steaming climate, Cole vowed he would not imbibe until his tour was over. Drinking was one of the few diversions for the flight crews, and many drank to excess when not in a cockpit. Sartz looked wistfully at his bottle of scotch and, after a pause, proclaimed that he too would voluntarily go on the wagon until the end of the tour. The bottles were laid carefully in the pilots' footlockers.

Lt. Jim Segel was another Burma Roadster who flew with Cole out of Chabua. Segel was featured in a *Collier's* article about the early days of the Hump. In the turgid style of the day, the writer described a typical flight, when the temperature on the ground was 110 and the flight crew wore moccasins and shorts, and gloves were required in the oven-like cockpit where the controls were too hot to touch. Between eight and ten thousand feet, it was time to pull on flight coveralls and perhaps a sweater or sweatshirt. At fourteen thousand feet, it was time to don the sheepskin clothing.[6]

It was difficult to dress for the wide range of temperatures that the aircrews encountered. In the summer, temperatures soared, often topping 120 degrees; metal surfaces of the aircraft would sear the hands of ground and aircrews alike. Pilots frequently wore shorts on the ground at Chabua and the other bases in Assam and carried additional clothing to pull on as they climbed into the icy regions of fifteen to twenty thousand feet. Sheepskin jackets, pants, boots, and hats were in short supply but prized by the Hump pilots; they were usually carried aboard, dumped in a heap behind the pilots, and pulled on when the temperatures slowly dropped as the cargo planes clawed for altitude.

Oxygen was necessary for flying the Hump as well, although oxygen equipment was in short supply in mid-1942. Frequently, crews simply gasped for air at the highest altitudes, but then tanks and breathing equipment became available and a requirement for flights above ten thousand feet. At first, Cole used a "pipestem" system, with a mouthpiece clenched in his teeth; later, masks were issued. They were uncomfortable, and ice tended to form in the flexible tube. Fliers had to periodically crush the tubing to prevent complete blockage of the vital oxygen.

Ice was an even bigger threat when it built up on the wings, since often no remedy was available. Flying through the thick, moisture-laden clouds above fifteen thousand feet caused water droplets to stick to the metal skin of the wings and freeze. This had two potentially disastrous consequences: the accumulated ice added critical weight to the already overloaded cargo planes, but, even worse, it also altered the shape of the wing. The curvature of the wing surfaces was precisely calculated by aeronautical engineers; the decrease in air pressure just above the wing surface, caused by an increase in velocity of the air passing over it, was the genie that provided lift and allowed a heavy machine to fly. When ice altered the equation, the airplane first became sluggish, requiring more power to remain at a given altitude; as more ice built up, the plane simply was not capable of continued flight. Hump crews faced this challenge on every flight. Deicing equipment had been added to the airplanes, but it tended to wear out quickly and replacement parts were in critically short supply. Ice could kill flight crews as surely as an enemy fighter or antiaircraft fire.

Two kinds of ice affect aircraft in flight: rime and clear. Rime ice is white and granular, easily seen and fairly easy to eliminate. It forms when the cold surface of a wing (or propeller) comes into contact with the moisture in clouds. Clear ice is more difficult to discern, particularly in the dim light available inside storm clouds, and is the result of freezing rain contacting the airplane.

Segel, a Boston native and MIT graduate, had a nerve-racking flight in which his wings accumulated so much clear ice he could not maintain his altitude despite full power and 2,450 rpm. On a return flight from Kunming carrying five thousand pounds of tungsten ore, Segel and his copilot, Lt. Bob Spector, were flying through the typical instruments-only weather when they were startled out of their daydreams by the horrific sounds of something pounding the outside of their cockpit. It sounded like large rocks, and for an instant Segel was certain they had scraped the top of one of the unseen peaks. It was Spector's first flight over the Hump, and he looked at Segel as though certain it would also be his last.

Segel realized quickly that the loud thudding was caused by chunks of ice slung from the propeller blades. Part of the deicing system provided for fluid to be pumped to the propeller hubs and then through centrifugal force dispersed to the spinning blades. That part of the system was working well, but Segel knew that ice on the props undoubtedly meant ice on the wings as well. He peered through the gloom and saw clear ice building on the fronts and over the top of his wings. He cursed the supply officers and the paperwork and the lack of parts. The wing deicer system was an inflatable rubber "boot" attached to the leading edge of the wing; when air was sent through the system, the boot flexed to break up accumulated ice. Clear ice was difficult at the best of times to break away from the wings; forming in sheets, it tended to flex as well, but the system was the best they had. The boots wore out quickly in the tropical climate and when they began to disintegrate were removed because of the drag they created. On Segel's plane that day, the boots had been taken off, and no new parts were available.

The plane was on the verge of stalling, despite being at full power, and the pilots quickly agreed that they needed to throw out the tungsten ore, an extremely valuable cargo used in war production of steel. With one man flying and the other helping the crew chief manhandle the sacks of tungsten, they pitched out thousands of dollars of valuable ore, the entire five thousand pounds of cargo. The C-47 was lighter, and the airspeed began to build slowly. But it was a temporary gain; ice continued to form, and once more the cargo plane was struggling to stay airborne.

As Sartz and Scott earlier, and no doubt countless other pilots as well, they knew they needed to descend to warmer temperatures to melt the ice. If they didn't, they understood the inevitable end as the airplane simply ceased being a flying machine and transmuted into a falling object. And, as for Sartz and Scott on their memorable flight, a small light area in the clouds revealed a patch of ground below. Well aware of the dangers of a "sucker hole," as pilots dubbed such seeming beacons of safety, they dove for the earth. Flight training usually advises against such actions, since the hole in the cloud can quickly fill in, leaving the pilot and his airplane in the same conditions as earlier but now at a much lower altitude.

The ice melted, Segel and Spector were able to climb once more to clear the peaks of the Hump, and they lived to tell the tale.[7]

In those early days of the Hump operation, such flights created an atmosphere of derring-do that permeated the organization. Pilots decorated the fronts and sleeves of their jackets with colorful leather patches handmade in Calcutta and sewed American flags to the back. Blood chits—cloth or leather flags with Chinese figures that promised a reward for the safe return of the flier—were carried in pockets or sewn inside the jacket. The crusher, a soft-billed, unstructured hat specifically designed to accommodate the headset of fliers, was worn with all the bravado of fighter pilots. As military-trained pilots who had survived the rigors of flight school and the unceasing winnowing of cadets, they considered themselves an elite species, and if they hadn't been designated to fly fighters or bombers, they were not willing to concede any diminution of their status. The pilots and flight crews were young and many terribly inexperienced. Planes with their young crews regularly went missing. The Hump was the subject of many magazine and newspaper articles that stressed the danger and the bloody awful conditions, and that didn't hurt their image either. So the pilots made the best of it.

# CHAPTER 17

By September 1942, the routine of flying the Hump was fairly well established for the pilots of Ferry Command. Cole celebrated his twenty-seventh birthday, but there was no time off and no facilities or provisions for a party, so it went by largely as any other day.

The weather for the next two months would be some of the best for flying. The monsoons had largely dissipated, along with the drenching rains of June, July, and August. Temperatures were milder, the humidity was bearable, and only an occasional afternoon thunderstorm interrupted the otherwise smooth return trips from Kunming. Cole, Sartz, and the other Hump pilots at bases in Assam had settled into a kind of scout-camp existence, where they were learning to be self-sufficient. If problems arose with the aircraft, or when foul weather ambushed them, they would be the ones to pay the price.

Weather reports were provided by the pilots themselves. If a plane ran into turbulence or icing or severe storms, he reported those conditions to the weather officer at Chabua, who would make that information available to the next flight out. Similar reports were made at Kunming and often en route to other aircraft.

Cargo for the majority of Hump flights into China consisted of drums of aviation gasoline for Chennault's air force operating out of Kunming—the AVG, which evolved into the China Air Task Force, which became, in time, the 14th Army Air Force. Drums containing the fuel were strapped into place on the reinforced deck of the cabins to prevent shifting in flight; the straps were not strong enough to prevent their being hurled forward into the cockpit in the event of a crash landing, however. Mules were also a frequent cargo into Kunming for use with the Chinese Army; in that event, the cabin was strewn with hay and the mules secured in makeshift, easily removed stalls. The cabin of the transport smelled like mule urine for weeks after such a haul. Frequently, large sums of money—paper Chinese currency printed in the United States—would be flown in, as well as spare aircraft parts, ammunition, and, most important for the Americans in China, mail from home.

They seldom returned to Chabua empty. Frequently, they ferried Chinese soldiers over the Hump for training in India. Tungsten, tin, and hog bristles—for Navy paint brushes—were common cargo items carried out of Kunming, but they carried virtually anything vital to the war effort.

Between flights over the Hump, which were generally every other day, Cole and his buddies didn't have much to do. One nightly event was the ubiquitous poker game, found everywhere on the globe that American troops could conjure, steal, or manufacture a deck of cards. The stakes could be matchsticks, or money. In India the currency was the rupee, and too often the airmen considered the brightly colored paper bills the equivalent of Monopoly money. It was too garish, too *foreign* looking, to be real. Many of them lost their monthly checks to the sharks waiting for them at the table.

Cole didn't play, but Sartz did. After losing badly a couple of times, the easygoing Sartz commissioned Cole to be his banker. He gave the quiet man his monthly pay, and at the onset of a poker game Cole doled out three rupees. If Sartz won in the first hands, he stayed in the game, gambling only his winnings during the long evening. If he lost quickly, he threw in his hand and came to the other side of the barracks, where Sartz the gambler and Cole the banker settled into a game of hearts. No stakes.[1]

There were other, more serious, games of hearts, and often the stakes were agonizingly high.

In a letter home, Cole described one wall of the poker room. Apparently, someone had sent him a letter that contained news clippings of weddings and engagement announcements around Dayton. Cole's description of the poker room in a letter to his mother is sad; there is a touch of resentment and anger behind the words: "*I like to get those clippings. We have lots of fun over them, the wall of the room where the boys play poker is reserved for pictures of 'gal friends' who got married to draft dodgers since the boys came overseas. Boy! You ought to see 'em now. They drew mustaches and beards on 'em. Some fun. It's quite a large club by now and growing every day. Sure lots of good boys disappointed."*[2]

Dear John letters were a common complaint among troops in every theater. As the war went on, there would be many more of them. For young men in the war, the award of wings had given them instant status among women, and while they were home and in uniform they were able to date girls who formerly might not have looked twice at them. That changed, however, when they left for war zones. There were always plenty of men around, either in military training or else in jobs protected from the draft. It was a galling circumstance, and the "it's over" letters induced deep sadness and depression among the pilots and aircrew. That they were able to turn the rejection around and publicly transform their hurt and humiliation into a kind of communal game was no doubt excellent therapy.

Not all the letters from loved ones at home were heartbreakers, however. Cole was still awaiting his first letter while continuing to write home.

*Because we don't get much news over [here], we are all interested in getting mail. Most always when one of us get a letter from home (not me yet) or friends they either read it out loud or let all of us read it. This may sound funny but it is really a good feeling to read a letter from "back there." Lenard Rippy the boy who bunks next to me is married and his wife had a baby May 20. She sent "Rip" some pictures, has red hair. He is undoubtedly the proudest man in the world. Every time we come to the barracks he gets out the letter, reads it, and then looks at the picture making some comment or wisecrack about it.*[3]

Like the American Wild West, life on the frontier of the war produced colorful characters. Jim Segel tells of one, a cowboy from Amarillo, Texas—every unit in the Army Air Forces had a "Tex," he says—who was enamored with Segel's .45 revolver. A shortage of 1911 .45 automatics, standard sidearms for fliers, had resulted in Segel's being issued a model 1917 .45 revolver, a large and unwieldy piece of personal armament. "Tex" Weston, who wore cowboy boots with his khakis tucked into the tops, lusted for the revolver, which more closely resembled the sidearms of Old West characters. He continually pestered Segel to borrow it. With the revolver strapped to his waist, Tex practiced his fast draw for hours. Tall, lean, with sandy hair and a perpetual squint, he looked the part of a lawman—or a desperado.

Finally, Tex suggested a swap, Segel's revolver for Weston's .45 auto. Segel was more than happy to accommodate. The trade was made, and shortly thereafter Tex was once more practicing his fast draw in the basha he shared with three other pilots. The revolver was loaded. As Weston twirled it around one finger before reholstering it, the handgun went off, narrowly missing the cowboy's prized boots. The bullet went through the floor and into the first level, where two Indian houseboys were preparing meals for the fliers. They screamed and ran from the bungalow, thinking they were under attack by the Japanese. Segel and his housemates banished Tex to outside the living area to practice his fast draw and warned him to always unload it. It cost them many rupees to persuade the houseboys to return.[4]

Cole, the shy boy from Dayton, worked hard not to be a colorful character. He was quiet to the point of annoying some of his flying mates. Segel had been among the first group of Ferry Command pilots sent to India specifically to fly the Hump, and his personality was outgoing, even brash at times, the polar opposite of the taciturn Cole. Segel often tried to begin a conversation.

"So, what did you do in theater before you joined this outfit?"

"I was in a B-25 group." A short silence followed.

Segel again: "Why'd you transfer to the Burma Roadsters?" It was one of many nicknames for the men who flew the Hump.

"Too many pilots, not enough planes. Wasn't getting any flying time."

Other attempts at conversation were equally frustrating for Segel; the older pilot was competent and friendly, but not gregarious in the way of so many military fliers. Segel finally stopped trying to learn Cole's background.

One day after landing back at Chabua, another first pilot asked Segel how he liked hanging out with a celebrity. Segel looked puzzled, and the other pilot pointed out Cole, who was going into the Operations Office for a weather report. "Right there. Cole." They had been flying together for several months, and it was only now that Segel learned that the quiet man was Jimmy Doolittle's copilot on the Tokyo Raid. At that time, the raid was still seen as one of the biggest, most spectacular events of the war, and those who participated were lionized not only in hometown newspapers but in officers' clubs and operations shacks across the CBI and Europe, where many had been sent following their return to the States. When questioned directly by Segel about the Tokyo mission, Cole shrugged and replied that it was quite an ordinary event.[5]

"I never wanted to be a blabbermouth," Cole said many years later. "For all I knew, if I'd been talking about things I'd done in the war, the guy I was talking to would turn out to be a Medal of Honor winner."[6]

On an early flight into Kunming, Cole and his copilot were in a cantina run by the AVG, a shack known as the Tiger's Lair. A delay in loading their transport for the return flight to India meant they would RON— Remain Over Night. Cole was wearing his AAF-issued A-2 leather flight jacket, with his name tag and the Thunderbird patch of the 34th Bomb Squadron on the left chest. It was the jacket he had worn on the raid. An AVG armorer ordered a drink and began a conversation with Cole. The armorer was wearing a Navy flight jacket, which was standard issue to the Tigers. The Navy jackets had mouton (lamb fur) collars, with an inside pocket in addition to two external ones.

The AVG enlisted man recognized Cole and his squadron patch— news of the raid was everywhere now—and offered to trade jackets. Cole wanted the additional comfort of the fur collar as well as the convenience of the internal pocket. In the end, he swapped jackets when the other man sweetened the pot by throwing in a large Flying Tiger emblem painted on a four-by-four-foot sheet of plywood. It was the famed depiction of the winged tiger jumping through a Japanese flag, originally designed by the Disney group.[7] Cole eventually gave the emblem to Tex Hill, a leading ace of the Flying Tigers, who presented it to a museum in San Diego. Years later, the museum burned and the artifact was destroyed.

Even after the Hump pilots were issued sheepskin flight jackets in addition to the lighter horsehide or goatskin A-2s, Cole continued to wear his Navy jacket for many years. He never attached any squadron patches to it, or decorated it in any way, which in its own way made him stand out in the CBI.

The base at Chabua was growing. More permanent buildings were constructed, and the runway was improved. An alert device was constructed: a hinged pole to which was attached a large red flag. When an attack by Japanese was probable, the pole was pulled straight up with the flag at the top; when the attack was over, the pole was lowered, the flag dangling near the bottom.[8]

And finally, the post exchange was receiving shipments. *"Our first PX supplies arrived today, got 1 Coca Cola—course it was hot—but tasted fine. Also some peanuts, chocolates, 1 can of fruit juice and a box of sardines."*[9]

Conditions were improving at Chabua, and supplies were dribbling in. But this was not a ragtag airline run on a shoestring, with the attendant problems of domestic transportation and fierce competition. It was a war, a fact that was brought home to Cole all too clearly. He made new friends, but lost some old ones.

# CHAPTER 18

Lt. Bobby Cook went missing near the end of his tour. He was one of the original AMMISCA pilots who roomed next to Cole at the Chabua flight crew basha and whom Cole knew well. Cook took off from Chabua in a C-87 and made it to China, where his cargo was unloaded; his airplane was then reloaded with tungsten for the trip back to Chabua. He never made it. For a time, it seemed to Cole that a plane disappeared about once a week, and early in the airlift operation few of their crews made it back alive.

So far as Cole and others knew, no trace was ever found of Cook's C-87, like so many others who disappeared over the Hump. Before and after Cook, fliers went missing with a frequency that should have alarmed higher brass. But there was a war on, a big war, and the Hump operation was considered high priority, possibly the highest in the CBI. It had to go on. Besides, everyone knew that flying was itself inherently unforgiving. No one raised a hue and cry when young cadets were killed in training; by war's end, an estimated fifteen thousand young men had died trying to earn their wings.

For Cole and the other Hump pilots, Cook's empty bunk was cause for sadness, a time for silent mourning. But that's the way it was. There was no body to view, no funeral at which to pay last respects. In truth, many of them—including Cole—were grateful that it was not them, not this time anyway. "It was our way of coping. You don't get anywhere brooding. That was my job, and you just had to go on, or you would never put your foot in an airplane again," Cole said many years later.[1]

But the Hump pilots were not merely fatalistic automatons programmed to fly. Knowing that the route was extremely dangerous if they were forced down or had to bail out, they began to fashion kits that they hoped would enhance their prospects of survival. One pilot, Al Boll, designed a vest with multiple pockets in which he stuffed so much gear that the others teased him aloud. "We called him Dumb-Boll, like dumbbell, the heavy weights used in gyms. We guessed he had about 50 pounds of gear," Cole recalled. But soon others began assembling their own survival kits. Cole clearly remembered bailing out of his B-25 over China with few provisions. He made a vest from an old blue denim farm jacket with the sleeves removed and had his Indian houseboy arrange for numerous pockets to be sewn onto it, much like a modern fly-fishing vest. Now, he never flew without several candy bars, a couple of C rations, the large knife that he had used while hunting as a boy, a pocket knife, a small fishing kit with line and hooks and wooden bobbers, several pocket compasses, matches, and a signal mirror. In addition to his issued .45, he also carried an Army canteen on a web belt and a small first-aid kit. Soon most other pilots had fashioned their own walkout gear. In a pocket of his flight suit, Cole carried a small folded cloth blood chit, a promise written in several languages that if the airman was returned safely to Allied forces, a reward would be paid to those who brought him in. While the aeronautical research laboratory at Wright airfield in Dayton worked on survival gear, including the famous C-1 Survival (sustenance) Vest, fliers in India were already designing their own.[2]

Those who sent young men out to fly over hostile and forbidding environments were not ignorant or insensitive to the dangers faced by aircrews. Several booklets were printed during the war to aid downed fliers in a variety of conditions. One, the so-called Red Book, was titled *Survival: Jungle, Desert, Arctic, Ocean*, and was printed by the AAF's Office of Flying Safety. It was small, with a red cover, and intended to be included as part of the C-1 Survival Vest issued late in the war. Another, with the succinct title *Survival*, was published by the Air Lines War Training Institute, initially for use by the many airline pilots who had been requisitioned for the war effort, and the Allied air forces in the Pacific collaborated on another called *Survival Hints*. Both of the latter were printed in 1943.[3]

All contained some good advice for fliers who didn't make it back to their base and included tips for those who had descended under a parachute canopy and those who had crash-landed their airplanes. The Allied *Survival Hints* pamphlet was targeted mainly for those flying in New Guinea, but contained some generally useful information for all aircrews. The 8.2-ounce chino long-sleeved shirt and trousers were recommended for jungle survival, as well as a leather flying jacket for nights at higher elevations. Sturdy shoes, the high-top GI style, neither too tight nor too loose, would serve best. Two pairs of socks should be worn on every flight; after landing in the jungle, the outer pair should be removed; each night they should be washed and a clean pair used the next day. The parachute could be used for a tent or a sleeping bag, or even for making signal panels. A machete should be strapped to the lower leg, and each flier should carry a hunting knife, a pistol with extra ammo, a compass, matches, a mosquito net, and leather gloves. Downed fliers should try to stay on trails, no matter how faint or narrow, rather than hack through jungle growth.[4]

Not all the advice would have been met with confidence, however. In a section dealing with animals, the writer of the pamphlet notes that crocodiles are the most dangerous beast in a jungle setting, and their behavior is likely to be unpredictable. If attacked by a crocodile, the booklet suggests, try jamming your thumbs in its eyes.[5]

Luckily for Cole and his flying buddies over the Hump, there were no crocodiles in the jungles of northern Burma. Farther south, in the mangrove swamps on the island of Ramree just off the coast of Burma, however, saltwater crocodiles were manifest. In a horrific incident in January 1945, British troops landed on Ramree to establish an air base; the thousand or so Japanese defenders retreated into the mangrove swamp, and over the course of several nights perhaps as many as five hundred of them were killed and eaten by the fierce carnivores. Survivors reported that the nights were filled with screams of terror and the sounds of attacking crocodiles in feeding frenzies.[6]

The absence of crocodiles in northern Burma was of little comfort, however. In the glades and beneath the green canopies of the hundred-foot teak trees could be found the Asian two-horned rhinoceros, wild water buffalo, sun and moon bears, tigers, clouded leopards, and wildcats. While most of these were not often dangerous to humans, tell that to a stranded and possibly injured downed flier. If the mammals were not enough to give pause, there were plenty of reptiles, including about forty poisonous vipers—notably the cobra and a variety of kraits—as well as the Burmese python, which can grow to more than twenty feet.[7]

Once in a while, a flier downed over the Hump route made it back, and it was big news. The American Army (and Air Forces) troops in the CBI theater received a weekly official newspaper beginning in September 1942, not long after Cole began flying the Hump. Breezy and informal, with photos of starlets, cartoons, and short pieces about the ordinary GIs fighting a war so far from home, it was a favorite of Cole and his flying buddies. The 31 December 1942 issue of the *CBI Roundup* detailed the harrowing experience of Cpl. Matthew J. Campanella, a crewman on a 47 flying back to Assam from China. Campanella and co-pilot Lt. Cecil Williams spent twenty-three days in the jungle of northern Burma before being rescued. Their transport had experienced some kind of distress—the *Roundup* story does not indicate the exact cause—and the pilot had ordered the crew to bail out.

The crew members of transports ordinarily did not wear their chutes during flights, donning them only when necessary. Campanella strapped on his parachute, grabbed his .45 pistol, a flashlight, a unit of K rations—an unsweetened chocolate bar—and a canteen. Standing at the open rear door of the Gooney, Campanella and Williams looked at each other. "Who's going first?" The copilot said, "We'll jump together." They locked arms and leaped from the aircraft. Campanella evidently struck the tail of the aircraft and was knocked unconscious. He was unable to remember how his chute opened, but somehow both men landed in the top of the same seventy-five-foot tree. They climbed down, leaving their chute canopies in the treetop, hoping they would be spotted by friendly aircraft. It took hours in the dark to descend from the tree.

Taking stock the next morning of their situation and their supplies, they realized they did not have much. The shock of a parachute deploying can cause items not securely fastened to scatter into, literally, thin air. Lieutenant Williams had lost his .45 as well as both of his flying boots and was now barefoot. Campanella lost one flying boot but retained his shoes. Together, the pair had a dozen matches, quinine pills (to combat malaria), iodine (to purify water), some fishing line and hooks, one compass, two flashlights, a large jungle knife, one canteen, three K rations, Williams's wristwatch, and Campanella's .45, with seven rounds of ammunition. Campanella gave Williams his remaining flight boot, and the copilot used a leather glove for a second shoe. Rocks quickly sliced the glove to ribbons, and the flight boot, made of sheepskin and not intended for walking, fared little better.

It was late November, and at twelve thousand feet they were bitterly cold. That night they huddled against each other for warmth, but the cold, fear, and shock prevented sleep. The next night, they stopped for a cold interlude of restless, intermittent sleep. Hunger was a constant companion; they ate only a few bites of their meager chocolate ration each day and supplemented the tasteless survival bars with a few wild, wormy lemons they found. By the fourth day, they were out of food and matches. Despair filled them, and Campanella at one point began eating grass that he discovered growing between rocks along the stream. They had fishing gear, but saw no sign of fish. On the fifth day, they stumbled across three small deer ahead of them, drinking from a small pool. Campanella hid behind a log and waited for the deer with his .45; he emptied his pistol at them but failed to bring one down. They were now out of food, matches, iodine for drinking water, and ammunition.

Walking now seemed the only option to sitting down to die. After a week or so, their path was blocked by steep cliffs; they needed to cross the stream, which had grown wider and deeper as they continued down the slope of the mountains. Campanella had tied his shoelaces together and swung them over a log, which he used as a float; midway across, the log rolled and his shoes went to the bottom of the river. Williams lost his lone tattered flying boot a couple of days later, and the pair now limped barefooted across razor-sharp rocks and earth that was covered with burrs. They were both in agony and relied on walking sticks to remain upright. Discouragement was taking a heavy toll on their minds, and both were beginning to doubt they would survive. That morning the exhausted men, bruised, cut, and lame, dropped to their knees and prayed, plaintive cries for help from any source.

That evening four men with their hands on knives approached the airmen at their temporary camp. The two exhausted fliers sat down and motioned that they were hungry. The native men handed each of them a ball of warm rice wrapped in large leaves. When the two had finished eating, the native men helped them walk about a mile to a small village of about forty people, where they were shown into a small bamboo hut. For the next several days, while the two recovered from their exhaustion and torn feet, the villagers brought them food while attempting to communicate through hand signs.

They wrote a note, and a runner headed out with it, bringing hope of a speedy rescue to the airmen. He returned with the note undelivered, and the next day more runners set out. After eight days in the village, they heard the sound of a transport plane flying low overhead. Campanella and Williams ran outside and waved their arms at the plane. It turned and circled back. From its rear door they could see bundles emerging, and soon two chutes were drifting down toward the village. The eager fliers opened the packs and found shoes and socks, food rations, rifles and ammo, a flare gun and flares, mosquito head nets, heavy flying boots, field jackets, first-aid kits, blankets. One bundle even included a Christmas card.

The next morning, their twenty-third day in the jungle, a transport plane again appeared overhead, accompanied by a PT-17, a biwing, two-place training airplane. The trainer reduced power and disappeared behind the trees. Soon a man in a flight suit was walking through the tiny village.

Maj. Paul C. Droz had landed the PT-17 in a nearby rice field. He flew Campanella out first and then returned that afternoon to haul out Williams. The lieutenant gave all of the supplies previously air-dropped, plus a reward of one hundred silver rupees, to the villagers. Campanella learned that one of the runners named Salong Lot had found a Ghurka camp, who transmitted the message to the nearest American air base.[8]

Major Droz rescued another Allied flier a few weeks later. His trainer was the only search-and-rescue airplane available in the first months of the Hump operation. It was nearly a year later that a formal S&R unit was formed. Before that, volunteer crews commandeered any available aircraft to launch a search. It seems incredible today that no formal unit existed to locate and rescue downed airmen, but apparently that was something that no one had considered. No one except the fliers themselves, that is. It is doubtful that flight crews and aircraft were available in the first year of the Hump airlift to form a dedicated unit, but there also does not appear to have been a keen sense of urgency on the part of commanders at the time to push for one, either.

One of the most colorful of the early S&R pilots was Capt. John L. Porter, widely known as Blackie. In October 1943, he was named "flying safety and rescue officer," the first such position in the theater. His men called themselves "Blackie's Gang," and they launched when an aircraft failed to return from a trip over the Hump. Using C-47s for search missions, augmented by a few B-25s, Blackie's Gang was responsible for locating many downed crewmen and dropping supplies by parachute. Eventually, small L-4 and L-5 airplanes were used to carry out fliers who were not too far into Burma. By late in the war, medics or surgeons made perilous jumps into the jungle if an airman was badly injured or wounded. His own S&R unit couldn't help Blackie Porter in the end, though. He was shot down and killed by Japanese fighter planes in December 1943, on a mission in the Fort Hertz region of northern Burma. Only the copilot survived.

But for the entire time that Cole was flying his cold, underperforming C-47 from Chabua to Kunming, he and his fellow Hump fliers were largely on their own should their plane go down. Preparing for a forced landing or crash was considered their own responsibility by the pilots and aircrews; their homemade multipocketed vests and the provisions and gear they held were the closest thing available to survival gear during Cole's stint as a Burma Roadster.

In truth, it took a major newsworthy event to convince the brass that an S&R squadron was even a necessity. On 2 August 1943, a C-46 transport carrying CBS newsman Eric Sevareid and twenty others, including John Davies of the US State Department, who was political adviser to Gen. Joseph Stilwell, departed from Chabua, en route to Kunming. Shortly after leaving India, the left engine failed, and the pilots tried to return to the base in Assam. Soon the right engine overheated, and the pilot ordered them all to bail out. The copilot was killed, but everyone else survived, although they were in rugged terrain inside Japanese-occupied Burma. The radioman had stayed with the plane as long as possible, sending out messages of their location and actions taken.

Within a couple of hours, a C-47 appeared overhead, circling around the smoking wreckage of the plane. Many of the survivors, including Sevareid, had struggled through the undergrowth and were in the area of the wreckage. When the crew of the circling Gooney spotted them waving in a clearing, they immediately kicked out a couple of packs of supplies along with a note advising them to stay near the aircraft wreckage and avoid the natives, who were believed to be fierce, head-hunting Naga tribesmen. A party would be sent by land to lead them back to India.

A supply plane appeared almost daily and air-dropped more supplies, including a radio and carbines and ammunition for the entire party. The aircraft radioman, who had so valiantly stayed with the C-46 until the very last, had broken his leg badly in the jump. When they radioed that medical attention was needed, Lt. Col. Don Flickinger, a medical doctor, and two enlisted assistants parachuted from the next plane. They were able to set the radioman's leg, and of course they were then committed to staying with the group until they could walk out.

Despite the potential danger of the tribesmen turning on them violently, their proximity to a village made it impossible to avoid contact. The entire group was led by tribesmen to the village and housed in rough bashas. For nearly three weeks, they lived in an uneasy state of dependence and distrust, until a young Englishman leading a column of Indian troops arrived and led them on a weeklong trek back to India. The radio operator was carried in a stretcher by native bearers.[9]

In all, it was an extraordinary event, and the resultant effort to recover the men would undoubtedly have been made regardless of who was aboard. But the coverage of Sevareid's adventure and the subsequent news stories that followed were doubtless goads to the military brass to establish a formal system of search and rescue.

Of course, an S&R effort could be counted successful only if the plane and crew were located. Many never were, including Bobby Cook and his plane. James Segel, one of the original AMMISCA pilots who flew with Cole in those early days, rode with Cook and copilot Marv Siegel to China on that fatal day in May. Jim Segel had just finished his tour of Hump flying and was given two weeks' R&R (rest and recuperation) leave before heading back to the States. Cook and Siegel had been chosen to fly the C-87, a job initially much coveted by some of the early Hump fliers for its perceived high-altitude performance, and they invited Segel along to ride the jump seat. Segel had an 8 mm Kodak movie camera, and Cook promised him that because the weather was good, they would fly far north of the regular route so that he could film Chhogori, or K-2, the famed peak second only to Everest in height. As it turned out, the peak was shrouded in clouds, so Segel did not get the spectacular view he had hoped for.

At Kunming, instead of flying back to Chabua in the C-87, Segel was asked to fly as copilot in a C-47; the scheduled copilot had been stricken with "Delhi belly," or severe dysentery. From the cockpit of the Gooney, Segel forlornly watched as his friends took off in the C-87. A few minutes later, cockpit checks complete, the C-47 was cleared to take off. When Segel arrived at Chabua, he learned that Cook's plane never arrived. Late that night, the plane was listed as missing.[10]

# CHAPTER 19

Although each of Cole's flights over the Hump was different, frequently laced with new challenges and fresh terrors, a routine developed: predawn awakening, preflighting the aircraft in the early-morning darkness, and coaxing the tired and overworked aircraft into the thin air. This pattern was both comforting in its uniformity and dangerous in its ability to lull the inattentive into a false sense of safety. Decades later, Cole described a typical flight out of Chabua, over the Hump, and into Kunming.

He felt the hand on his shoulder and a tentative, almost gentle shake. It was the young American corporal charged with the unenviable duty of waking pilots and aircrews for the day's flights over the Himalayas. Cole was already awake; lately, he had been waking hours before the faithful corporal appeared. "Captain Cole, Sir. It's oh-five-hundred, and you're on the board for 553 today." Hump pilots flew whatever aircraft was ready; the corporal had a list of pilots and the tail numbers of the planes they were to fly that day. As always, they would fly alone, no formations, no fighter escort, just individual aircraft making their way to China.[1]

"I'm ready." Cole was already awake and alert, unlike some of his flying buddies, who often drank late before rising early. No throbbing head or cottony mouth for Cole. Since arriving first at Dinjan, then Chabua, both sited in the center of British colonial tea plantations in northern Assam, he and his roommate, Jake Sartz, had kept their vow of not drinking alcohol until they rotated home. It frequently took the corporal several minutes before some of the pilots—most no older than a fraternity man in a university—were roused enough to plant their feet on the floor of the basha. When both soles touched the ground, the corporal's job was finished. He lived in constant fear of being slugged by a half-asleep, hungover pilot; he was relieved to retreat from the thatched-roof bashas.

As was always the case, the sun was still far below the horizon. Flights over the Hump began in the cooler hours of predawn, both to escape the heat as well as to avoid being caught on the runway in the light of day, when Japanese bombers might be expected to pay the primitive airfield at Chabua a visit. It didn't happen often, but the threat was constant.

Cole pulled on his khaki shirt and pants, tied his boots, grabbed his gear bag and AVG-issue leather jacket, and headed for the pickup area, where flight crews waited for their six-mile ride to the base. The 6th Squadron of the 1st Ferrying Group had a busy schedule, flying their overloaded C-47s an average of three times a week. It was grinding work, flying over enemy-held jungles that were terrifying enough even without the threat of capture; sometimes the weather was so severe that it left first-time copilots in a state of silent terror. If they made it to Kunming, they were on the ground just long enough to refuel, oversee the loading of the plane with tungsten ore or Chinese soldiers headed for training in India or some other war-related cargo needed in India or the United States, and then take off to repeat the trip in reverse. After a while, it almost seemed routine, although the lack of sleep never did; the nights of tossing and turning, the pilots too tired, too hot, or simply too miserable to sleep, merely added to their exhaustion. In the hotter months, pilots often fell into their cots fully clothed, sometimes kicking off their boots but not always. Cole knew the hot season was still ahead, and he was hoping to be gone before it arrived with its usual vengeance.

At last the ancient bus arrived, and Cole boarded it for the rough, bouncing trip to the airfield. Aircrews were housed far from the airfield to protect them in the event of a surprise raid by the Japanese. It worked well for that, but the snaillike pace of the bus and the washboard surface of the road made the trip seem agonizingly long. At Chabua Cole went first to the chow hall for breakfast. He was in luck this morning. Real eggs, not powdered. A glass of milk but no coffee—he rarely touched it—and a small bowl of oatmeal. There were only a few men in the building, most eating quietly, trying to clear the alcohol-induced cobwebs from their brains. Most looked weary and hollow-eyed, but exhaustion was such a common malady that no one commented on it.[2]

Cole checked in at the operations basha, a low, roughly fashioned building with a thatched roof. There he picked up the Form 1—the

"squawk sheet" on which problems with the aircraft would be noted—
from the duty officer and listened to the meager weather report, already
several hours old and based primarily on pilot reports. A front was
brewing; he could expect poor visibility and turbulence. What else was
new? He grabbed a parachute and headed out to his plane sitting on the
ramp in the darkness.

There the copilot, flight engineer, and radio operator were already at
work, preflighting the airplane, turning the propellers through several
rotations, visually checking the fuel in the tanks, and supervising the
loading of the last of the cargo. The crew was different for each flight,
each crewman drawn from the pool of available men who were not sick
with dysentery or any of a dozen other ills that struck with such frequency. This morning Cole recognized their faces and knew their names
but was not close to any of them.

The C-47 was loaded with drums of high-octane aviation fuel for the
23rd Fighter Group in Kunming. It would make a tremendous fireball
if it went down, but Cole refused to let his mind consider that scene.
Pilots and ground crews did their jobs, every one doing all they could to
ensure that the planes would fly safely.

The ramp was illuminated by lights powered by a portable generator;
the lights created harsh yellow holes in the black night, bringing into
sharp focus everything in their circle. Three men were rolling drums
of fuel up a ramp and through the large cargo door, a feature of the
military version of the DC-3. The flight engineer was on the right wing,
peering into the fuel tanks to ensure that they were topped off. Cole did
his walk-around, looking critically at each potential source of problems.
An early flight instructor back in East St. Louis had told him that each
item on the checklist was someone's epitaph. Something hadn't been
checked, and someone died. Cole paid special attention to the brakes,
checking for dripping hydraulic fluid, and carefully inspected the tail
wheel, including the lock, before climbing up a ladder to the small door
on the left side of the cockpit. The cabin was now crammed with gasoline drums, and access to the cockpit was easier this way, even carrying a
parachute and the rest of his flight gear. The cockpit smelled of fuel from
the drums, but Cole ignored it; all of India was odoriferous to Americans, and av gas was at least a familiar if pungent olfactory assault.

Cole grinned at his copilot and handed him the worn binder containing the many detailed checklists. His reticence was well known among
the crews. Cole was friendly but never garrulous; if a word were equal

to a sentence, he used a word. If no word was required, a gesture and a smile worked just fine. Together, they went through the familiar rituals of the prestart checklist. By now, the myriad of gauges, switches, instruments, levers, cranks, and controls that filled the cockpit had long since become like old friends. Above all, flying such a sophisticated machine was challenging and fun, an adventure acknowledged by all who sat in the cockpit. There was a deep satisfaction in knowing what all those controls and monitors were for and being able to control and direct such a complex machine.

Just to start the engines was a multistep routine, but seemed straightforward and surprisingly simple to Cole after so many hours in the Gooney Bird's cockpit. Both pilots adjusted their seats until they were looking squarely through the center of the windshield, and then the co-pilot turned on the battery switches, checked to see that the landing gear levers were down and locked, and checked for five hundred pounds of pressure in the landing-gear pressure gauge. The landing-gear light was green, and the warning horn emitted a shrill tone when the gear lever was moved side to side. Cole nodded approvingly.

The copilot read from the checklist, and Cole responded with a crisp "Checked!" The autopilot hydraulic valve was verified in the "off" position. Fuel supply was always critical and varied by mission. For a trip over the Hump, they wanted full tanks, both main and auxiliary; full tanks would mean six hundred gallons of usable fuel. The copilot moved the fuel selector valve to each tank and checked the appropriate gauge as Cole watched carefully. He turned his attention to the control pedestal between the pilots, which bristled with levers. A pair closest to him (marked "P") controlled the pitch angle of the propeller blades; Cole ran them through their range of motion and returned both to the low pitch setting. He did the same with the center pair, the throttles (marked "T"), slowly pushing them forward and then pulling them back, leaving both one quarter open; the mixture control levers, on the right (marked "M"), were also checked and returned to the full-back position of idle cutoff. Cole set the elevator trim wheel, on the left side of the pedestal, to neutral and then ensured that the oil shutters, two small levers forward on the left of the pedestal (marked with an "O"), were in the full forward position. The carburetor air-temperature control was set to the "cool" position.

On the front side of the control pedestal were the aileron and rudder trim cranks, and the gauges that accompany each were set to "zero." The autopilot was checked to ensure it was in the "off" position, the deicer control behind the copilot's seat was set to "off," and the parking brake was pulled on. The fuel cross-feed valve was on, and the static electric valves were set to "top."

The pilots turned their attention to the instrument panel, with its many round, black faces and white numbers. Cole set the altimeter to 367 feet, the field elevation at Chabua, and tapped the glass face to ensure there was no friction causing the needles to become stuck; he checked that the airspeed indicator and the tachometer were both registering "zero" and then coordinated the eight-day clock to his wristwatch, which he had set to the clock in the operations shack. Flight controls were checked: the rudder pedals adjusted for each pilot and pushed to ensure full range of movement; the rudder, elevators, and ailerons all moved smoothly by means of the pedals and the control yoke; each pilot verified that the movement of the ailerons on his side was correct. They looked to the flap indicator to ensure the flaps were up and then to the engine cowl-flap gauge to verify they were open. The cowl flaps needed to be fully open to avoid overheating the engines while on the ground.

Finally, they were nearly ready to start the left engine. The copilot read from the checklist, while Cole confirmed the instructions: Left engine tank selector to "left main" and the right to "off," propeller levers at low pitch, throttles one-quarter open, mixture control to idle cutoff, carburetor air temp on "cold." Overhead was the main ignition switch; Cole now turned it to "on" and ensured that the left engine switch remained at "cold." The copilot operated a wobble pump, located on the left side of his seat, and brought fuel pressure up to 10 psi (pounds per square inch).

Safety first. Cole opened the left cockpit window and shouted, "Clear!" It was the signal for everyone to be clear of the propellers. A ground crewman stood nearby, with a fire extinguisher ready. Cole indicated he wanted the copilot to proceed with the start, and the right seater moved the left mixture control lever forward and back to prime the left engine and then moved up the left starter switch and safety switch. The propeller began to turn, slowly at first, then more rapidly, and when it was spinning at its peak the starter was "meshed" and the spinning propeller mated with a series of gears that began turning the engine. As the engine fired, there was a series of loud pops and a cloud of smoke, and Cole motioned for the copilot to move the mixture control forward to "rich" and pull the throttles back to 600–800 rpm. Both pilots watched the oil-pressure gauge to ensure that it showed upward movement. Assured that the engine had adequate oil pressure, Cole pointed to the checklist and indicated to the copilot that he should advance the throttle to 1,000 rpm.[3] With the cockpit window open and the radial engine roaring, it was now impossible to speak in the cockpit, and both pilots pulled on their radio headsets to dampen the noise. They could feel the vibrations of the radial engine up through the metal seats in which they sat; it made the airplane seem alive.

They repeated the sequence to start the right engine, and Cole gestured that the next checklist, that for taxiing, should be followed. There were additional checklists for takeoff, cruise, landing, and emergencies, all as detailed as that for preflight and starting engines. Cole enjoyed the complexity; his high school experience of rebuilding an aircraft engine and his subsequent years of training left him confident in his understanding of the mysteries of flight and of the internal combustion engine.

On this still-black morning, the engines were running smoothly, and the cockpit crew completed their run-up and called the tower. A jeep headed down the runway to shoo off any stray animals that might have wandered onto the strip during the night. Cows, considered sacred by the local residents, frequently roamed onto the flying field. The driver then turned around and flashed his headlamps at the Gooney at the far end of the runway. The unofficial rule for flying at Chabua was if the pilots could see the jeep's lights, the weather was good enough to take off.

Cole applied power to the right engine and stepped on the left toe brake at the top of the rudder pedals, being careful to keep the inside tire rolling slightly and not locked in place; the heavily loaded bird slowly swung left. Before the nose reached the direction he wanted, Cole eased off the power and let momentum carry the plane through the turn and then deftly, smoothly, applied power to both engines, and the plane began to roll forward. They taxied to the end of runway 5—meaning it was constructed in a direction of 50 degrees, or northeast—and lined up with the strip. Cole did a final check of the instruments, once more checked that the altimeter was set to 367 feet, set the gyrocompass to 050, and locked the tail wheel. An unlocked tail wheel made departures very exciting events if there was any crosswind at all.[4]

They were cleared by the tower—still in a tree—for takeoff. Cole looked to his copilot, who nodded his readiness. A quick check of the control levers to verify that the propellers were in low pitch and the mixture controls rich, and then he slowly pushed the throttles forward, taking a full five seconds to go to full power. The Gooney began to roll, very slowly, down the rough runway, with both pilots pushing forward on the yoke. With the plane on its tail wheel and its nose up, Cole was unable to see down the runway, so he watched the lights on the side of the strip. He glanced down at the airspeed indicator on the panel in front of him: 30, then 40. The tail came up, and now the pilots could see ahead; Cole eased the yoke back to neutral. The speed continued to increase, and at 80 mph he pulled back slightly on the control wheel and the cargo ship rose a few inches, settled back onto the runway, and then lifted again into the mild Indian air. In an instant, the cargo plane transitioned from an awkward earthbound beast of burden into a graceful, birdlike creature. Cole gave a quick thumbs up to his copilot, who raised the main landing gear to reduce drag. His mind flashed back to a similar signal from Lt. Col. Jimmy Doolittle to a young lieutenant as they lifted from the deck of a Navy carrier.

Departure procedure for cargo planes bound for Kunming was to climb in a circle over the air base until they reached four thousand feet and then turn east and continue climbing at three hundred feet per minute in order to clear the eight-thousand-foot Naga Hills, east of Chabua.

They turned left and continued a climbing turn in the now semidark sky. Cole reduced power slightly and made another quick scan of the instrument panel. He looked back at the flight engineer, who gave him the thumbs-up. In a few minutes, they turned east one final time and settled in for a steady climb to fifteen thousand feet. The air in the cockpit was beginning to cool now, and Cole motioned for the copilot to take the yoke while he slipped on his leather jacket. As he settled back in the bucket seat and indicated to the copilot to continue flying, Cole looked ahead at the eastern sky. A far-off bank of clouds was now infused with gold, reflecting the rising sun and painting a magical picture. It was, he knew, one of the reasons men wanted to fly, to experience such beauty and perfection. But, of course, men didn't speak of such things; most could not have found the words. When flying together in a small cockpit, the silence spoke for them.

Cole carried maps of the route, folded to reveal his course of 110 degrees to Kunming. It was his preferred course, known as the southern route, and he knew it by heart. Later, established paths were set and instrument landing charts published. But in the early days, the pilots were largely on their own to find their way to Kunming. Cole's route took them over the Naga Hills, which would have been labeled mountains had they not been in the shadow of the Himalayas. The land was wrinkled, and the map showed elevation lines close together, black indexes that impersonally and without fuss indicated the extreme ruggedness and the sharp rise and fall of the land. He had marked the course on his maps, a long, straight line drawn in pencil over the mapped symbols of the earth over which he must fly. He would cross the Chindwin River, with Fort Hertz somewhere off his left wing, and then the west and east branches of the Irrawaddy in Burma.

One hundred and ten degrees from Chabua to Kunming, 290 to return. Five hundred miles each way. He had marked the course at fifty-mile intervals, noting the distance flown, the miles remaining. Cole carried the maps in a clipboard, the penciled course aligned with the plane's longitudinal axis.[5] The tactile and visual comfort of the maps was illusory, Cole knew. Today, as most days, the first leg would be in darkness and the majority of the flight in clouds, with no visual contact with the earth three miles below.

But he was able to project in his mind's eye the trip ahead. The route was nearly always the same, although each flight was different as weather and winds issued new challenges: Over the Khasi Hills, then the higher Naga Hills with their fierce headhunting tribes, followed by a long, almost eerie stretch of unpopulated jungle over northern Burma. The Kumon Range of mountains, with tops approaching fourteen thousand feet, rose to greet them; on rare clear days, crews could look down and marvel at the two-mile drop from the peaks to the valley floors. The Salween River was next, with the Sanstung Mountains of the Himalayas sitting between it and the Mekong River; some of the Sanstung (Nu Shan on Chinese maps) peaks were more than fourteen thousand feet as well. The Salween marked their unceremonious entry into China, and the narrow distance between the Salween and the Mekong marked the midway point of the five-hundred-mile flight. They would pass the north end of Er Hai Lake, with the monastery town of Tali (Dali) on the western shore, and Mount Tali (Dali), a prominent landmark. The land below would become less forbidding now, the mountains giving way to rolling hills. Finally, Kunming, on the northern shore of Dianchi Lake, nearly six thousand feet higher than Chabua. The airfield was older, more organized than Chabua, and lacking its just-built sense of raw newness as well as impermanence. Cole had flown the route many times now, in both directions, and had developed a feel for his position and for what lay so far below him.

With few weather reports or radio beacons, Hump pilots could only trust and hope that they had not been blown far north into the higher peaks or perhaps had hit a headwind that might mean letting down on the wrong side of the mountains. The cockpit became an isolated place, a small haven crammed with instruments, awash with the acrid smell of aviation gasoline in the drums crammed into the cabin. At ten thousand feet, they went to oxygen, pulling the straps tight and smelling the vulcanized rubber of the mask that covered their nose, mouth, and chin. The mask was uncomfortable. No conversation could take place except for necessary communications regarding the flight itself.

There was a cloud bank ahead, the leading edge of a front building quickly, a living thing fed by heat and water vapor. There was no way around it, nor could they climb over it; ducking under it was a fool's choice. They would plow straight into the ominous ethereal range and ride it out. Cole checked his heading and turned the plane right about 15 degrees to account for the wind he expected. He was convinced that most of the bad things that had happened to pilots on the Hump route were the result of wind—high-velocity unseen currents of air that came up from the Bay of Bengal and pushed aircraft, traveling blind in the clouds, far north of their intended route to smash against the granite peaks of the higher mountains there. Sometimes the unseen wind reached speeds of more than 100 mph, forcing aircraft far off their course, unknown by the men in the cockpits.[6] On a couple of rare flights that were above the clouds instead of in them, Cole had seen the tops of mountains off to the north; snow was being ripped off the peaks by winds and hurled horizontal in thick columns that resembled smoke from industrial stacks.

Cole made a last check of all his instruments, noting the altitude, airspeed, and direction. Oil temperature and pressure are equally important. Flying blind is a poor time to lose an engine. He eased back the throttle, knowing that the aircraft would be subjected to less stress at lower speeds. In minutes the C-47 entered the wall of clouds, crossing into a nation-size aerial kingdom of white vapor, a swirling opaqueness that rose higher than the overloaded plane could climb and extending downward lower than they could safely fly. As they penetrated the clouds, Cole and the copilot tightened their seat belts, and Cole motioned for the right seater to notify the other crewmen. They knew that inside the altocumulus mass might be vicious turbulence, upward and downward currents that could toss the airplane around like a toy thrown by a young boy. More than one crewman had been injured, some severely, in such conditions.

They hit an updraft, and the Gooney shuddered slightly; the vertical-speed indicator showed them climbing at six hundred feet per minute. It caused his stomach to drop, but Cole thought it was no worse than riding a fast elevator; the pilots rode it out, and it quickly dissipated. Another one, this time a bit stronger, and Cole watched as the altimeter climbed despite his nosing the plane slightly downward. He glanced at the copilot, an experienced flier who had flown several trips with Cole, and noted with approval that he was watching the gauges intently and ignoring the swirling tendrils of moisture crawling upward across the windscreen. Believe the instruments! The mantra of the flying instructors and the Link operators had been pounded into their brains. Vertigo, caused by a lack of reference to the ground, can set in quickly; the body tells the brain that the plane is turning right when in fact it is in straight and level flight, and soon the pilot is ill, too dizzy to function and unable to recalibrate his impaired senses. Cole also concentrated on the flight instruments before him and saw that they were now climbing at nearly fifteen hundred feet per minute. He didn't fight it, instead striving only to keep the plane level. He knew that soon they would experience an avalanche of air that could hurl them earthward at an appalling rate. They would be okay, he reasoned, so long as there was enough sky below them. And he was right; soon the plane was plunging earthward, one thousand and then fifteen hundred feet per minute, now two thousand, and again Cole tried only to keep it right side up and level. The rate of descent slowed, then stopped, and soon they were climbing again.

Rain began to slam against the windscreen; the clouds now were a greenish black. Gone was the golden-tinged painting of a morning's promise, and the two pilots grimly held onto the yokes while still letting the airplane go with the turbulence. To fight it would only induce critical strain on the wings and control surfaces. For the next hour, the plane and its crew were tossed on the waves of wind that swirled and howled within the storm. Cole could feel the strain in his shoulders; his muscles ached; his hands hurt. He tried to relax. It wasn't possible.

The turbulence decreased slightly, and the sky outside was a shade lighter. Cole knew they must be nearing the far edge of the storm. He tuned in the radio and heard only a steady crackling of static.

They crossed over the Salween River, far below and unseen. They were halfway through the flight, in China now, with no fanfare, no radioed report, and soon were over Er Hai Lake, so named because it was said to resemble a human ear. In a couple of hours, they would be in Kunming. When Cole was certain they were well past the last ridge of the Himalayas, they began to let down, keeping power up but trimming the nose down slightly. The airspeed picked up about 10 mph. Kunming sits at six thousand feet, much higher than Chabua, and is ringed by mountains to the west, north, and east. They broke through the clouds over Dianchi Lake, the landmark south of Kunming that was impossible to miss, and the copilot contacted Kunming tower. They were cleared to land.

At the operations shack, Cole and his copilot paused and grinned to each other at the sign that greeted them and every Hump flier who landed at Kunming: "You made it again! Good work." Now all they had to do was fly the same route back to Chabua.

# CHAPTER 20

The China-Burma-India theater was a kaleidoscope of changing seasons, new experiences, and fresh new terrors. For Cole and the other Hump fliers, it was one surprise after another. Spring and summer of 1942 had brought the monsoon winds and the attendant fierce storms. Winter into 1943 brought relief from the unremitting heat and sodden days and nights. And throughout Cole's time in Assam, the political tensions of Indians seeking independence from Great Britain combined with a drought in parts of India sparked deadly riots that were hard for the Americans to understand.

The Japanese continued their periodic raids on the airfields in Assam, causing little damage but making life a bit more miserable for the Americans. "*Things are pretty much the same, the 'Slant Eyes' haven't been around for about a month,*" Cole wrote his family in December 1942. But they had wreaked some personal havoc in a previous raid. Cole's government life insurance policy had gotten misdirected somewhere, and he had attempted to obtain a new certificate, which he had requested to be mailed to his parents. It had been sent to him in Assam instead. The new certificate and "*the card you sent from the bank for me to sign—were blown sky high by the 'Slant Eyes.'*"

The winter brought better flying weather, but more misery to the fliers in their bashas. "*It gets so cold at night that we wish we had some of that hot sunshine of a few months ago. Seems funny to be nearly in the middle of December—winter—and have green grass, trees, and etc. We still get fresh fruit—bananas, oranges, pineapples, and coconuts. Guess the season never ends. Monkeys still seem to be in season, too.*"

Cole had gotten a rare letter from his father and took the opportunity to gently poke fun at his loyalty to the St. Louis baseball team. Listing the letters he had received in a bundle, Cole is obviously pleased that he got *"one from the 'Ole Timer' praising the Class 'C' ball club called the 'St. Looie Cards.' Also proves he can write a swell letter, if he wants to."*[1]

On 29 April 1943 by Special Order 79 from Headquarters, India-China Wing of the Air Transport Command, Cole, Sartz, Segel, Walker, and eleven other first pilots were "released from assignment." They were to leave Chabua by "first available mil[itary] or commercial ap [airplane] water transportation or rail, or any other means available fr[om] Chabua, India, to Continental United States."[2] The syntax was pure military, the spelling and grammar strictly soldierese, and the music the sweetest they had heard in a year. Cole had left the United States on 2 April the previous year. After a perilous first-ever mission over Japan, several ad hoc bombing missions to targets across Burma and Hong Kong, and nearly a year flying the Hump, he was finally going home.

That evening Cole and his roommate, Jake Sartz, opened the two bottles of scotch that had remained unopened in their footlockers during their flying assignment and went to work draining them. They spent much of the night "seasick in the tea bushes."[3]

Cole had been in India and China since bailing out of his B-25 on 18 April 1942. He was ready to see his family, eat some Midwest American home cooking, sleep in a soft bed with clean sheets, and not worry about malaria-carrying mosquitoes, Japanese bombing raids, or flying over forbidding terrain in stomach-churning weather. He had earned another Distinguished Flying Cross and an Air Medal, although they had not been formally presented yet. That would come later, but the awards didn't particularly interest Cole.

He was keenly aware that the airlift from Assam to China had come at a very high price, and the bill would continue to be paid for years to come. By war's end, 910 air crewmen had given their lives flying the Hump; 594 aircraft were lost.[4] In exchange for China agreeing to stay in the war against the Japanese, the American political and military establishments had determined that the price in young lives was worth it. Some of the factors that entered the equation were military: China, despite its lethargic record of actively engaging the Japanese army, was vital to the war effort simply by tying up hundreds of thousands of enemy troops. Other factors could be seen as political: Chiang and Madame Kai-shek were masters at manipulating public opinion in the United States as well as applying pressure on President Roosevelt and top military brass to continually increase the amount of cargo flowing into China over the Hump or risk losing their support against the Japanese. There were other elements that contributed to the carnage that the Himalayan airlift caused. One might be considered, charitably, as those making decisions being unfamiliar with and therefore out of touch with the realities of the conditions in which American fliers were asked to perform.

Terrain similar to the Himalayas (but not as high or as extensive) might possibly be found in the mountain regions of the United States, and the threat of enemy aircraft was found in every theater. Poor weather might be expected at any place on the globe. And perhaps, as some Air Force commanders suggested, there was a tendency to exaggerate the dangers and the conditions over the Hump by writers and some of the pilots themselves. But no place in the United States had the jungle regions of Burma, with all the attendant dangers; virtually every other theater had fighter escorts not only for transports but for heavily armed bombers as well; no place on the planet had such unremitting rain, storm clouds, and high winds as the Hump routes; the lack of aids to aerial navigation, the inaccuracy of available maps, and the absence of a search-and-rescue unit to recover downed fliers made it particularly hazardous; and the number of missing and crashed airplanes is no exaggeration—the dangers were very real.[5]

Perhaps the best weapon against all of the forces working in unison to thwart the Hump fliers was experience. But there was very little of that. While many of the earliest pilots flying the Hump were airline pilots drafted into service, with thousands of hours in a cockpit and vast experience with instrument flight in adverse weather conditions, a large number of military pilots assigned to the theater were barely out of flight school. Cole, considered an old hand, had fewer than five hundred hours' total flight time when he transferred to Ferry Command and only a couple hundred in multiengine aircraft. But he had listened to those more experienced; he had been meticulous in his preflight preparations; he had made a conscious effort to understand the forces of nature, particularly the monsoon winds; and he had worked assiduously on perfecting his instrument flying. And while all of those efforts had paid off, there was one more element that he readily acknowledged:

Lady Luck continued to ride on his shoulders.

# PART III
# THE INVASION

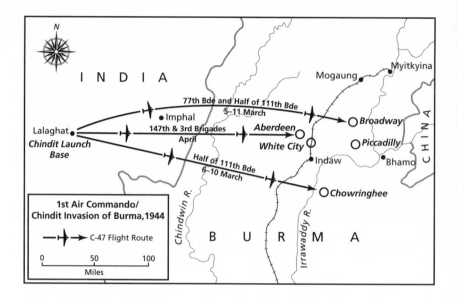

The aerial invasion of Japanese-held Burma by an Allied force; the first contingents of British and Commonwealth troops were taken into clearings in the jungle by glider, towed by Air Commando C-47s. Cole was among the fliers going into the area code-named Broadway. (Map by Chris Robinson)

By early 1944, the war against Germany was tilting in favor of the Allies; soon the cross-Channel invasion that had been building for a year would be launched, and hundreds of thousands of young men would be engaged in a fierce battle for the future of Europe. On the other side of the world, in Burma, the Japanese were still holding on, hatching their own plans to invade India, eliminate China from the war, and score what they hoped was a knockout victory against the Allies in the China-Burma-India theater.

An unorthodox British major general had his own ideas. Orde Wingate had gained experience in harassing the Japanese behind their own lines in Burma in 1943. With his Special Force, nicknamed Chindits, he had blown up bridges, railroad tracks, and lines of communication and scored some significant victories in a theater that was sorely lacking in good news for the Allies. But his success had come at a high price: hundreds of British and Commonwealth troops in Wingate's command had to be left behind when they were wounded or ravaged with illness.

A second incursion was envisioned by Wingate for early 1944, but this time he sought American aid. If the United States could provide aircraft capable of evacuating his wounded and ill troops, the joint effort would provide enormous dividends, he argued. The top brass believed the Japanese could be foiled in launching a possible attack on India or China and the region kept secure for launching the long-range B-29 Superfortress raids on the Japanese home islands, which they reasoned would end the Pacific war. The Joint Chiefs of Staff of the United States and Great Britain approved the project, and Gen. Hap Arnold appointed two young fighter pilots to head the American effort. Col. Phil Cochran and Col. Johnny Alison expanded the original plans to include fighter and bomber air support, cargo aircraft and gliders to carry troops and equipment, and light aircraft for liaison and air-ambulance duties. They would operate in one of the world's worst environments in which to fight a war: thick jungles, wide rivers, extreme heat, and sodden humidity.

Capt. Dick Cole had returned to the United States from a year in the region, flying his C-47 over the Hump from India to China across northern Burma. He had been back just three months when Alison called him in Tulsa, Oklahoma, where Cole was test-flying new aircraft. The colonel promised him nothing; it was a secret mission, it would involve combat, and it would mean another stint overseas.

# CHAPTER 21

On 28 May 1943, Capt. Dick Cole sent a brief but joyous telegram to his parents in Dayton: "*Ten days granted.*" For the first time in more than a year, since his B-25 had first lifted off the deck of the *Hornet*, the young man who had always dreamed of flying was coming home to the States, with a week and a half leave to spend at home in Dayton. That telegram was followed by another on 2 June, equally ebullient: "*Back in God's country. Will call later—hope to see you soon.*"[1]

Cole's orders were to report to the Transitional Ferrying Group at Rosecrans Field in St. Joseph, Missouri, following his leave. It appeared his war was over: a one-way trip to Japan, followed by a short assignment to a bomb squadron in India, and then a year of hauling cargo over the Hump. He had faced Japanese air defenses in the raid on Tokyo and bombing raids on Hong Kong, endured horrific weather and unholy terrain flying the Hump, lived through raids on his base at Chabua, watched as friends and comrades crashed around him or simply disappeared. Cole had survived unscathed and wore two DFCs and a row of combat ribbons as testament to his active service in combat.

But on the flight from India to the States, he feared he was going to die, the victim of American pilots. The irony was not lost on him, but it was completely unappreciated.

It was a long flight from Karachi to Khartoum in North Africa. Cole and other Hump pilots who had completed their tours were jammed into a C-47, wearing their khakis and leather jackets, slumped into canvas seats that lined both sides of the cabin. Their B-4 bags had been loaded aboard; heavier gear would be sent by ship. It was a relief to be going home and away from the misery, the oppressive heat, the incessant rain of India. On this day, the weather was fair, and the C-47 carrying Cole and the others flew on through blue skies, crossing over the Levant and the eastern end of the Mediterranean. It should have been restful, but to Cole being relegated to the role of cargo was galling and uncomfortable. However, it was a quiet unease, not alarm, and Cole attributed it to so much time spent in the cockpit, flight after flight, day upon day. The cabin seemed like a foreign place, strange and familiar at once. It was, after all, he told himself, a bit of a relief to not be the one in charge of the aircraft, to not be the one to monitor the instruments, to let someone else make decisions about the weather and the route to fly. At this stage of the long flight, the two men in the cockpit, although quite young, seemed competent. They were, like him, products of an intensive course in flying conducted by Uncle Sam, a course filled with instructors who allowed little room for error and were implacable when eliminating aspirants.

But upon touching down at the dusty airfield at Khartoum, the C-47 ground-looped, running off the runway and causing havoc in the cabin. The tail of the airplane started swinging to the right, and in a flash the airplane made a complete circle, dust rising in a storm as it plowed off the runway. Inside the cabin, the passengers were thrown to their left by centrifugal force, as they grabbed their crusher hats and held onto the sides of the seats. The two pilots were both flight officers—flying warrant officers—and very young, perhaps still in their teens. The airplane was unhurt, but Cole was left unimpressed with the flying ability of those in the cockpit. The next morning, they lifted off early to avoid the heat and landed hours later without incident near Lake Chad to refuel. The next stop would be in about six hours in Dakar, the final point in Africa before heading across the South Atlantic to Natal, Brazil. Cole dozed and when he awoke looked out the window, watching the sun sink slowly below the horizon; a veil of darkness descended upon the land below. He checked his watch. They would be in Dakar in another hour.

The transport droned on. Cole crossed his arms and dozed some more, as did most of the others in the darkened cabin. But he suddenly jerked awake, as his pilot senses kicked in. They were circling, but had not descended. He looked out at a totally black carpet below them. Not a light to be seen. The C-47 continued to circle, cutting a large arc through the night sky. He looked at his watch and realized they should have landed a half hour ago. He nudged Willis Grube, who jerked awake and stared at Cole, startled. Cole cocked his head toward the window and the blackness outside, then tapped his watch. "These guys are lost." The two sat for a few minutes longer, and the plane continued to circle.

"That's it. Let's go." Cole and Grube, both captains and three ranks higher than the flight officers, walked to the front of the C-47. Cole tapped the pilot and copilot on the shoulder. The two pilots looked around, and Cole could read the concern, bordering on fear, in their faces. He motioned with his thumb to the cabin. "Out. We're taking over." The two young pilots did not protest. They vacated the front office, and Cole and Grube slipped into the left and right seats. It seemed like home. They found the frequency for the airfield at Dakar and radioed for them to turn on their homing beacon. The tower operator informed them that the beacon was turned off at 1800 (6:00 p.m.).

"Well, you are going to turn it back on now. We're coming in—turn on the homing beacon!" The operator at last consented, and Cole and Grube guided the Gooney over the dark African landscape, finally landing at Dakar without further incident. They reported to operations there that the two assigned pilots were not competent and needed to be relieved from flying duties until they received further training.[2]

Ten days was not much leave for one who had already been in combat zones for more than a year, but Cole was glad just to have the time to get reacquainted with his family, with clean sheets, with American food. It was a bit of a whirlwind, actually, since it was now well known that he had been on the Doolittle Raid. He was a hometown hero, a celebrity back from the war. The local press wanted interviews, and a seemingly endless string of visitors filed into 747 Faulkner.

But there was a war on, still raging across Europe, the Pacific, and the CBI, and the ten days passed all too quickly. He received new orders to report to Love Field in Dallas, to the 62nd Ferrying Squadron, 5th Ferrying Group. The group of friends from the Hump airlift, who had sweated out flights, drank whiskey together, mourned comrades who died or disappeared, played poker, and self-consciously made fun of their Dear John letters were now being split up. Jake Sartz went to Rosecrans Field in St. Joseph, Missouri; Paul Conroy to Mobile, Alabama; Joe Walker to Nevada; and Herman Luske and Cole to Dallas. Shortly thereafter, Cole received word from Sartz that he had gotten married again.

June in Texas was hot, but not as bad as the temperatures in India. Cole found the rooms cleaner and the food better. In addition, he could finally buy things with the money that had been stacking up while he was on overseas flying duty. He had to rent a room off base with another pilot because the bachelor officers' quarters at Love were full.

"*We have to do our own cooking—trouble is, the points go too fast,*" he wrote to his parents in June. Rationing with a point system was in effect even for military officers. He wasn't entirely happy with his quarters and began looking for something better, but not having a car limited his search. "*Have priced some cars and they want on the average of $1300 for them. I'll walk before shelling out that much for a car.*"[3]

At last he found something that suited him. On 5 July, his parents received a telegram, typically brief: "*Bought car have bank send $800 to Mercantile National Bank Dallas Texas immediately.*" A week later, in a letter, he described his purchase, a 1941 blue Ford convertible. A flashy ragtop was a bit out of character, but he explained his decision to his parents: "*Has only 9000 miles, just like new. I didn't especially want to get a convertible, but I looked and looked at lots of cars and most of them had lots of miles and worn tires. Finally I found what I wanted in the Ford— low mileage and five original tires. The spare has never been used at all.*"[4]

Now that he was back in the ZI—the Zone of the Interior, or the good old USA—he needed to spruce himself up a bit as well. New uniforms were high on the list, and he asked his parents to forward his medal ribbons to sew on his blouse, as the dress uniform jacket was called. At this stage of the war, DFCs and Air Medal ribbons were frequently seen on uniforms; not so common was his Chinese medal. In requesting that his parents forward his ribbons, he underlined "*especially the Chinese medal ribbon.*"

Cole was notified that his DFC for his flights over the Hump was to be awarded at a ceremony at St. Joseph, Missouri, where he had originally been ordered to report. Cole thought this was a rather puzzling situation, since it could easily have been done at Love Field. A picture and story in the newspaper indicated that Cole and Herman Luske were to receive their medals but were "too busy" to go. Cole was disdainful of the official explanation. "*Don't believe the story about us being too busy. They gave us permission to go to St. Jo, but not much time or a way to get there—so we had no choice except just not to go—that's all.*"[5]

There was not much for Cole to do in Dallas. On 3 July, he was issued a certificate for passing the Ferrying Group's "blind flying" course. The informal certificate was typical of the unofficial paper awards of the day. Below a fanciful heading "Institute of Blind Flying, Fifth Ferrying

Group" was a depiction of a blindfolded man sporting an oversize wing badge and carrying a cane and cup. Cole was commended for "barely" completing the prescribed course "without peeping." In truth, flying on instruments without severe updrafts and downdrafts or icing was child's play for Cole after his Hump flying.

But things were about to become less boring, once more. On 4 August, he cabled his parents: "*Have been transferred to Tulsa address later got ribbons.*"[6] Tulsa was home to Air Force Plant No. 3, on the municipal airport, where Douglas Aircraft had a plant to build C-47s. Cole was designated a test and acceptance officer. His job was to fly every third or fourth C-47 that rolled off the line, putting it through a series of maneuvers and testing the engines, fuel system, controls, and other components of the airplanes. Additionally, the company was tooling up to produce B-24s and the A-26 twin-engine attack bombers. It was a good job, he was able to get plenty of flight time, and he didn't need to look for enemy aircraft. There were no raids by enemy bombers, and the weather was generally good. If it looked otherwise, he didn't fly.

He celebrated his twenty-eighth birthday on 7 September, consuming a cake sent by his mother for the occasion. "*Got cake, ate same. Thanks a lot. It was very good, but didn't last long.*"[7] In the same letter, he apologized for not having written sooner, but explained that there wasn't much to write about. He was flying; Jake Sartz had been through the previous week, still sold on married life; letters were coming in from his siblings and relatives. He had gotten "*pipe mania*" and purchased a new one and promised to send his old one to his father. "*It's a good one,*" he advised.

He obviously was thrilled with his new job, testing new flying hardware. "*Still flying these new airplanes. Lots of fun. Sure is hard to take—flying new airplanes—ho hum!*"

Later that month, Cole's life changed dramatically. One day about mid-September 1943, he was in the operations office when the phone rang. It was Col. Johnny Alison, who identified himself to Cole. Alison was well known, a legend in the CBI, a fearless fighter pilot who had commanded the 23rd Fighter Group, successor to the AVG, or Flying Tigers, while Cole was flying the Hump. Alison was an ace, credited with downing seven Japanese aircraft, including two bombers. He shot them both down in one night, the first time anyone had attempted night interceptions in that theater; for the feat, he was awarded the Distinguished Service Cross, second only to the Medal of Honor.

"Jake Sartz said you might be interested in something we're putting together." Jake had called Cole a few days previously with sketchy information about a secret operation involving a lot of flying; would Dick be willing to talk with Alison? Sure, why not? Cole affirmed his earlier conversation to Alison, who continued: "We're forming a unit to go back to the CBI. It's a special unit. Would you be interested in going?" No details, no promises, no enticements. Dick had been to the CBI, knew about the weather, the miserable living conditions, the lack of equipment, the slow and uncertain mail, the high accident rate for transports.

"Sure, I'll go. Sign me up." There was a war on, and someone had to go, and if his buddy Sartz was going, Cole would too. He had no compelling reason to avoid further combat. No wife, no children, and no prospects. Alison said he would send orders to Cole's permanent duty station at Love Field in Dallas. Cole was to report to Seymour Johnson AAF Base in Goldsboro, North Carolina, about the middle of October.[8]

In his current job, in addition to test-hopping new C-47s rolling out of the Douglas plant, Cole was also charged with testing new modifications and equipment changes to a variety of aircraft coming through the AAF Plant No. 3 on the field at Tulsa, across from the Douglas plant on the east side, beside a new, long runway. For Cole, "it was an ideal job."[9] The job was flying, a lot of it, in a variety of aircraft. Contractors in the AAF Plant were hired to develop and build new equipment or to modify existing aircraft systems; Cole's job was to fly the airplanes and see that the contractors had performed the work and that the modification did what it was intended to do. So he had gone from bombing the capital of a nation at war with the United States to flying the most dangerous route in the world to the equally dangerous job of flight-testing large, complex warplanes.

On this particular day in late September, Cole had been tasked with flying a modified B-24. The nose turret had been taken out and a radar unit installed in its place. His job was to take the heavy bomber to thirty thousand feet to determine if it could hold pressurization. Having flown C-87s, or the cargo version of the B-24, over the Hump, Cole was familiar with the type of four-engine aircraft.

Cole was at the field early and walked out to the heavy, slab-sided Liberator sitting awkwardly on the ramp. No one ever called the Liberator graceful; it squatted on relatively short main gear and a nosewheel, an arrangement that placed the fuselage close to the ground; its twin tail and long, thin Davis wing gave it a mismatched, awkward look. It gave the impression of weight, a lot of it; it was hard to resist a comparison to a dump truck. It was only in the air that it began to appear that it would fly, and fly well.

For these test hops, Cole as the test and acceptance officer for the Army Air Forces was the only military member of the flight crew. The copilot and flight engineer were civilians, as was a tech rep who would be going along on this flight.

Cole arrived early and began the walk-around inspection of the big bomber. As he looked over the brake lines and tires, a young woman rode up on a bicycle. She was tall, slim, dark-haired, with high cheekbones and dark sparkling eyes. She watched the pilot for a moment; he was only vaguely aware of her presence.

"I'm taking flying lessons at Spartan," she announced. The flight training school was on the opposite end of the field, and she pointed to the brick building. "I want to fly in a big airplane." The young woman looked over the Liberator, appraising it and evidently judging it to be worthy of her interest. "I'm going to be a WASP." Women Airforce Service Pilots delivered new aircraft to military bases around the country, flying everything from trainers to heavy bombers.

Cole was friendly but absorbed in the preflight inspection. "Well, I'd be happy to oblige you, but this is a test hop and we can't take people on test hops. Another reason is we don't have a parachute." The airplane was equipped with four chutes; there were no provisions for additional passengers. The young woman was silent, still taking in the size of the bomber, and eventually she drifted off as Cole completed the walk-around inspection. He entered the airplane and opened the bomb-bay doors, allowing the relatively cool morning air to enter the cabin and cockpit. The two pairs of doors were the normal entrance for the flight crew. It was a short step onto an I beam, and then crew members moved either to the rear compartment if they were aerial gunners or forward to the stations for the flight-deck crew, navigator, bombardier, and flight engineer if they were a full-combat crew.

The copilot and flight engineer arrived along with a Western Electric technical representative, Austin Harrison, who would monitor the radar installation and the pressurization test. Cole advised them he had completed the walk-around, and it was time for the prestart and engine start checks. The cockpit of a B-24, like most complex military aircraft, is jammed to overflowing with instruments, controls, levers, switches, radios, and knobs. Each of the four engines monitors the performance and health of the power plants through separate gauges measuring oil pressure, oil temperature, and fuel flow. Just checking all of the instruments and controls before starting the first engine is a complex operation requiring coordination among the pilot, copilot, and flight engineer. When at last they completed the checklist, they closed the bomb-bay doors and signaled to a young man standing by with a fire extinguisher that they were ready; slowly, the propeller of the inboard left engine began to turn and quickly became a spinning disk, and with a loud bang and a pop a blue cloud of oily smoke belched from the exhaust. The roar of the huge radial engine settled into a smooth and steady rhythm, and they repeated the procedure for the other three engines. Cole radioed the tower for clearance, taxied to the runway, and took off.

The flight crew was carefully monitoring the performance of the bomber, and particularly noting whether the modified radar unit in the nose was affecting the pressurization in the cabin. They were climbing straight out and passing through twelve thousand feet when Cole was suddenly aware of someone standing between the two seats in the cockpit.

It was the young lady he had talked to on the ramp. She smiled charmingly, but Cole was not amused. The mission had to be scrubbed, and they turned back to the Tulsa airport. After landing they sat in the cockpit after shutting down the engines while Cole filled out the Form 1. The copilot, who was about fifty and divorced a couple of times, still had an eye for pretty women. He began to lecture the stowaway and slyly suggested that an investigation might follow. He pulled a matchbook from his pocket and told her to write her telephone number on it so she could be contacted if further action was to be taken.

The woman dutifully wrote down her name and number, while the copilot watched with a small smile. Big-eyed, she looked squarely at the copilot with a look of concern. She then turned and handed the matchbook—and her phone number—to Cole.

He was perplexed and embarrassed. It turned out that the young, good-looking woman worked at the Douglas plant, and he did not want her to lose her job. He also was taken by her spirit and her desire to fly; she had already accumulated nearly thirty hours of flight time toward her goal of becoming a WASP. He and the tech rep from Western Electric decided that no harm had been done, and they agreed not to take it further.

Her interest in Cole was obvious, but in his own words, he was not very interested in chasing women. Flying had been his first love since he was a small boy, and he had pursued it with a passion that left little room for Cupid. But this young lady seemed far different from any of those he had casually dated while in school or as a cadet. Yes, there was definitely something about her that intrigued him. Beautiful, to be sure. High-spirited, without a doubt. Self-confident, in spades. And she wanted to fly! But first he had to overcome his shyness.

Cole eventually called Marta—that was the name she wrote on the matchbook—and asked her out. He fell hard; after three dates in two weeks, he asked her to marry him.

Lucia Marta Harrell, daughter of a Scottish engineer from Louisiana and a Mexican mother, was nineteen. She was from El Paso, Texas, and had attended the Texas School of Mines (now the University of Texas—El Paso, or UTEP) for two years. Her older sister, Christina, had married a Navy pilot who was killed early in the war. Christina and Marta had traveled to Tulsa to visit Christina's grieving in-laws, the Barretts; they ended up staying, living with the dead pilot's parents, and both obtained jobs at the Douglas plant.

Mart, for that was what Cole called her, was Catholic. When the couple went to a priest to make the necessary arrangements to marry, he refused to perform the rites. Cole was not Catholic, and Cole later recalled that the priest told him he was going to hell. She called her mother for advice, and her mother called Mrs. Barrett in Tulsa. Together, the two women reckoned that under the circumstances, the couple could be married by a justice of the peace, or JP. Dick had agreed to report to Seymour Johnson Army Air Force Base in Goldsboro, North Carolina, in a matter of days. They were running out of time.

So at 11:00 p.m. on 11 October 1943, Dick Cole and Mart Harrell called a justice of the peace to plead for a wedding. It was wartime, they were young, and he agreed to perform the ceremony if they would drive to his house. He met them at his front door wearing a long flannel nightshirt and a cap that made him look like a stage character playing the part of Scrooge. The ceremony was brief, the JP signed the marriage license, and they left. No white wedding gown, no bridesmaid, no best man. But they were legally married, in the eyes of the law if not of the church. They went back to his small apartment and the next morning packed the blue Ford convertible with all of their earthly possessions—which were almost entirely her few dresses and Dick's uniforms—and headed to Seymour Johnson AAF Base. They took five days, honeymooning along the way through the Appalachians.

Cole was apprehensive when he reported to Seymour Johnson. Alison had promised to send official orders to Cole's permanent base in Dallas—Tulsa was considered a temporary assignment—but they had never arrived. Officially, he could be considered AWOL. He asked for and found Alison, who laughed off any suggestion that Cole might be in trouble and quickly got him the necessary paperwork that made his presence legal as well as setting up arrangements for allowance for Mart. Housing would be a bit of a problem, as it was around the country for the millions of newly minted troops, but they would figure something out.

The next stop was to call on the base chaplain, a lieutenant colonel who was a Roman Catholic priest. Cole related their civil ceremony and Mart's desire for a church wedding before he had to leave for his new assignment. His bride wanted her union with her new husband blessed by a priest. The padre, as Army chaplains are often called, listened sympathetically, smiling with reassurance at the beautiful young bride and the shy, beaming pilot.

He suddenly rose and walked to the doorway of his office. Three or four young soldiers were walking past, and he stopped them. "You and you and you—come in here." The men, with wide eyes, wondered what they had done to irritate a lieutenant colonel. "You are going to witness a marriage here," he told them. They were clearly relieved and cast admiring glances at the lithe, dark-haired beauty sitting with the young captain wearing silver wings and a row of combat ribbons.

With no further fanfare, the padre donned his vestments, asked the young couple to stand before him, and performed the traditional rites of marriage in the Catholic Church. The young soldiers signed the document of marriage as witnesses and were dismissed. Dick and Mart had now been married twice in five days.[10]

# CHAPTER 22

Johnny Alison's mysterious phone call was part of the recruiting effort for Project 9, a top-secret plan that originated in the jungles of Burma, was approved by the president of the United States and the prime minister (PM) of Great Britain at a conference in Quebec, and directed by General of the Army Air Forces Henry H. "Hap" Arnold from the Pentagon. Capt. Dick Cole was once more involved in one of the military's most secret plans for operations in World War II. Project 1 had been the raid on Tokyo, for which Cole had had the best seat in the house; Project 7 was the use of airline personnel and equipment for the Hump airlift, and he was there for that. Cole would have an equally good seat for this operation.

It would be several months before Cole and the rest of the 523 men gathered for Project 9 would learn what it entailed. The plan had been the brainchild of the eccentric and brilliant British army general Orde Wingate. Alison and his friend Col. Phil Cochran had expanded the role of the Army Air Forces with the encouragement of General Arnold. Alison and Cochran had been tasked by Arnold with supplying Wingate's Long Range Penetration Group—called Chindits—on their incursion into Burma. Wingate's first foray in early 1943 behind Japanese lines in northern Burma had been deemed a success in harassing the enemy, blowing up bridges and railroad tracks, and severing lines of communication. But it had come at an appalling price: Unable to evacuate wounded or sick, they had to leave behind hundreds of Tommies, propped against trees in the jungle, each man with a rifle and a bit of food. Their eventual fates were the stuff of nightmares, particularly for their friends who had been forced to abandon them.[1]

What was needed for a second campaign was a way to evacuate these gallant wounded and ill troops. The British had very few light planes that would be capable of landing in rough jungle clearings to carry out the wounded and sick. The Americans had plenty of liaison planes—L-birds—that would fill the bill very nicely. Would it be possible for the Army Air Forces to cooperate in a joint operation?

Prime Minister Winston Churchill was a great admirer of Orde Wingate. Born in India to a career officer, Wingate had already successfully tested his theories of irregular warfare in Palestine and Ethiopia. In the late 1930s, he had been posted to Palestine, where the conflict between the Jewish Zionists and the Arabs had flared into violence. Wingate's sympathies were with the Zionists, and he organized them into Special Night Squads that struck in the dark. Soon, Arab attacks on British troops, Jewish settlers, and oil facilities were significantly diminished. Wingate's efforts earned him a Distinguished Service Order (DSO), virtually unheard of for a captain not on frontline duty. When World War II started in 1939, Wingate was sent to Ethiopia, where he organized troops there to engage the occupying Italian army in irregular, guerrilla-style actions. Again, he was recognized by the British government with a second DSO, a promotion, and then posting to Burma.[2]

Wingate had arrived in Burma only a week or so before Rangoon fell to the Japanese in March 1942. The British forces there as well as the Chinese troops under Gen. Joseph Stilwell were routed and withdrew, largely on foot, to India. Wingate, in India, trained a force of British troops, together with Indian, African, and Burmese soldiers, and led them into Burma in early 1943. Their exploits earned him a third DSO, the envy and possibly the enmity of many in the officer corps, who viewed him as undisciplined and a bit of a showboat, and the admiration of Churchill, who summoned him back to England. The plucky Wingate was to accompany the PM on his secret sea voyage to Canada, where Churchill, President Franklin Delano Roosevelt, and the Combined Chiefs of Staff of the armed services of both nations were to meet and plan the next phases of the war. The Quadrant Conference of August 1943 was in Quebec; it was there that Wingate detailed to the Combined Chiefs his plan for another behind-the-lines incursion into Burma, with a much larger force of Chindits.[3]

Burma by itself would not have been terribly important in the grand scheme of the war. However, China was, and Burma was key to ensuring that China remained in the war. The vast nation had been largely cut off by the Japanese from receiving aid through any of its ports, which left only land routes. One of them was through Russia, but Russia and Japan had signed nonaggression pacts that shut down the northern route. The Burma Road was then the lifeline to bringing in thousands of tons of much-needed materiel, but it too had been cut off by the Japanese conquest of northern Burma, and of course that initiated the airlift known as the Hump operation in which Cole had flown in its dangerous first year. Wingate had been in the jungles of northern Burma harassing the Japanese while Cole and friends flew overhead on their way to China.

The Combined Chiefs liked Wingate's new plan, Roosevelt and Churchill approved, and Arnold had been tasked with aiding the British general in his campaign to once again make life miserable for the Japanese in Burma. Arnold was an airpower booster; he saw in the Wingate mission the opportunity for the Army Air Forces to show what they were capable of doing in a war unencumbered by traditional thinking of ground and sea officers. Alison and Cochran were both innovative tacticians, with brilliant combat records, Alison in China and Cochran in North Africa. "The hell with paperwork—get out there and fight," Arnold told them.[4] The training in North Carolina would reveal just how innovative they were and how much the initial request for light-plane support had evolved into an entirely new concept in joint-force operations.

Light planes to carry out the sick and wounded would be provided, but Cochran and Alison had submitted a plan that would also involve transport planes and cargo gliders to carry in Wingate's troops and P-51A fighters to provide close-air support. Additionally, they had commandeered four YR-4 helicopters to use in plucking downed aircrews from the jungles where no landing site was available. They were the first helicopters ever used in combat operations. And eventually, B-25s carrying the massive firepower of eight .50-caliber machine guns in the nose as well as a 77mm cannon would be added to the air task force in support of Wingate. The group, which would devise new tactics for supporting a ground force as well as stimulate forward thinking on unorthodox warfare, would become one of the most colorful combat groups in the war.[5] Dick Cole would be a member of the unit that became known as the 1st Air Commandos. He reported to his new assignment 18 October 1943, shortly after marrying his new bride for the second time.

The airfield at Seymour Johnson turned out to be a perfect location for a highly secret project that involved hundreds of men and, at that point, dozens of aircraft. It was a center for soldiers being deployed overseas, so it had a constantly changing population. Set in the piney woods of North Carolina, it had runways that allowed for a variety of unorthodox activities without evoking a lot of questions.

Cole looked out the windscreen of the low-flying C-47; ahead, he could see the long runway at Seymour Johnson and, at the near end, a large cargo glider. This was a new ball game; despite his many hours in a Gooney, he had never participated in the aerial snatching of a glider. He couldn't see the poles that he knew were in position about a hundred yards in front of the glider. The twin poles were fifteen feet high but less than two inches in diameter. Connected by a horizontal bar, they resembled a football goalpost, around which was a large loop in the towline that was connected to the nose of the glider on the runway. His job was to set up the Gooney Bird at an airspeed of 130 mph, slightly nose down, and to pass over the twin poles at an altitude of twenty-five feet, where a long hook projecting back and down would snag the loop in the towline. As they passed over the poles, Cole would shove the throttles full forward and begin to climb. If they were successful, they would know quickly: both pilots would be thrust forward in their seats as the transport plane slowed under the sudden addition of a five-thousand-pound cargo glider.

This was far different from the ground-based tows they had practiced for the first few days. This snatching of gliders from the ground was a harbinger of what they would be doing in Burma: gliders would be flown into remote jungle clearings by C-47s, known as tugs, but if they were to be used again would have to be snatched out because there would be no runways long enough for C-47s to land and take off with a glider in tow.

The tug pilots at Seymour had started with normal single-tow takeoffs with one glider in tandem and then double tows in a V, with one glider on short tow, the second one seventy-five feet behind and to the right. Neither had seemed particularly difficult to Cole. The transport was slower to build to speed, and it ate up more runway. Steep banks were to be avoided, and every change in direction, attitude, or altitude had to be made with the gliders in mind. But in all, regular towing, with one glider or two, was not difficult for experienced pilots. After shackling the towropes to a hook on the tail of the C-47 tug, the tow pilot inched forward to take up the slack in the cable. A series of signals between the glider pilot and the tug driver had been worked out, including the indications of an emergency, in which case the glider was to release immediately. The rope could be jettisoned by either the tug or the glider; it was infinitely better for the glider if it was released by its own cockpit crew, so that the cable did not fly back and wrap around a wing, a potentially serious occurrence.

Because communication between the pilots of the tug and the gliders was so vital, the fliers attached a phone cord to the towrope to be able to communicate directly, cockpit to cockpit. At first, they taped the cord to the towrope but forgot one thing: the rope was nylon and would stretch, but the cord didn't. That didn't last very long.[6]

Training for the tugs and gliders had two goals: one was to orient the tow pilots to a variety of conditions involving single and double tows. Gliders were loaded in various configurations and weights and towed into flight from grass strips to simulate the primitive conditions they would face in any theater. Transport pilots were told to take off and climb with gliders in tow to a predetermined altitude—one to three thousand feet—directly over the field. Glider pilots had to make the decision on when to release and then safely put the Waco onto the grass field below. There were, of course, no go-arounds in a glider. They had to be right the first time.

On takeoffs, after receiving word that the glider was ready, the tug pilots began their takeoff roll down the runway. The gliders, especially empty ones as used in training, were airborne before the transports, and the glider pilots had to immediately push forward on their control yoke to keep the Waco just a few feet above the runway. Rising too high too quickly meant pulling up the tail of the transport before it could take off. The result would be disastrous.

In a double tow, the left glider was connected to the tug with a 350-foot line; the glider on the right was hooked to a 425-foot rope. They had to stay in an inverted-V formation even while taking off to prevent the snarls that would ensue if they were in a straight-line formation. At the start of the takeoff roll, there was insufficient air over the rudder for it to be effective, so the glider pilots had to maintain their positions by tapping on the appropriate brakes—left for the forward glider, right brake for the rear glider. It was the duty of the pilot on long tow to keep his Waco from creeping up and smashing into the forward glider, whose pilot had a restricted view behind him.[7]

As tricky as all this was, particularly for the glider pilots, aerial snatching was rather more intricate.

Glider snatches were not unheard of, even in October 1943. Gliders had been successfully used by the Germans in the invasion of Belgium, and it was a widely known secret that the Allies would use them in some capacity when they launched the invasion of Nazi-occupied Europe. The technique of snatching was developed to be able to reuse the glider. It was a new experience for Cole and the other tug pilots, and they found it quite a challenge to hook the large Waco CG-4A gliders on the fly and jerk them into the air. The secret to not pulling the nose off the glider or pulling down the tug was a complex bit of machinery installed in the cabin behind the bulkhead, known as the Model 80-X Glider Pick Up System. It was built by All American Aviation in Baltimore and consisted of a nylon cable more than 1,000 feet long, wrapped around a revolving drum. The line was attached to a hook at the end of a long arm that extended through a hawse pipe on the left side, forward of the cargo door. The cable played out at first, to reduce the shock to both the tug and the glider, and then the drum began to reel in the line, pulling the glider to within 350 feet of the tow plane. It was also equipped with an emergency line cutter operated from the tug cockpit.[8]

They were closer now, and Cole checked with the assistant flight engineer, young Ray Roberts, from Vermont. The nineteen-year-old was standing by the open cargo door with a long wooden boat hook, ready to push the nylon rope off the C-47's tail surfaces if the line should loop over. That was a disaster waiting to happen if they should lose control of the elevators in the tricky maneuver. A cargo net had been slung over the lower half of the door opening to keep Roberts from falling out.

Cole looked at his copilot, 2nd Lt. Ralph Bordley, who was keeping a close eye on the airspeed and calling out the numbers to Cole.

"134, Captain." Cole nodded, and raised the nose almost imperceptibly, while simultaneously reducing power ever so slightly. He did not take his eyes from the glider.

"130." The transport was lined up just to the right of the glider. The poles were clearly visible now. In seconds, they were directly over the glider, and it was no longer in sight. The poles were just ahead, and for just an instant the nylon tow cable that was looped around them was clearly visible. Cole glanced outside to his left, judging his height above the terrain, knowing his experience in this was more valuable than an altimeter. He began to smoothly apply power and pulled the nose up to a shallow climb. Suddenly, the plane seemed to sag. Cole and Bordley both felt their hips pressed hard against their seat belts. It was good—they had snagged the glider. It was hard to suppress a grin.

In the cockpit of the glider, Flight Officer Charles Turner, a twenty-one-year-old from Texas, had felt as much as heard the roar of the Gooney Bird as it roared just a few feet over his head. He braced himself for the shock he knew was coming despite the size of his glider, an awkward, ungainly flying machine. The Waco CG-4A had thick, untapered wings and a squat, square fuselage capable of hauling thirteen combat-ready troops or a jeep, cannon, or small bulldozer. The manual and the instructors both insisted that when it was snagged from the air, the g-forces were quite mild, far less than those experienced by Navy pilots who were launched from a carrier's catapult. When it came, Turner was surprised, not at the low g-loads he experienced but that it worked at all. It seemed improbable that the five-thousand-pound Waco could be snatched into flight without a long runway. But seconds after Cole's tug flew over, Turner found himself airborne, rising quickly over the pine woods of Wayne County, North Carolina.

There were far more improbable flights in the future, for Cole and Turner as well as the others selected for Project 9.[9]

The selection process for the secret project headed by Cochran and Alison had continued even as the tow planes and gliders were already at work. Each member of the team—which would variously be known as Project 9, CA-218 (for the suite at the Hay-Adams Hotel in Washington where Cochran and Alison planned the enterprise), 5318th Provisional Unit (Air), No. 1 Air Commando, and the 1st Air Commando Group—had to possess skills and attributes that would be useful in the upcoming campaign. Although three hundred of the men were pilots, all had to have secondary and tertiary skills, making it possible to function well with a very small number of multitalented troops. For Cole and Turner, it had been their mechanical abilities. Cole was selected to head up the engineering unit of the transport section; Turner was a good glider mechanic in addition to his rating as a pilot.

Shortly after training began at Goldsboro, each man was issued a .45 pistol and either an M1 .30 carbine or a Thompson submachine gun. Many were given the brand-new M1A1 folding-stock carbine, developed for the airborne troops. Alison had learned of the new weapon and made a strong case that they would be ideal for aircrews, as they would be easily stowed in a cockpit. In the conditions they expected, he reasoned, anyone could quickly find himself fighting the Japanese in the jungle. Now, when men were not in training classes, or flying, or doing physical training, they would be at the firing range, practicing with the weapons. There would be little letup in the rigorous regimen; they had only a limited time before shipping out.

Cole and the others didn't know precisely where they were going other than the CBI, or what the assignment was. They had been told it would involve combat, it was for only about six months, and they could expect absolutely no gain from it other than contributing to winning the war. But it wasn't hard to guess, from the equipment they were issued, that they would be in a tropical jungle environment. Marine jungle boots, made of canvas and rubber, were to replace their leather footwear. Additionally, airborne jumpsuits—pants with voluminous pockets on the legs and a top resembling a bush jacket—had been given to flight crews. Classes were held on avoiding malaria and a host of other tropical diseases.

Only Alison and Cochran knew the full plans. Capt. Bill Taylor, who had been assigned to head up the glider section of the new unit, and his assistant, Lt. Vincent Rose, had been stationed previously in Panama, where they had done some experimenting with flying gliders into jungle clearings. Cochran and Alison had questioned them closely about their experiences; they no doubt had some idea of the unit's destination, but never voiced their thoughts.

Training continued at a killing pace, beginning early each morning and continuing late at night. "Heads Up" classes were held on living in a jungle environment, respecting indigenous cultures, survival after bailout, and very technical classes on servicing and adjusting the complicated 80-X Pick Up system. Each tow pilot made three or four takeoffs with a single glider and then advanced to double tows. The additional weight was obvious, but the C-47 pilots quickly learned to accommodate by extending the takeoff run. Glider pilots were already proficient in being towed into the air, so the training here was for the tug pilots.

When tug pilots were judged proficient in tows and aerial snatching, they were told that now they were going to try something never done before: night snatches.

Flashlights were rigged to the tops of the same poles used during daytime training. Additionally, colored lights that replaced the panels of symbols used during daylight flights were placed at specific intervals on the approach end of the pickup zone. Cole, who had racked up considerable night-flying experience over the Hump, was not intimidated by the new requirements. "It really wasn't that hard to find the pickup zone. You could see those flashlights for miles. You just came in like normal, and watched your airspeed and altitude."[10] Right. Piece of cake. The knowledge that it had never been done before was simply an acknowledgment of history. It was not intimidating to Cole, nor, as it turned out, was it to the other experienced tug drivers.

Often the pilots flew early in the morning and again in the afternoon or late at night. Because they still were awaiting the bulk of their C-47s, some days they did not fly at all. The Glider Pick Up System was often balky, and a tech rep from the factory was there to advise how to adjust the complicated machine when it failed to perform as it should. The rep, a man named Gephardt, often flew with the C-47s and frequently with the gliders. Cole heard later that he was killed in a crash at the factory's home field in Baltimore.[11]

There occasionally was time for socializing. Bill Cherry and his wife, Bobbi; Jake Sartz and his new bride, Betty; and Dick and Mart were having dinner one night at the Officers Club at Seymour Johnson. Bobbi was sitting on Cherry's lap when the base commander, a brigadier general, came in, swagger stick and all. He saw the group of young pilots and their wives and made a beeline for their table, his face red.

Cherry, who had survived twenty-four days in a life raft, bobbing around with his B-17 crew and Eddie Rickenbacker in the South Pacific, was not one to be intimidated. He smoked a pipe and enjoyed a good joke. When the general motioned for him to rise, he did so, slowly, looking the general squarely in the eyes.

Pointing to Bobbi, the general vented his anger at Cherry. "That is not a practice at this base! That will never happen again!" When Cherry explained that the woman who had been sitting on his lap was his wife, the brigadier was not placated. "I don't care whose wife she is. That will not happen in this club again." The pilots found other places to eat after that.[12]

The men at Seymour Johnson soon learned that while the C-47s and the Waco gliders were working at a frantic pace, another group was training at an equally killing speed at nearby Raleigh-Durham Army Air Field, fifty miles east. The original plans to supply Wingate's troops and to evacuate wounded with light planes had expanded many times over, as

Cochran and Alison, with the blessing of Hap Arnold, designed an autonomous and independent unit that would not only provide transportation but also include aerial firepower. The C-47s and gliders were to take the British troops behind Japanese lines instead of walking in from India; light planes, primarily L-5 Sentinals as well as a few L-1s and UC-64s, would provide resupply, liaison, spotting, and ambulance duties. A contingent of thirty P-51A Mustangs had been assigned to the new unit, which still called itself Project 9, as well as 100 L-5 Sentinel light planes and a dozen each L-1s and UC-64s. A few two-place TG-5 training gliders had been added, with the primary role of constant training, but also with the idea that very small combat teams might be inserted behind enemy lines by glider. And, of course, there were the helicopters, the acquisition of which had caused howls of outrage by the staff at Wright Field, where they were still undergoing testing and evaluation.[13]

The fighter pilots and the L pilots (L for "liaison") at Raleigh-Durham were flying a series of training exercises and maneuvers that would prepare them for the rigors of combat and the realities of war in the jungle. To head the fighter section, Alison had chosen a tall, dark-haired veteran of twenty-five whom he knew from his days in China. Gratton "Grant" Mahony was fierce and focused, already recognized with the Distinguished Service Cross and with four Japanese planes to his credit. He burned with hatred toward the Japanese for what they had done in the Philippines and China, where downed Allied fliers could expect little mercy from Japanese troops. Many of the fighter pilots selected for Project 9 were also combat veterans, but many were selected from fighter squadrons that had yet to deploy overseas. Mahony set a demanding schedule to prepare them all for combat in the skies over Burma.

Equally frenetic was the schedule that Clinton Gaty and Andrew Rebori set for the light-plane section. The pilots, most of whom had flown only the relatively simple L-2 class of liaison aircraft made by Piper, Aeronca, and Taylorcraft, were now in larger, more complex airplanes with more power, variable speed propellers, flaps, and equipment for instrument flight. While the fighter boys were dogfighting and practicing aerial combat tactics, the liaison guys were finessing short-field landings and takeoffs, shortening the published distance for becoming airborne by a few hundred feet, and carrying far more weight than the manuals recommended. The light planes, after all, were the original heart of the project, the aerial means of resupply and evacuation requested by Orde Wingate. The L pilots were creative and had much the same spirit as the cocky and more celebrated fighter pilots. At one point, a pilot rigged two Thompson submachine guns to the wing struts of his airplane and fired them at a ground target by means of wires running to the triggers from the cockpit. It was determined that the vibration from firing the .45-caliber automatic weapons was too severe to be effective, however. Another man rigged a wire-tripped rack to the struts, a rack that could carry bags of supplies or perhaps a small bomb.[14]

The monsoon season, which would turn the jungles of Burma into swamps and trails into muddy slides, would begin in May. Any planned assault would have to take place long before then, and that fact was heavily on the minds of the two men in charge of this new operation. In early November, Cochran and Alison announced to the men that they would be shipping out, destination unknown, and training would continue under conditions vastly different from North Carolina.

For Cole and his new bride, it was far too soon. Although work had been intense and nearly around the clock, Dick and Mart had managed to settle into the sweet and blissful routine of the young and newly married.

# CHAPTER 23

As it turned out, Cole and the other transport pilots and crews had more time in North Carolina than the other pilots, ground crews, and support personnel. The fighters and light planes were sent by ship, as were the gliders, which were disassembled and shipped in crates. Most of the men were sent by air, with top priority on any aircraft bound for the CBI.

Dick and Mart, married for less than two months, said their good-byes. Mart and Bobbi Cherry would drive Dick's 1941 Ford convertible to Dallas, where Bobbi lived, before Mart went on to her parents in El Paso. The newlyweds promised to write every day, but Cole was under no illusions about mail delivery from and to the CBI.[1]

Cole and the C-47 flight crews were the only ones to fly their aircraft to India. The crews had been formed while in training at Seymour Johnson, and for Cole the men he would fly with were his copilot, 2nd Lt. Ralph Bordley, from Baltimore; engineer, T/Sgt. (Technical Sergeant) William Ecklar, Nelliston, New York; radioman, T/Sgt. Kenneth J. Alexander, Kokimo, Indiana; and assistant engineer, PFC (Private First Class) Maurice Raymond "Ray" Roberts, Poultney, Vermont. After loading their gear, they left Saturday morning, 11 December, going the southern route from Florida to Puerto Rico to British Guiana and on to Natal, Brazil. Fitted with extra fuel tanks, they departed for Ascension Island, a speck in the South Atlantic, where they refueled before heading on to Accra, on the west coast of Africa. They rested and refueled and then departed for a British air base at Lake Chad. The next day, on to Khartoum, and from there to Bashiyah, in Iraq, where they spent a final night before departing for Karachi in western India. It was a long, tiring flight, taking nearly ten days. The thirteen transports departed in two groups, with Cole leading one section of six for the long haul, and Bill Cherry the other.

Monday, 13 December, Cole wrote his mother, with "enroute" denoting his location. *"Our 'Hairless Joe' runs like a top. We should cross the equator soon. It's already pretty hot. Have been getting up at 3 and 4 o'clock to beat the heat and the midday tropical thunderstorms that hang around in this area."*[2]

"Hairless Joe" was the name Cole and his crew had christened their C-47, after a character in the comic strip *Li'l Abner*, by Al Capp. In the strip, Hairless Joe and Lonesome Polecat brew and peddle their own concoction, Kickapoo Joy Juice, the fumes of which can melt the rivets off battleships. On the flight from the States to Karachi, the crews were repeatedly asked about the strange hooked arm extending from a hawse pipe forward of the wide cargo doors. Unable to reveal its purpose, the crews painted a blue question mark on the vertical fins of each plane, with a blue circle enclosing it. "We're the Question Mark Squadron," they told inquisitive ground crews wherever they landed. "Don't ask us any questions." When they arrived in India, the transport-section crewmen had leather patches made that replicated the tail markings and sewed them on their flight jackets as the unofficial emblem of the transport section of Project 9, now being called the 5318th Provisional Unit (Air), a much more awkward designation.[3]

On 21 December, still "enroute" but now somewhere in India—probably Karachi—Cole again wrote his mother. Jake Sartz had left the States with Cherry's group four days earlier than Cole's section of six; somewhere they had evidently experienced trouble, for now they were only a single day ahead, he wrote. Cole probably revealed too much about his destination: *"Lots of land and water have passed under our wings, and we're still not there. Tomorrow is the last lap to the mainland, are going to the same place we were stationed while flying the 'Hump.'"*

At twenty-eight, Cole was nearly ancient in the wartime flying game. Most of the men in his section were much younger, and it showed in their high spirits. *"This place is real noisy. All the boys are playing 'Black Jack,' a gambling game, with rupees. First time they've seen them. Most of them are getting a bigger kick out of going places, more than I did. Maybe it's cause they're a good bit younger. Sure are a peppy bunch,"* he wrote.[4]

Younger, and decidedly more culturally insensitive. Somewhere in their training, some had missed the classes that stressed the importance of respect for dress, religion, and traditions among indigenous people in the CBI. Before crossing into India, somewhere in the Middle East, the young crew chiefs had been sprucing up the planes. "*Last night the crew chiefs were working on the airplanes. A couple of Arabs were cleaning it out. One of the crew chiefs jerked off one of their turbans and started polishing the ship with it. Well! We almost had a race war.*" Cole was able to defuse the incident, but it did not lend to good relations between transient flight crews and local workers on the airfields.[5]

At Karachi the men waited for the ships carrying the fighters and light planes, where they were carefully inspected by the ground crews. The gliders, each packed into five crates, went to the port of Calcutta on the southeast coast of India. From there they were taken by truck to Barrackpore, fifteen miles north, where the glider pilots assembled them. Tools were in short supply, and a vital one missing was a tensionometer, a device that measured the tautness of the bracing wires in the Wacos. F/O (Flight Officer) Charles Turner had a good ear for music, and he was able to tune the gliders by plucking the wires and memorizing the sound. He then flew one that he deemed ready; it performed as it should, and he then became the unofficial tuner of the gliders.[6]

For several weeks, the flight crews had no permanent home. The transports had flown to Bengal in eastern India, and the fliers spent the days towing gliders and practicing pickups. The transports and gliders would eventually move to a former RAF emergency airfield near Lalaghat, in Assam, while the fighters and light planes would go to Hailakandi, ten miles south of Lalaghat. But neither base was ready to accommodate the group; the flying fields needed work, and structures for housing, operations, and administration had to be constructed. Until the bases were ready for occupancy, the men of Project 9 were homeless, living from base to base and moving often.

On 2 January 1944, Cole wrote his parents a reassuring letter. "*Everything is O.K., all we are doing is just flying around. Do not have to fly the 'Hump' at all, just around 'romantic India.'*" "Hairless Joe" was down at the moment with a dead cylinder in the left engine; they were awaiting parts and hoped to be in the air again in a day or two. He lamented the lack of a permanent place to spend nights: "*This moving around is really getting monotonous. Different place every night, sleeping in the airplane, not shaving, showering, just moving. Just bought four sheets and two pillow cases. Drew some blankets, so it won't be so chilly tonight. Don't like to sleep in my clothes. Also got a mattress for a rope bed.*" And, music to a mother's ears, the food was much better than when her son had been in India previously. He requested razor blades and toothbrushes, which were difficult to obtain in theater. He also noted that he and his new bride were writing each other every day.[7]

On 4 January, Cole and his crew left Barrackpore shortly before two in the afternoon. They flew northwest, landing at Panagarh forty minutes later. For the next couple of days, Cole and the other transport pilots did a series of short hops, testing the planes and fine-tuning the glider pickup system. The next day, they flew up to Lalaghat to deliver supplies and equipment. His assistant flight engineer, Ray Roberts, recorded in a diary: "Hundreds of natives around Lalaghat. Cows seen from plane." On the seventh, back at Panagarh, they began practicing double glider tows, doing that several times until the tenth. On that day, Cole's and other transports towed two gliders each to a large rice field, where they were going to rig up poles and practice snatching the gliders on the fly once more, at night. They ended up circling the field for several hours, while the ground crews experienced a series of setbacks as they rigged up the equipment and sought to get the lights set correctly.

It was a long night. They departed from a small airfield at Lalipur a few minutes past four for the exercise and returned the next morning at a quarter past three. Along the way, the C-47s became lost, and the home base sent up flares to guide them in. Roberts recorded: "Very little gas left."[8]

In the meantime, work was proceeding to build more or less permanent facilities for the group. At Lalaghat and Hailakandi, work went on virtually around the clock. The location of each was on tea plantations that had been there for more than a century; they were flat, flood-prone depressions among cone-shaped hills. Hard runways would not be necessary; all of the aircraft would use the grass field itself, which at Lalaghat was sixty-three hundred feet and at Hailakandi forty-five hundred feet. But living quarters, operations shacks, dining halls, ordnance dumps, fuel depots, dispersal areas—everything necessary for an air-combat organization—had to be constructed.

Luckily for the group, Capt. Andrew Cox had been unofficially assigned as an engineering/construction officer. Cox, who had a background in operating heavy equipment, was officially assigned to the coast artillery and therefore could not be attached to the Air Force. Cochran simply arranged for him to be assigned to the Southeast Asia Command staff of Adm. Lord Louis Mountbatten and then sent on "temporary assignment" to the Air Commandos, for that was what they now were calling themselves. Cox, a tall, unassuming man of quiet competence, immediately took stock of the sites at Hailakandi and Lalaghat and organized construction details based on priorities. Things were a bit better at Hailakandi, where several buildings from the tea plantation were pressed into service, including the tea-processing shed, which became a commissary, and the tea planter's cottage, which became the unit hospital.[9]

First on the list for both fields were bashas for barracks, constructed of bamboo, with thatched roofs and dirt floors. Privacy was only a memory; men slept in hammocks in open bays, each hammock draped in mosquito netting. A place to sleep was not only good for morale but imperative for protection at night from the hoards of mosquitoes that carried malaria. Slowly, the large, flat field was transformed into an operational air base. Runway lights were installed, a control tower built.

As planned, the Cole newlyweds wrote each other daily, but delivery in both directions was far more problematic. On 26 January 1944, Cole wrote his mother on colorful CBI stationery and poked gentle fun at the sequence in which he received Mart's letters. His pride and happiness are evident. *"Mart has written just about every day. Course they don't arrive like that (wish they would), but I get them eventually just like before. The first ones arrive last and the last ones arrive first. Most of the time I've no idea of what she is talking about."*

And in the way of the just married, he was eager to talk to his parents about the girl he had wed.

*[Brother] Ralph didn't have much to say except a general razzing about getting married. Everybody so far has razzed me. The only reason why that I can think of is the fact that most everybody thought me a woman-hater and I'd probably never get married. The fact is I wasn't at all. Guess I was just afraid of 'em. You know that I would have gotten married a long time ago, had I met Martha. Somehow I knew it would happen someday and often wondered why it took the time it did. Now that it's here I'm more than glad things turned out like they did. You are right—she is tops.*

The weather had been cool, he reported, and not much rain. Oh, and Jake Sartz had lost about fifteen pounds: *"He could spare it. I'm just the same."*[10]

Finally, on 10 February, the crews began arriving at Lalaghat. Ray Roberts, Cole's assistant flight engineer, drove a jeep in a convoy traveling through mountains and crossing the numerous rivers by ferry, two trucks at a time, arriving at the forward base on 11 February, about noon. Captain Cherry, head of the transport section, gave Roberts and the rest of the enlisted men the day off after their herculean efforts to move the group to Lalaghat. But since there was nothing to do at the most primitive base, Roberts and his buddies drifted out to their aircraft that afternoon, reinstalling empty deicer tanks in the C-47s and then flying when Cole determined that more glider tows were necessary. On 13 February, the crew of "Hairless Joe" left Lalaghat early, flying to Tezgaon to pick up more needed supplies and then made the same trip in the afternoon to pick up a small bulldozer and trailer.[11]

The next day, 14 February, proved to be disastrous for the Air Commandos. On that day, Cochran himself led a flight of P-51s to attack a target at Mandalay, Burma. For a couple of weeks, the fighter pilots had launched probing attacks into Burma, striking at bridges, railroad tracks and rolling stock, suspected fuel depots, communications centers. They had done a certain amount of damage, but more important had become familiar with the area. Their mission would be to support Wingate's Chindits as they began the long-range penetration campaign far behind Japanese lines. The mission this day exceeded that charge, and the Air Commandos paid a heavy price for a series of bad decisions.

Cochran had been asked if his new group might be willing to destroy a Japanese supply depot in northern Mandalay, in a complex of metal-roofed buildings. The thirty-four-year-old fighter pilot, who had been itching for combat and kicking against an assignment to a "back-alley fight" in the CBI, quickly agreed and at eight o'clock on the morning of Valentine's Day led a flight of thirteen Mustangs from Hailakandi, bumping the fighter section leader, Grant Mahony, from the command position for the mission. The general target was easy to find, on a major bend of the Irrawaddy River, but the precise building would be difficult to spot among a cluster of similar structures. The 51s were loaded with .50-caliber shells on long belts laid into the wings as well as two five-hundred-pound bombs each attached to hardpoints—reinforced attachment rings for a variety of ordnance—under the wings. When they arrived over the target area, Colonel Cochran—an experienced fighter pilot with three German aircraft to his credit—failed to assign a top cover for the dive-bombing Mustangs. It was an elementary and fatal mistake.

The Americans, all looking down on the target, were bounced by a flight of ten Hayabusa Ki-43s, dubbed "Oscars" by Allied forces, from the veteran 50th Sentai. They were on patrol, looking for the newcomers in Mustangs who had lately been staging raids into northern Burma. In the ensuing attack, two Mustangs were shot down immediately. 1st Lt. Carl Hartzer was killed; Capt. Donald V. "Red" Miller was captured after bailing out of his crippled fighter. Cochran, knowing that the Commandos were caught unaware from above and that the mission exceeded his orders from Hap Arnold, ordered all the American pilots to break from the fight and head back to Hailakandi. The young fighter pilots were furious with Cochran, and the incident might have seriously jeopardized the unit cohesion and esprit de corps that had been so carefully built up during recruiting, training, and shipping out to India.

Cochran was a savvy commander, one who had already made his mark in North Africa and in the comic strips. He was the real-life model for the character Flip Corkin in Milton Caniff's popular *Terry and the Pirates* that was carried in hundreds of American newspapers. He was the opposite of a by-the-rules popinjay. His good looks, quick sense of humor, and easygoing command style had made him a favorite among his men in numerous military assignments. Cochran dispensed with salutes, was not concerned with personal appearances, and called everyone "Sport." His acceptance of responsibility for the Valentine's Day Massacre over Mandalay carried the day when the fighter pilots gathered to debrief and to voice their disgust and dismay over "cutting and running."

There was plenty of blame to pass around. Cochran admitted he should not have taken command of the mission from Major Mahony and that he specifically should have assigned a top cover. On the other hand, the tactic of providing several fighters to keep a lookout and be prepared to attack enemy fighters from above was so elementary that it should have been second nature to the American fighter boys. Second, he told them, they needed to show more discipline in the air. It took far too long for them to heed his orders to break from the fight and head back to base.

One upshot of the disaster was an erroneous report that Cochran had been shot down and killed. When the details of the aerial battle became known, Wingate asked and American commanders ordered that Cochran fly no more combat missions. He was too valuable and knew too much about the upcoming Chindit campaign to be killed or to fall prisoner to the Japanese.[12]

It was the first combat blood shed by the Air Commandos, but it would not be the last. And others would die in horrible accidents.

# CHAPTER 24

Combat, particularly aerial combat, is intended to be a deadly endeavor, at least for the enemy. There are so many ways to die inside an aircraft—fragile human bodies ripped apart by machine gun or rocket fire from other aircraft or exploding shells from antiaircraft batteries on the ground or roasted alive while trapped in a burning airplane as it takes its final plummet to meet the hard earth below. Even if an airman is able to extricate himself from a damaged airplane—no easy task in World War II flying machines—and hurl himself into the too thin air, he still must hope that he will not be shot in his harness as he descends under a silk canopy or that the airplane he just left will not come around and snag his parachute or light the thin fibers ablaze. Necks are delicate parts of the human body and easily broken in a bad parachute landing; men have been caught in trees, unable to free themselves, and died.

But men who chose to fight in the sky accepted all those risks. They understood that some would not come home from missions. They knew that the enemy—Japanese or German or Italian—would be trying hard to ensure that their families received a telegram: "We regret to inform you . . ."

Very few, however, understood clearly that just taking off or landing or any of the dozens of changes in altitude or attitude required of airplanes, all airplanes but especially of warplanes, might just as easily result in their early death. More than fifteen thousand young men were killed in training accidents in the United States, youngsters just as eager to earn their wings as Dick Cole and Jake Sartz and Bill Cherry and Charlie Turner. Just as eager, but perhaps not as skilled. Or perhaps just not as lucky.

The day after the Mandalay mission, Cole and his crew made two round-trips to Tamu, just inside Burma, bringing supplies to Stilwell's men. Because Tamu was in Japanese-controlled Burma, the flights counted as combat missions. That night a double-tow exercise was on the schedule. This time, the gliders would be filled with Chindits.

Cooperation, even admiration, had been building between the some-times cocky Americans and the tough Commonwealth soldiers who were going to be transported and supplied by them. The Chindits were a varied lot: Englishmen, Indian troops, Gurkhas from Nepal, a few troops from British colonies in West Africa. It had taken a bit of time for the two Allies to come around. To the British, the Yanks were often loud, overbearing, and far too confident; worse, by His Majesty's stan-dards, they were vastly overpaid. Most of the Chindits were infantry-men, which in the king's service were among the lowest paid of those in uniform. A disproportionate number of Americans were officers, whose base pay was already many times higher than an enlisted Tommy. Add-ed to that was another 50 percent for flight pay and an allowance for overseas duty. To the Americans, the British seemed distant, distrust-ful, and very difficult to understand. At one point, the Air Commandos were instructed not to discuss money, America, or Texas around other Allied troops.[1]

A couple of joint exercises had begun to heal the breach. At a night exercise held near Gwalior, the Americans had towed twenty-four glid-ers into a field, silently and precisely on schedule. Mountbatten and Wingate had been dumbstruck; the gliders touched down and rolled to a stop in front of where they stood in a wooded area as if it all had been scripted. The next morning, the gliders had been snatched out by the tugs in a display of American skill that amazed and delighted the Brits, many of whom clamored to board the gliders to be snatched from the field. Wingate was among them.

For glider pilot Charlie Turner, it was memorable for two reasons: he was reprimanded by Wingate, and he had to abort the snatch take-off. Wingate and his aide had boarded Turner's Waco to experience the unorthodox takeoff, and Turner turned around to inform him that he could not be aboard for the risky maneuver.

"Young man, I can do whatever I choose. I command this group," Wingate informed Turner. "I will never ask my men to do something that I won't do." With that settled, Turner prepared for the snatch and the impending increase in g-forces during the sudden acceleration as a tug flew up behind him. He had done this many times and was considered to be quite proficient on the maneuver. But something went wrong that day; the left wing of the glider struck one of the poles on which the towline was looped, cutting it to the main spar. Turner released the line, and the glider skidded to a stop. Wingate apparently was unfazed; he boarded another glider, one flown by Taylor and Cochran, and was airlifted back to the British base. Turner spent the night at the maneuver field after repairing his glider. He was pulled out the next day.[2]

The nonchalance of the American flyboys as they demonstrated extreme skill and daring in the joint maneuvers could hardly fail to impress the Chindits. It was, then, that on the night of 15 February, Wingate's Special Force troops (the official name of the Long Range Penetration Groups) boarded the Waco gliders in full kit and in high spirits.

There is nothing prosaic about a night takeoff involving gliders; it is dangerous, demanding work that calls for the highest degree of alertness and an extreme level of precision and coordination on the part of the tug crew and the glider pilots. Add a second glider in a double tow behind one transport plane, and the dangers increase exponentially. Visibility is severely limited; none of the gliders had external position lights, so it was difficult at the best of times to see each other. Other factors compounded the difficulty and danger. The towlines must be inspected for any indication of wear or weakness, and they must be connected to the tow plane and each glider correctly, with the left glider on a short line of 350 feet, the right one 75 feet longer, without the lines crossing. This has to be done in darkness, so lights don't affect the night vision of the pilots. Tactile and auditory senses come into play. Did it feel right? Did it sound right? And in the air, the two gliders had to respond differently to the same maneuver. If the tug turned to the left, the glider on the short tow was on the inside of the turn and had to bank sharply; too steep a bank would result in a stall, and the glider had to quickly release and hope for enough altitude to recover. In the same turn, the pilot of the glider on long tow had to precisely gauge the degree of bank to account for the slightly increased arc through which he must fly. For three ugly sisters of the air, all double-tow flights had to become aerial ballets executed with beauty and precision.

For this night exercise at Lalaghat, the tugs would tow two gliders into the air, turn left, then turn left again to bring them all to the downwind leg of the traffic pattern. The glider pilots were to release at 1,000 feet about midway down the field and then set up their landing so that both could touch down on the landing portion of the field, well marked with lights. Wacos had been pulled by small tractors into lines on each side of the takeoff strip, wingtip to wingtip and facing the grass runway. The Chindits stood in small groups, laughing, quietly smoking, teasing each other and the American crews. As each C-47 pulled onto the runway, the empty gliders were pushed into position behind the tug, one from each side of the strip. As the Yanks attached the towlines, the Chindits quickly filed into the Wacos through the cabin door on the right side and took seats on the wooden benches built along each side of the fuselage. A baker's dozen, thirteen heavily armed and equipped troops strapped themselves in and craned to see what was going on in the cockpit and beyond. The tug was a few hundred feet in front, just visible by the bluish glow from the exhaust and, since it was a training exercise only, the red and green lights that marked the left and right wingtips of the tow plane.

They had practiced rapidly boarding and disembarking for days, an officer standing by with a stopwatch timing the ingress and egress of the fully kitted-out troops. Tonight boarding went smoothly; the Chindits quickly and efficiently stepped into the gliders and took their places on the benches. They were in high spirits. This was an adventure.

In the cockpit of one of the gliders that night, Lt. Kenneth Wells and F/O Bishop Parrott made a final check of the spartan cockpit. Trim wheels set to neutral, all flight controls free and clear, with full range of the yoke. Big rudder responding to the pedals. Altimeter set to field elevation. They turned to give a quick look and nod to PFC Robert Kinney, a glider mechanic along for the adventure and the flight pay. Wells and Parrott were on short tow that night, left of the centerline of the tug. Seventy-five feet behind them on the right was another fully loaded Waco piloted by Lt. Donald Seese, with F/O Troy Shaw as copilot.

The light signal was given for the tug to ease forward and take up the slack in the towlines; ground crew, many of them glider pilots as well, checked to see that the lines for both gliders were equally taut. A minute passed, and then the green light to take off was flashed to the tug and the gliders. In another minute, all three were airborne in the night sky above Lalaghat. In unison, they turned left while continuing to climb to one thousand feet. A half mile away, they started to turn again. That's when the rope towing Seese's glider broke; stretched like a rubber band, it shot forward and wrapped itself around the wing of Wells's CG-4A, causing considerable damage and leaving the pilot unable to control his glider.

Wells released, but could not recover. The glider went straight down. Seese was able to put his Waco down safely.

Wells, Parrott, Kinney, and four Chindits were killed instantly, others badly injured. Parrott, a tall, handsome young guy from Nebraska, was a basha mate of Charles Turner.[3]

As awful as the crash was, it seemed incredible that the Air Commandos had been able to go as long as they had without a catastrophe. Night training in the gliders was hazardous in the extreme, and they had been incredibly lucky up until now. Cochran and Alison were upset about the accident and mourned for the lost lives of both Americans and British. They were also worried that the fatal crash would undo all of the trust and camaraderie that had so painstakingly been built up among the Allied troops.

The dead Chindits were all part of Dah Force, under Lt. Col. D. C. "Fish" Herring. (A dah was a machete-style fighting knife used in India.) The next day, Herring sent the American colonels a handwritten note: "Please be assured that we will go with your boys any place, any time, any where." Cochran posted the message on a bulletin board outside of the operations shack at Lalaghat. Concerns about loss of trust vanished, and the note became the motto of the Air Commandos: Any Time, Any Place.[4] Glider pilot Charles Turner related the incident seventy years later. "It was quite a compliment. I still cannot talk about it without getting emotional."[5]

# CHAPTER 25

In the initial planning for the combined operation of American airpower and British ground troops, the Royal Air Force had agreed to provide close air support to Wingate with light bombers, perhaps Beaufighters, that were in theater. But early in 1944, RAF commanders informed the British leader of the Chindits that they did not have enough airplanes to dedicate to his campaign. Cochran and Alison quickly agreed to cover that as well. A cable to Hap Arnold in Washington produced a dozen B-25H Mitchell bombers, similar to those flown by Cole and the other Doolittle Raiders from the USS *Hornet* back in April 1942.

These were decidedly different animals, however. The glass nose of the B-25B in which a bombardier had sat, armed with a .30-caliber machine gun and a toggle switch to release the bombs, had been replaced by a hard nose, slightly shorter because of increased weight. The nose now held eight .50-caliber machine guns, arranged in two vertical rows and hinged to tilt upward for access to the compartment. Additionally, each of the Mitchells carried a 75mm cannon, originally designed as a tank gun, that extended through the nose and far back into the airplane. The shells, each more than two feet long and three inches in diameter, could be loaded singly by a crewman inside; it was fired by a button controlled by the pilot. Aiming was easy; the pilot simply pointed the bomber at the target and pressed the button. The cannon was a phenomenally lethal weapon, with a recoil that stunned flight crews with each round fired. Some swore that the bomber stopped in flight when the 75 was fired, but of course that wasn't true. It just felt like it.[1]

Cole might have been considered an ideal candidate to fly the medium bomber. But he hadn't flown one in combat in a year and a half while

240

becoming a masterful pilot of the C-47. In addition to his hundreds of hours flying the Hump in every conceivable kind of weather, he was one of the Gooney drivers who had practiced for hours towing and snatching gliders—in daylight and at night—and was thus doubly valuable. The plan, when it was launched, was for the thirteen C-47s of the Air Commandos to tow gliders into Burma and to snatch them out again. They would carry the pathfinders, the assault troops of the Chindits, as well as equipment and personnel to build rough airstrips. Additional C-47s from the Troop Carrier Command in the CBI would then be used to carry in thousands of additional Chindits, as well as mules and tons of supplies, but only the Air Commandos would work with the gliders. With his training and experience as a tug pilot, Cole was too valuable to switch flying assignments now.

Cochran and Alison had other ideas regarding the cannon-equipped B-25s. The cockpit crews that brought the Mitchells to Hailakandi were green, never having been in combat, and the Air Commando leaders immediately reassigned them as copilots for the C-47s. No, they reasoned, these bombers would be used far differently than anything for which the young, untested pilots had been trained.

Cochran and Alison tapped Maj. Robert T. "R. T." Smith to be commander of the new bomber section, with Maj. Walter Radovich as his deputy. Their selections were telling: Smith and Radovich were fighter pilots to the core. Smith was already an ace, having flown with the original American Volunteer Group, or Flying Tigers. Both protested vehemently; they were placated when Cochran assured them that they could retain their P-51s and continue to fly fighter missions when not on bombing runs.

The B-25H, with its colossal 75mm cannon, needed to be flown like a fighter by a seasoned fighter pilot, reasoned Cochran. And so they were. On many occasions after the start of the Chindit campaign, they were called in to hit specific targets—"the house with the red roof a hundred yards north of our position"—and did so with devastating accuracy. Smith and Radovich would frequently fly a fighter sweep in the morning against Japanese airfields or positions and then return to the same area in the afternoon flying a B-25.[2]

So Cole stayed in the cockpit of his C-47, content to fly as a transport pilot and let the fighter guys drive the Mitchells. It did not mean he was not constantly in harm's way, however. As the weeks passed and it became obvious that the big assault into Burma was imminent, flying of all kinds increased dramatically. There were more practice tows, both day and night; more practice snatches, including nighttime grabs; flights to a variety of small airfields to procure more needed parts or equipment; occasional hops into Calcutta; and forays into positions in Burma. Always there was the danger of Japanese air attacks, both in Assam and of course anywhere in Burma.

When they were not flying, there was a seemingly endless list of backbreaking jobs that needed to be done. Buildings were constantly being erected, repaired, or expanded; Cole helped install runway lights and erect a control tower when he wasn't flying. Convoys of trucks were driven to the nearby rail station, where equipment, fuel drums, and supplies were unloaded from ancient boxcars and wrestled onto the six-by-sixes. Ordnance was stacked in an area among the trees. The aircraft constantly needed work, with routine twenty-five-, fifty-, and one-hundred-hour inspections requiring hours of labor. The glider section crews were continually fiddling with their aircraft, testing possible new equipment. At one point, Flight Officer Turner and his friend Harry McKaig experimented with mounting flexible .50-caliber machine guns in the noses of their gliders, weapons they could swivel in any direction, knowing that they would be landing in Japanese-held territory and possibly surrounded by enemy troops.[3]

But it wasn't all work, as much of that as there was. While the fighter boys and the L guys, together with the new section of Mitchells, operated out of Hailakandi, Lalaghat was very much the base of the tug crews and glider pilots. Surprisingly, or perhaps not so much, the two groups seldom socialized, preferring birds of their own feather. In particular, those with glider wings felt themselves a group apart. "We were very much a tainted bunch," recalled Turner. "The Gurkhas called us 'neigh punca wallah' or 'No Fan Man,' because we didn't have propellers."[4] Glider men had been trained as infantrymen as well as pilots; part of the original thinking in the glider program was that the pilots would fly troops into combat arenas and then act as groundpounders until they could work their way back from the front lines and be returned to a base to do it all again. The wing badges of glider pilots bore the letter G. To a man, they swore that it stood for "Guts."[5]

Both the transport section and the glider group had its share of characters and even celebrities. The C-47 pilots were glad to welcome John Kelly "Buddy" Lewis, who had been an All-Star third baseman and right fielder for the Washington Senators, and they were always looking for a pickup ball game against all challengers.

Lewis, a tall, lanky, dark-haired man from South Carolina, had been a rookie in 1936; he and Joe DiMaggio had been considered the top freshmen that year. He was selected to the 1938 American League All-Star team and then in 1941 was drafted into the military. Lewis went through aviation cadet training and was sent to fly the Hump. Later, he was invited to join the Air Commandos. The ballplayer was older than most of the fliers; at twenty-seven, he was just eleven months younger than Cole. He was quiet, not given to a lot of high jinks, but he was capable of stepping outside the batter's box on occasion. When he left the States to begin the long haul to India the first time, he had buzzed Griffith Field in Washington while a game was in progress. It was a farewell to his teammates; apparently, no one thought to get his tail number and report him, although most probably knew it was him and didn't mind at all. Buzzing by young military pilots was common and largely accepted during the war. Lewis named his transport "The Old Fox" after Clark Griffith, the owner of the ball club. In India he had flown more than 350 missions over the Hump into China.[6]

There were others, of course. Cole was a bit of a celebrity himself; the Doolittle Raid was still a huge event in the conduct of the war. He rarely talked about it, and then only when pressed and only in short responses to specific questions. Irrepressible, pipe-smoking Bill Cherry was widely known as the pilot who survived twenty-four days on a raft in the South Pacific with Eddie Rickenbacker, the top American ace of World War I and, in 1942, president of Eastern Airlines. Jake Sartz was the guy, everyone knew, who in the early days of the Ferry Command had made numerous flights into "Mitch"—Myitkyina, Burma—to evacuate people from that city as it was about to fall to the Japanese and frequently flew with Robert Scott. For his heroics in the evacuation, Sartz had been awarded the Silver Star. He, like Cole, had also earned a Distinguished Flying Cross and Air Medal clusters for his dozens of hazardous trips over the Hump.

In the glider section, the most recognizable name was John Leslie "Jackie" Coogan, who in the 1920s and 1930s had been the biggest child star in Hollywood, earning several million dollars while starring with such icons as Charlie Chaplin (in *The Kid* and others). As he grew out of his youngster and preadolescent cuteness, Coogan was offered fewer parts; his last movie was with Betty Grable in 1939. He was now twenty-nine, a balding, broad-shouldered cutup who often offended those around him with his bawdy tales of sex with the young starlets who appeared in the movies so avidly watched in the evenings. He seldom let anyone forget that he was married for a time to Miss Grable, the favorite pinup for GIs.[7]

But the glider pilots didn't need to be international stars to display their individuality. They already possessed that quality, in spades. Thanks in part to the casual approach to leadership taken by Cochran and Alison, so long as the job was completed and done well, the Air Commandos were as colorful as any group in the military during the war. The word *uniform*—meaning consistent and unvarying—became an antonym at Lalaghat and Hailakandi. Men wore bits and pieces of a variety of uniform items, including British issue. Headgear in a single group of men might be the shapeless, beaten-down "crusher" cap made available to fliers so that a headset might be worn over it, the fore-and-aft overseas cap, a pith helmet, a ball cap, a mechanics cap with the bill turned up, an Australian-style bush hat, with one side of the brim snapped up. Or, more commonly, no hat at all. Charlie Turner had purchased a classic "Mountie" campaign hat at March Field in Riverside, California, in 1941, while undergoing training. It was obsolete at that time. In India he refashioned the crown and rolled up the sides of the brim to create a cowboy hat. Turner was from Texas, after all.[8]

The climate and conditions in India, and later in Burma, were factors directing the style of dress. As the days heated up, many of the men wore shorts. Glider pilot James "Mickey" Bartlett was photographed wearing baggy shorts, a sleeveless T-shirt, and mosquito boots (soft leather roper-style boots that fliers frequently bought in Natal as souvenirs). He wore a pith helmet with an eagle on the crown and was armed with a .45 pistol and a large knife. Standing with him was Lt. Vincent Rose, deputy commander of the glider section, similarly dressed and armed, but having added a short-sleeved khaki shirt to his ensemble.[9]

Even Cole was not entirely immune from the need to express individuality. Despite being an Army Air Forces captain, he continued to wear his Navy-issue flight jacket, with the mouton fur collar. Otherwise, he usually wore khaki pants and a long-sleeved khaki shirt with the sleeves rolled up above his elbows.

As time drew near for the anticipated invasion of Burma, General Wingate made frequent visits to Lalaghat and Hailakandi, and as was his wont, he began growing a full beard. Many of his men did as well, so it did not take long for some of the Americans to try their hand at facial hair. The lack of hot water and scarcity of razor blades at the forward bases were perhaps a partial justification, together with the hectic schedule of training and constant work. Cochran himself was often careless of personal appearance, dating back to his days in North Africa at the Allies' most forward base. There, he frequently had gone many days without changing out of his grease-stained flight suit, neither shaving nor washing as he flew mission after mission. In India his usual attire was a crusher hat well back on his head, a khaki field jacket, khaki pants rolled up past his ankles, and boots. Alison was equally informal, rarely wearing a hat and virtually living in his paratrooper pants. The beards and long hair affected by some of the Air Commandos would eventually lead to reprimands by brass in the theater and result in one of the strangest memoranda posted by any commander during the war.

Brig. Gen. William Old, commanding the Troop Carrier Command transport aircraft temporarily assigned to Operation Thursday, stayed over at Hailakandi during the invasion segment of the mission. One week into the campaign, he came upon a group of Air Commandos struggling with barrels of fuel; the fuel had proved to be contaminated with bits of rust, and they were straining it through cloth. It was a nasty, messy job; the men were dirty and oil soaked and had gone without shaving or bathing since the start of the operation. Old ripped into a junior officer overseeing the fuel decontamination. The next day, Cochran posted on the board outside operations the following memorandum:

To: All Personnel and Attached Organizations:

Look sports—the beards and attempts at beards are not appreciated by visitors.

Since we can't explain to all strangers that the fuzz is a gag or "something I always wanted to do" affair, we must avoid their reporting that we are unshaven (regulations say you must shave) by appearing like Saturday night in Jersey whenever possible.

Work comes before shaving. You will never be criticized for being unkempt if you are so damn busy you can't take time to doll up. But be clean while you can.

Ain't it awful.

(signed)

P. G. Cochran,

Colonel, Air Corps,

Commanding[10]

Old was not a martinet, usually leading his men from the cockpit of the first plane in any dangerous assignment. Realizing that the men were overworked, a couple of days later he pitched in to help with loading and unloading fuel and was soon as filthy as they were. He apologized to the young officer he had reprimanded earlier.

The entire group was aware that they were somehow "special"; they were getting equipment that was in short supply elsewhere, they had been issued weapons and uniforms that previously had been limited to distinctive units such as the airborne, and they were outside the normal chains of command in the CBI. That this resulted in some hard feelings from other units only added to their sense of privilege. It didn't take long for them to design insignia that would proclaim their elite status. The glider section had patches made up in Calcutta that were among the largest and most recognizable unit badges of the war: a mule's head sprouting wings and clutching a kukri knife in its mouth, superimposed on a large numeral 1 that bears a striking resemblance to the nude torso in profile of a well-developed female. These were sewn to the left front of their leather flight jackets; the back was often decorated with a large leather American flag, and "blood chits," with writing in Chinese and local dialects promising rewards for safe return of the airman, were often sewn inside as pockets. CBI insignia—a shield with red and white vertical stripes topped with a blue field displaying a white star and a white sun—were added to jacket sleeves. Many of the same insignia had been devised and worn by Hump pilots, another group of CBI veterans who were proud of their status. The fighter section of the Air Commandos devised its own unit badge—a flying horse—and many in the transport section wore the question-mark badge they had devised on the flight over.[11] Cole had gone along with his crew and purchased a blue-and-white leather patch, but he never had it sewn onto his jacket.

The colorful nature of the special unit was not lost on the folks back home, who were aware that the comic strip *Terry and the Pirates* was at least loosely based on the Air Commandos and their square-jawed commander. Many of the men in the unit became characters, renamed, in the strip. Cochran, of course, was well known as Flip Corkin, and the Army Air Forces had made good use of the pop-culture fame of one of their own. Advertisements appeared in newspapers around the country before the unit's formation with the headline "Meet: Lieutenant Colonel Philip G. Cochran, United States Army (The Real Flip Corkin)." Johnny Alison was Little John in the strip; R. T. Smith was Big John; Lt. Charles

Russhon was Vanilla Joe. The pilots in the cargo section looked forward to the strip sent to Cole by his mother: "*Thanks a lot for funnies. Just about everyday someone comes in and asks 'Has your mom sent any more Terry and the Pirates?' They sweat 'em out as much as I do.*"[12]

Cochran had gone to Ohio State University with Milton Caniff, the strip's illustrator; after Cochran became a fighter pilot before the war, the two had become friends. Caniff was fascinated by the swagger, the flight clothing, the jargon, and the love lives of the pilots in Cochran's squadron when he was posted around the East Coast and had been permitted to hang around the fliers to nail down the details of their lives and accouterments. As repayment, apparently, he invented Flip Corkin and introduced him to the story line. By the time the Air Commandos arrived in India, the strip was in full swing, with Colonel Corkin rooting out Axis spies, F/O Terry Lee rescuing young and beautiful damsels, and Japanese pilots taking a beating from General Chennault's 14th Air Force. By May the strip would approximate the events coming up in Burma, delayed only by a couple of months, and federal agents would pay a call on Caniff. Where was he getting his information? Everything in the strip had already been in the news, he informed them.[13]

Despite the varsity-team atmosphere engendered by the leather jackets and gaudy insignia, men at both camps understood what they were there to do. *Terry and the Pirates* was high adventure, and the good guys always won, but it was sheer fiction. Cole and his flying buddies enjoyed the comic strip, but understood all too well the dangers they faced in real life. Without knowing the exact date of the invasion—a decision to be made by the commander of the joint Third Tactical Air Force, Jack Baldwin—the Air Commandos knew it would be soon. The weather was good, their training had them at peak readiness, and time was passing that they could never get back. Monsoon winds would bring a deluge beginning in April or May, so there was little time in which to conduct the actual mission. On 27 February, Cole wrote his parents a letter in which he apologized for not writing sooner—"*We've been pretty busy*"— and hinted of things to come: "*Things are still pretty much the same. Have lots of work coming up soon, will be very interesting.*"[14]

Combat missions had begun as early as 3 February, when Cochran led a sweep of P-51s over Japanese-controlled Burma. This was eleven days before the disastrous Valentine's Day mission to Mandalay. A technique for ripping out telegraph and telephone lines had been envisioned—some said by Cochran himself—that called for a large weight to be attached to a metal cable. The cable and weight were coiled around hardpoints on the underside of the fighter and could be released from the cockpit to hang three hundred feet below the Mustang. Roaring along at high speeds (the Mustang was capable of more than 400 mph), the weighted cabled could easily rip out lines and on one mission across Burma did just that.[15]

The tows and gliders were also busy before the invasion was scheduled. One part of the overall plan to harass the Japanese called for a column of Chindits under Brig. Bernard Fergusson to enter Burma by foot, in coordination with Gen. Joe Stilwell's troops in the North. Fergusson left Ledo on 1 February but by the end of the month was on the west bank of the Chindwin, unable to cross the wide and swift-flowing river with his heavily burdened troops and mules. He called for assistance, and two Wacos, flown by James S. "Mickey" Bartlett and Vernon "Needle-nose" Noland, landed on a large sandy bank near Fergusson's encamped column. They delivered six folding boats with outboard motors, along with poles, paddles, and gasoline. The troops were able to cross without incident. The next day, 29 February, a C-47 flown by Capt. Edwin J. Coe and 1st Lt. William W. Johnson flew over and snatched Bartlett's glider into the air. It was the first time a glider had been snatched from behind enemy lines.[16]

Noland's glider had been damaged in landing but was quickly repaired. Cole and his crew flew to the Upper Chindwin and successfully snatched it out as well, leaving Lalaghat at 8:10 and returning with the glider at 12:30.[17] It seemed little different from the many snatches they had practiced since Goldsboro.

# CHAPTER 26

The balloon went up on 5 March 1944: the aerial invasion of Burma would begin that night. Air Marshal Sir John Baldwin of the RAF that morning sent word: "Weather suitable. Carry out Operation Thursday." The men and equipment were ready, and a three-quarter moon would provide plenty of light. It must be done soon, before the monsoon rains ended any possibility of ground operations. The weeks of preparation and training, of hard work and heartache, would come down to this: The C-47s of the Air Commandos would each tow two gliders over the eight-thousand-foot Chin Hills and into Burma, releasing them 150 miles behind Japanese lines, where they would land in two clearings in the jungle. There, British assault troops would secure the area, American engineers would quickly construct rough airstrips, and thousands of Chindits would be flown in by transports of the Troop Carrier Command over the next several nights.[1]

All day that Sunday, Troop Carrier Command C-47s under Brig. Gen. William "Don" Old had been flying the British forces into Lalaghat from their training base at Gwalior, and the former tea plantation was fairly bursting at the seams with airplanes, troops, gliders, and brass—American and British—who had come down for the big show. It would be a most extraordinary endeavor; nothing quite like it had ever been done before in the history of war. Soldiers of a confederation of Allied countries were going to invade another country entirely by air.

It would be dangerous in the extreme, of course. No invasion is free from the probability of casualties. But the hazard gauge had ticked up many notches with the addition of the cargo gliders. Adding still more to the lethal index was the cloak of night, which would make landing in jungle clearings far more problematic, while simultaneously adding a degree of cover for the invaders.

The first takeoff was set for 1700, 5:00 p.m. Bill Cherry would pull the first gliders, flown by Bill Taylor and Neal Blush; Jake Sartz would tow the second pair, with Alison flying one of the gliders himself and Donald Seese, who had survived the horrific accident three weeks earlier, in the other; the third Gooney off would be Cole's. His two gliders would carry Lt. Col. Arvid Olson, who would be in command at one of the jungle clearings, and Maj. Richard Boebel, the unit intelligence officer.

Two hours before first launch, the pilots—tug and glider alike—were summoned to a briefing by Colonel Cochran. Mission briefings for wartime pilots were ritualistic and informational. Expected weather en route, possible enemy resistance, headings and altitudes to fly, engine start times, green-flare (launch) times, emergency procedures, sequence of takeoffs, radio call signs, frequencies—all were covered by the briefing officers. Pilots, jocular and teasing until the briefing started, sobered immediately, some writing down details on the backs of their hands. The briefing this day was little changed from those given on countless bases across the globe, with a couple of important differences. This one was conducted outside, the pilots gathered casually around, some kneeling, others standing, a few sitting on the ground. And the map was pure CBI: unable to procure detailed, large-scale maps of the landing area, Cochran and Alison had drawn the location on a bedsheet, painting in details such as the surrounding terrain and jungle, as well as the elevations and known obstacles. The sheet was hung from a rough wooden frame, visible to all the gathered pilots.

Two clearings in the jungle, code-named Broadway and Piccadilly, for two main thoroughfares in New York and London, were displayed on the map, along with their coordinates. Half of the pilots were going to Broadway, the rest to Piccadilly. They were both deep inside Burma, far behind Japanese lines. Cole and his copilot, Bordley, along with the other pilots looked at the shapes of each, shown in light brown amid the green of the surrounding jungle. Cole squinted his eyes, trying to imagine how Broadway would look at night. It resembled nothing so much as a blob of chocolate icing on a chocolate cake.

Cochran was pure Flip Corkin for most of the briefing—breezy, informal, knowledgeable. Tugs would circle to climb over Lalaghat, flying out at eight thousand feet until they cleared the Chin Hills; return altitude was nine thousand. Cochran went over the procedures for inadvertent or early release of the gliders, as well as the need to observe radio silence unless an emergency arose. A sure identifier for locating the clearings was a bend in the Irrawaddy River. Broadway was north of the bend and Piccadilly north of there. He used a pointer, touching various places on the makeshift map. It was cool in the shade of a line of trees on the side of the flying field, and many of the pilots slipped on their jackets. Cole looked around at the pilots gathered for the briefing—most wearing their preferred headgear, strung with a variety of weapons. He glanced at Bill Cherry, who was wearing a .38 revolver in a shoulder holster and a .45 on a web belt and, he knew, had a small pistol in a pocket of his flight suit. Cherry made no secret of his arsenal: he had been caught unprepared once, he said. Never again. Most of the fliers had large jungle knives on their belts; a few had the curved, wicked-looking kukris so favored by the Gurkhas. Survival gear was evident in their pockets—rations, compasses, silk walkout maps. Just as important were the blood chits—Cole's was folded in his pocket—and the small stash of opium that would serve as cash in areas of Burma.[2]

"Now, is there anything anybody doesn't understand?" Cochran looked around at the gathering of pilots. No one spoke up. "If there is, let's get it straight now." Still no questions or comments from the pilots. They looked confident and ready. This was the payoff for the weeks of training and work, the sleepless nights, the poor food, the miserable climate. No, they had no questions. Let's go! was the attitude of the fliers.

Cochran suddenly dropped his cocky fighter-pilot mien. He looked serious, and for many of those grouped around him the sight was a first. "Okay, now just before I came over here, I had a final meeting with the British ground troops that you're going to take in there tonight. And I talked to the guy that's got the red flare that you know is going to be shot off if there's too much interference with the first few gliders that land. He tells me that flare's in an awful deep pocket, and it's going to take an awful lot of finding to get at it." Cochran paused, looking at the faces of the men before him. "So, if those guys have that kind of heart, and they got that kind of guts, it's up to us to get them in there so they can do their job, and get them in right."

Cochran was not given to locker-room pep talks, and this was a team that rarely needed one. But he sensed that the moment called for something to mark the occasion. After a pause, he continued. "Now tonight, your whole reason for being, your whole existence, is going to be jammed up into a couple of minutes, and it's just going to balance it there and it's going to take your character to bring it through. Now nothing you've ever done before in your life means a thing. Tonight you are going to find out you've got a soul." He paused for the briefest of seconds, perhaps slightly embarrassed by his words. "Good luck."[3]

With that, the fliers slowly dispersed, heading back to the flight line in small groups. Some were silent, a few nervously making jokes, the majority making small talk of the garden variety.

Cole and Bordley returned to "Hairless Joe," where Ecklar, Roberts, and Alexander were checking the equipment, items that had been looked over, inspected, and tested at least a dozen times in the past six hours. The two pilots stepped into the cabin through the broad double-wide cargo door and walked uphill to the cockpit. There, they did exactly the same thing as the rest of the crew, running through the checklist again, already knowing that each item had been checked and rechecked. Each then silently went through their personal equipment checklist: for Cole, it was a .45, a large Ka-Bar knife, two compasses, rations, a small fishing kit, a picture of Mart. Behind him, against the cockpit bulkhead, rested his .30-caliber carbine.[4] Cole checked his watch. A half hour to engine start.

A P-51 landed amid the swirl of activity on the grass field; a few minutes later, an L-1 touched down and rolled to a stop. Neither was cause for any comment. But in less than twenty minutes, someone yelled up to the cockpit that all pilots were to report to the briefing area immediately. Cole and Bordley looked at each other and shrugged and then rose from their seats, stepped through the door into the cabin, and made their way downhill to the door.

Back at the briefing area, Colonel Cochran stood on the hood of a jeep that was parked there. He was back in character, breezy and confident. "Say, Fellers, we've got a better place to go." Again, the crude bedsheet map of Broadway was displayed. This time, all the tugs would go to Broadway; Piccadilly was out for now. A new list of tugs and gliders was passed around; Cole and Bordley were still number three in the queue. Their task was unchanged, but others had to do some quick mental gymnastics to divert their focus from Piccadilly to Broadway. Among the glider pilots, there was a bit of a stir. Some of them, including Alison, had been bound for Piccadilly. In fact, Alison was to lead the gliders into that clearing and assume command of the operation there on the ground. Unwilling to be left behind, he bumped another pilot and took over one of the gliders towed by the second tug to leave. He would be second in command under Arvid Olson.

The reason for the sudden change in the battle plan was not given to the assembled pilots, but it had been riding in each of the two planes that had landed amid the bedlam on the Lalaghat grass field. The photo officer, Charles Russhon, had pestered Cochran early that morning for a recon flight over the fields, as part of the historical record of the unit. Overflights of the various target clearings had been expressly forbidden by Wingate, who did not want to alert the Japanese to their locations by aerial activity. Russhon's request made sense to the pilot in Cochran; Wingate, a ground officer, could not appreciate to the same degree the need for up-to-date recce photos. Thinking that Wingate would never learn of the secret flights, Cochran agreed that R. T. Smith, with Russhon aboard a B-25, could make a single pass over the various clearings designated for glider assaults. That afternoon at Hailakandi, as the photographer developed his film and printed large-format photos, Russhon gasped in disbelief as he stared at the field code-named Piccadilly. Strewn across the clearing were hundreds of logs, laid out in neat rows. Each of the logs—he guessed they were teak—was large enough to wreck a glider. In mass, they would destroy the entire fleet of Wacos scheduled to land there.

Russhon could not use the radio to call Cochran for fear the transmission would be intercepted. As he was dashing around looking for a jeep to drive the twelve miles to Lalaghat, over miserable roads, a P-51 landed. The pilot was lost; he was looking for Lalaghat. Russhon pressed the photos on the bewildered pilot, gave him a compass course to Lalaghat, and told him he must get the pictures to Colonel Cochran immediately. The fighter left, and as Russhon once more prepared to drive to the other field, an L-1 landed. Russhon gave that pilot no opportunity to refuse: Take me to Lalaghat, now!

Upon arrival, the excited photo officer rushed up to Cochran and Alison. He was convinced that the Japanese had discovered the operation and blocked the field at Piccadilly to force all the gliders into Broadway, where they would be waiting. The gliders, big and slow, would be easy targets even at night. Operation Thursday was going to be a bloodbath.[5]

"Who did this? Who flew over the landing area when I gave orders not to do so?" Wingate was furious, his deep-set dark eyes flashing as he stared at Cochran. The British general had a reputation for berating anyone and everyone when things went badly in his well-laid plans. Cochran was prepared. "I sent the plane over. I just had a hunch." Wingate's face softened. Hunches he understood. He'd had a career largely built on such metaphysical signals.

Cochran, Alison, Wingate, and several of his staff stood now, looking over the photographs brought by Russhon. Wingate stood with his hand on his hip, stroking his beard, looking down at the earth. The situation was clear: Piccadilly was out as a landing site, whether by happenstance or by carefully laid design. The question was whether Japanese forces had somehow winded the operation and were even now waiting to annihilate the assault force. No one spoke. The senior officers deferred to Wingate, upon whose head would hang glory or ignominy.

Cochran and Alison, who seemed to have the ability to communicate without words, almost like twins, had already reached their conclusion. Wingate finally looked up and asked Cochran: "Phil, what do you think?"

"Sir, I think we should proceed into Broadway."

"Right." So despite the loss of Piccadilly and the unknown that awaited them at Broadway, Operation Thursday was again given the green light.[6]

Back in the cockpit of "Hairless Joe," Cole and Bordley settled back into their seats and strapped themselves in. There was no conversation about the change of plans, no speculation about the need for a second briefing. They had a job to do, and some things simply didn't matter. They watched as the first C-47 was given the green light; there would be no radio communication for this mission. Slowly, Cherry's Gooney began rolling; to Cole and Bordley, it seemed much too slow. The two gliders, following the tug like two ducklings after their mother, inched ahead reluctantly. That something was wrong was apparent, but the cause was not. They watched as the nose of each glider seemed to dig into the grass and dirt of the field, and a crowd of men ran to hold down the tail, holding on as long as they could until the gradually increasing speed of the three aircraft left them behind. Even in the semidarkness, they could see the trio finally leave the earth at almost the same time. Normally, the gliders would have been airborne long before the lumbering transport.

Cole and Bordley didn't have time to consider what they had just seen. They began the long process of starting their own engines, carefully monitoring the oil pressure of each Pratt & Whitney after the banging and clouds of blue smoke had settled into a steady thrumming. Cole looked out through the windscreen and saw Jake Sartz pull his tug onto the grass strip, while the ground crew quickly linked two more gliders to the hook behind the tail wheel. The bizarre slow-motion dance was repeated, with the front skids of both gliders again plowing furrows in the grass. Once more, men ran to hold down the tail—the empennage—of each glider, and Sartz, after a long takeoff roll, slowly climbed into the night sky over Assam.

It was their turn. Cole gunned the left engine and applied a slight pressure to the right brake, swinging "Hairless Joe" precisely to align with the runway. Minutes passed, during which the towrope was attached, and they eased forward to take up the slack. They watched as Sartz and his two charges slowly disappeared in the dimming sky. Cole thought he could just make out a trio of tiny specks as the tug and gliders turned left. At last, the green light, and he slowly advanced both throttles. He understood why the two previous takeoffs had seemed like movies in slow motion; they were barely inching down the runway. He sensed, without seeing it happen, that once more the ground crew were running with the gliders, holding down their tail sections to prevent them from furrowing the field. The runway at Lalaghat was sixty-five hundred feet, far more than they had ever needed, but tonight he was glad they had it, for it seemed likely they would use it all.

Finally, reluctantly it seemed to Cole, "Hairless Joe" struggled into the sky, and they began laboring to climb to five hundred feet before making their first left turn, the start of a series of climbing turns designed to get them to four thousand feet over Lalaghat before turning east. They would need eight thousand feet to clear the Chin Hills; after that, it would be a long, slow descent toward Broadway, 168 miles distant inside Burma.[7]

Unspoken between glider pilots and the tug fliers was the understanding that whatever they found upon reaching Broadway, it would be a one-way trip for the gliders. The tugs simply didn't have enough fuel to tow them back. Cole wondered what was going through the minds of the men in the cockpits of the silent birds behind him.

"Hairless Joe" was working hard; it felt like they were pulling a pair of elephants. The oil temperature had climbed slightly, and Ecklar reported that they were using a lot of fuel. Cole could see the ominous tops of the Chin Hills now; they had finally reached eight thousand feet and would clear them. The rest of the ride would be a cakewalk, a long descent with the engines throttled back and the gliders riding easy behind them.

Cole reduced power after clearing the Chin Hills and settled into the leather seat. He checked the flight instruments, which were giving off a soft glow, comforting in the darkness. The transport was laboring less now, but still they could feel it jerk as the gliders crept forward on their towlines and the glider pilots maneuvered to take up the resulting slack. Never before had they had this kind of trouble hauling gliders, even on double tow. Cole suspected that the Wacos were loaded far more heavily than they had ever been during training flights.

Later investigation would prove him correct. In many cases, the CG-4As had been overloaded by more than two thousand pounds each, as the Chindits lugged more gear and ammunition and equipment aboard, each secretly fearful that they would not be resupplied as promised.

They crossed the Chindwin, far below them now. They droned on, still feeling the jerks and jolts of the gliders moving forward and falling back. Then, fifteen minutes east of the Chindwin, "Hairless Joe" stopped wallowing; the tug flew normally instead of like a team of draft horses pulling a sledge through mud. It could mean only one thing.[8]

Cole and Bordley looked at each other. "Oh, crap!" escaped them in unison, and they each looked out their side windows to catch a glimpse of the gliders, now descending into the darkness below. The towlines had broken. They would not be going into Broadway. Two seconds later, Roberts confirmed what they already knew. Stationed in the blister with a flashlight that had red and green lenses, the young assistant flight engineer had watched in horror as both gliders suddenly fell behind and began their long descent.[9]

"Don't touch that T-handle," Cole told Bordley. "We don't need any more trouble." In the event of an emergency, each C-47 equipped as a glider towplane had a handle mounted on the bulkhead behind the co-pilot; pulling it would release the towline. It was a last resort in the face of imminent disaster; the line, stretched to its limit, could shoot back into the glider causing serious damage or rendering it uncontrollable. It was what happened when the glider with Chindits aboard had crashed during a night training flight three weeks earlier.

Cole surmised that the line had broken under the severe stress of jerking and jinking the overloaded gliders. In that event, some of the line would still be attached to the hook on the tug. He didn't want anyone theorizing that Bordley had pulled the emergency release handle.

He turned "Hairless Joe" around and climbed to nine thousand feet and instructed Bordley to break radio silence to report they had lost their gliders. They returned to Lalaghat.

Cole's Wacos were not the only gliders lost that night. In all, seventeen had gone down somewhere in the darkness. Eight landed either in Assam or just inside Burma. However, three landed, with the most incredibly bad luck, almost on top of Japanese army headquarters. As it turned out, the crews and Chindit passengers of both gliders on Cole's first tow into Burma made it back safely after several weeks of avoiding Japanese patrols, crossing rivers, and hacking their way through thick jungle.[10]

When faced with the increasing loss of gliders, Cochran ordered all double tows suspended. When Cole returned to Lalaghat, a quick look at the stretched, frayed, and broken length of towrope with its metal eyehook still affixed to the hook of "Hairless Joe" told a story of stress clearly linked to the weight of the Wacos. Shortly after landing, Cole's tug was back in position on the field, and at 1:15 in the morning of 6 March, they departed once more for Broadway, towing a single glider.[11]

Unknown to everyone else, on the ground at Broadway things were going very badly. One of the gliders that broke from Cole's C-47 had carried Arvid Olson, designated as the ground commander for the air unit there. In his absence, Johnny Alison had assumed command. The glider with Olson had also contained the RAF radios that were to be the communications link with Cochran at Lalaghat. A second backup set was damaged in the heavy landing of Alison's glider, so they had no radio communication.

Japanese forces had not been waiting in ambush at the clearing, but something just as deadly had been. From the air, the clearing had looked smooth and free from obstacles, a perfect site for a night landing by heavy cargo gliders. But what the photos and aerial observations had not disclosed was that high, dense buffalo grass concealed logs, tree stumps, deep ruts, and water holes, invisible to overflights during the day and impossible to discern at night. It was a glider trap, not as obvious as Piccadilly but every bit as lethal.

Taylor's glider followed by that flown by Neal Blush were the first Wacos to touch down in the moonlight. Both wrecked. Alison, third to land, somehow managed to slide through the maze of obstacles unscathed. But succeeding gliders were smashing into logs and stumps, coming to a standstill in the middle of the designated landing area, where they were struck by incoming gliders. With no radio, Alison couldn't call them off, and a flare gun to fire a warning red signal couldn't be located in the jumble of equipment thrown about in the cabin. Glider after glider soared over the one-hundred-foot trees at the approach end of the clearing, silently bringing in more Chindits, only to crash horribly into the growing tangle of broken Wacos strewn over the field. Men rushed to each glider to help extricate the dying and badly wounded, who groaned or screamed in agony as they were moved. A sibilant rush of air indicated the approach of another glider, but in the darkness it was impossible to tell where it would touch down, so they crouched and waited for the sound of splintering wood to indicate a new crash location. The gliders were approaching at much higher speeds than normal because of the increased weight, and that extra speed was contributing to the severity of the crashes.

The invasion was turning into a disaster. Of thirty-seven gliders to eventually land at Broadway, thirty-four were smashed beyond repair. Far worse were the deaths of twenty-four men, including four Air Commandos. The dead included the American aviation engineer who was to oversee the construction of a rough strip for C-47s to follow on subsequent nights. They were to ferry in the majority of the Chindit troops and their equipment, including mules. Additionally, one of the gliders that had been carrying a small grader had come in too high and too fast, crashing into the jungle. Search parties had not been able to locate the wreckage in the dark.[12]

At last, Alison's men were able to repair the backup radio, and he sent a cryptic message to Cochran. Before the operation began, two code words had been assigned. If all was well, "Pork sausage" would be sent by radio; if there was fierce Japanese opposition at the clearing or some other catastrophe, "Soya link" was the code word. Soya link was the ersatz sausage despised by Tommies.

At 2:00 a.m. on 6 March, Alison sent his first message from Broadway. "Soya link" was broadcast three times before the radio died again.

Back at Lalaghat, Cochran was devastated, believing his friend Alison and the rest of the Commandos and Chindits had flown into a trap and were in the fight of their lives. Heartsick, he sent the word out to all the transports in the air, now towing single gliders, to return to Lalaghat and not release their gliders into Broadway.[13]

Cole and "Hairless Joe" were twenty minutes from Broadway when the radio crackled. The words were fuzzy with static, but the meaning was crystal clear: something was very wrong at the jungle clearing. Cole looked at Bordley and began a long, shallow bank while climbing to nine thousand feet, the assigned return altitude. They would return to Lalaghat once more, this time with their glider still in tow. That was possible only because they now were pulling just one.

# CHAPTER 27

The next morning, Alison, Taylor, and "Mad Mike" Calvert, the British brigadier who was to lead the Chindit assault force and then the assembling column out of Broadway, looked upon a scene of utter destruction. Smashed gliders were heaped one upon another. Most had had their landing gear ripped off in the deep ruts that scored the entire clearing, so the heavy Waco cargo haulers could not be pushed out of the way. Wounded men were being tended by the medical unit, led by Capt. Donald Tulloch, who had acted as Alison's copilot on the flight in. The dead were laid out by the edge of the jungle, covered by ponchos. It was a desperate and discouraging sight.

Then the sound of a diesel engine, chuffing through a cleared path in the jungle, arrested their attention. Lt. Robert Brackett was driving the small grader that had been carried in the glider that had soared overhead to crash somewhere in the jungle during the night. To accommodate large items such as jeeps or howitzers or small bulldozers, the front including the entire cockpit of the Wacos was hinged to tilt upward, opening the cabin to its full height and width. On this night, the glider pilot, Gene Kelly, had rigged a line from the dozer to the release handle for the cockpit. When the glider struck trees in the jungle, ripping off both wings, it had shot forward like a missile but was stopped quickly by the thick undergrowth. The dozer launched forward, the rope tripped the release handle, and the entire cockpit had flipped up while the heavy grading machine shot out like a cannonball, coming to rest on its side. The nose of the glider slammed back down, the two pilots largely unhurt save for a broken thumb of the copilot.

Brackett was second in command of the contingent of 900th Airborne Engineers flown into Broadway. On the death of Lt. Patrick Casey in the smashups at the clearing, he assumed command.

Alison, wearing his paratrooper pants and a camouflage-pattern sweater, approached him as Brackett drove up on the dozer. He swept an arm around the scene of destruction.

"Think you can build an airstrip here?"

The young lieutenant looked mournfully at the unpromising site. Yes, he told Alison. It could be done. Alison, looking hopeful at last, asked how long it would take.

The lieutenant assessed the scene and answered after a long pause. "Would this afternoon be soon enough?"

Alison wanted to hug him.[1]

That night the first C-47 landed by moonlight on the rough strip fashioned by the intrepid Brackett and the surviving Chindits and Air Commandos, who had worked like draft horses, pulling behind them logs to smooth the surface. Brig. Gen. William "Don" Old, commander of the Troop Carrier Command, flew the first one in, carrying additional Chindit troops. The most severely injured troops were loaded aboard, and Old departed quickly. Throughout the night, transports formed a steady river of aerial supply, often landing just seconds apart, unloading troops and supplies, loading on any wounded, and departing in a matter of minutes. Cole and his crew loaded "Hairless Joe" with Chindits and left Lalaghat at 1815 (6:15 p.m.). They landed at Broadway at 2005 (8:05 p.m.), leaving in just thirty minutes and returning to Lalaghat at 2240. It was a flight they repeated many times over the next week.[2]

On the night of 8 March, Cole and "Hairless Joe" towed a glider into another jungle clearing, this one code-named Chowringhee, named for a major street in Calcutta. The plan for the insertion of Chindits into Burma had always called for using multiple jungle airstrips, and no time was wasted after the initial success at Broadway, despite the loss of so many gliders and the deaths of twenty-four men.[3]

"Hairless Joe" left Lalaghat at 2035, or 8:35 p.m., part of a stream of a dozen transports towing single gliders. Pilot of the first assault glider was F/O Jackie Coogan. Despite his antics and a penchant for irritating his fellow pilots (he never remembered to repay his numerous debts), he was acknowledged as a "good stick" and fearless. As they approached the clearing, Coogan inexplicably released early. He was able to recover and landed safely.

F/O Charles Turner was second into the clearing. His Waco carried one of the machine guns poking through the windscreen that he and fellow pilot Harry McKaig had installed in their gliders. Although no Japanese opposition had appeared at Broadway, there was no guarantee that they would not be waiting at Chowringhee. As it turned out, the machine gun went unfired.

As Turner's glider touched down in the moonlight, he quickly raised his feet and placed them firmly on the instrument panel ("There was no protection in front, and none of us wanted to lose our legs if we hit something") and pushed forward on the control yoke to force the nose skid into the dirt and stop the glider. They came to a rest, and the silence was pervasive; all was still; there was no noise at all after the whistling wind and the thumping of the doped fabric that always created a symphony of flight in a cargo glider.

He looked at his copilot, a young Gurkha lance corporal who seemed to be carved of stone, staring straight ahead. Turner, still not certain they would not be fired on by waiting Japanese, shouted in his best Hindu, "Jilte Jow!"—Get out quickly! The lance corporal took him at his word, breaking out the side window and diving through. Staring back into the cabin, Turner watched in disbelief as the dozen Gurkha troops there suddenly pulled out their kukri knives and slashed through the sides of the Waco, ignoring completely the door in the fuselage.[4]

Despite the lack of Japanese resistance, there still were casualties. One of the gliders, flown by 1st Lt. Robert Dowe and carrying the all-important small bulldozer, sailed overhead, clearly visible to Turner and the others looking up into the starry night. It struck the tops of the one-hundred-foot trees at the end of the clearing and nosed straight down into the jungle. All aboard were killed, and the bulldozer destroyed. Once again, the engineers aboard several of the gliders were without the means to construct a landing strip for the C-47s that were to follow. When Alison heard the news, he dispatched a glider carrying the bulldozer from Broadway, while Cochran set about trying to obtain another one in India.

On 9 March, Cole and his crew carried troops into Broadway, landing on the improvised strip at 8:05 p.m. and leaving in just thirty minutes. The next night, they flew more troops and mules into Chowringhee, where the strip had been completed and was now available for transport landings. They touched down at 11:25 p.m. and departed at midnight, another quick, no-nonsense arrival and departure. Exhausted, the crew landed back at Lalaghat at 1:45 in the morning, where they were greeted with word that they must fly another round-trip to Broadway with additional Chindits. So "Hairless Joe" was refueled, the oil checked, and another load of British troops loaded aboard. They lifted off from Lalaghat at 2:30 a.m. and arrived at Broadway exactly two hours later. The soldiers quickly exited, and Cole left fifteen minutes after touching down.[5]

The sun was just peeking over the hills of northern Burma, and Cole was still climbing to get above the Chin Hills. It was 5:30 in the morning, and everyone aboard "Hairless Joe" was bushed. Cole's eyes burned, and he could feel the strain of so much flying in his shoulders. It would be good to get back to Lalaghat; there would be no more flying today until the light began to fade again in the evening. Years later, Cole did not recall the mission, but Roberts recorded in his diary a situation that must have frightened the young assistant engineer. For Cole, apparently, it was just another flight.

"Zeros, Captain!"

The voice of Roberts over the intercom jerked everyone into wide-eyed and instant alert. Cole remained calm, although his heart must have been racing. None of the transports was armed; they would be easy pickings for Japanese fighter pilots.

"How many, and where?" Cole's voice betrayed no emotion.

"Two, above and behind us."

"Thanks. Everyone hang on."

"Hairless Joe" was painted a dark olive green on the upper surfaces and top half of the fuselage and a light gray-blue on the under surfaces. The men in Washington said it would be difficult to see against the dark green of the jungle below; the crew of "Hairless Joe" hoped they were right. Cole pushed forward on the yoke, keeping the throttles open, and the transport quickly gained airspeed as it raced toward the earth. The terrain was hilly now, and Cole headed for a canyon, one of many that had been carved out of the mountains by the seasonal torrents of rain. He wanted to be low enough that the fighters—probably Oscars, and not Zeros—could not get beneath him. The narrow walls of the canyon would prevent their maneuvering, and he hoped the olive-drab camouflage would make them less visible to the enemy pilots.

For several minutes, they flew up the canyon, now more of a valley, and Cole continued to stay close to the deck.

"Do we still have company?"

"No, Captain, I think you lost 'em. Don't see them anywhere."[6]

For the next half hour, Cole flew low, just in case. By 6:30 they were back at Lalaghat, where the crew fell into a much-needed sleep for several hours.

The invasion continued unabated, with Wingate's Chindits pouring into Broadway and Chowringhee at the rate of hundreds each hour under the cloak of darkness. The 1st Air Commando Group, with additional transports and flight crews from Troop Carrier Command and four RAF squadrons, flew 579 sorties into the two rough airfields, delivering more than nine thousand troops, more than fourteen hundred mules and horses, and in excess of a half-million pounds of equipment and stores. For more than a week, they ferried Wingate's command into Burma, far behind Japanese lines, and were not detected. That wouldn't last forever, they knew, but for that week they enjoyed the relatively safe routine of landing cargo planes in jungle clearings by moonlight.[7]

The Japanese suspected something was up, and they were patrolling by air to sniff out the uptick in radio chatter and reports of aircraft. However, they didn't have airborne radar in their fighters, so nighttime interceptions were virtually nonexistent. Early-morning patrols scoured the area constantly, seeking Allied aircraft.

Wingate decided to shut down the operation at Chowringhee three days after it started, suspecting that it had been discovered. On the evening of the same day he evaded the Japanese fighters, Cole flew into Chowringhee and hauled out equipment that would not be used by the Chindits, who had already slipped away into the jungle to harass the Japanese. While Broadway was being built up as a stronghold, complete with a radar unit and antiaircraft guns, Chowringhee would serve only briefly. All that was left was a wrecked RAF C-47, several gliders that were heavily damaged on landing, and the runway lights.

That day the Japanese bombed and strafed the clearing. But there was no one home.

## CHAPTER 28

For the next two weeks, Dick Cole and his crew flew "Hairless Joe" across eastern India and deep into northern Burma, on some days keeping a grueling flying schedule that left them little time to rest but that ensured the success of the Air Commando and Chindit operation code-named Thursday.

On 11 March, they hauled barrels of fuel for the P-51s that were going to be stationed at Broadway to protect the incoming transports as well as provide a measure of insurance should the field itself be attacked. The next day, they carried another load of aviation fuel after unwanted excitement at Lalaghat. At midmorning loudspeakers on the field announced an alert: Japanese aircraft had been spotted, perhaps heading for the American forward base. Transports were ordered to take off from the field and fly west until it was safe to return; the C-47s would have been prime and easy targets sitting in the open. Ray Roberts, apparently not aboard "Hairless Joe," recorded in his diary that Japanese fighters showed up and were immediately hit by 51s; he watched as one of the enemy fighters was shot down and the others driven off. That night Cole and crew delivered more fuel to Broadway for the fighter section.[1]

The clearing in the Burmese jungle couldn't go undetected forever, and on 13 March the luck of the Air Commandos ran out. A formation of Japanese fighter-bombers showed up out of the East, coming in very low so they were not detected by the small radar set. Strafing and bombing, they destroyed three of the L-5s that were more or less permanently stationed there, killing one pilot who had been taxiing his plane and wounding another.[2] Several of the Japanese planes were claimed shot down. That evening Cole and his men delivered more drums of aviation fuel to the isolated field. Roberts recorded that they departed Broadway at 2250 (10:50 p.m.) and arrived at Lalaghat just before 1 a.m. on the fourteenth. "Very poor visibility, cloudy, but pretty nice moon," he noted in his diary.[3]

The next day, "Hairless Joe" made a quick hop to Hailakandi to load up with five-hundred-pound bombs, to be ferried to Broadway for the P-51s. But even in combat, aircraft had to be serviced regularly, and upon returning to Lalaghat Cole's transport was due for a fifty-hour inspection. The bombs were loaded on another C-47 for delivery to Broadway, and the next day Cole and the crew flew to Barrackpore, near Calcutta, to pick up another glider. Evidently, it wasn't ready, because for the next three days they sat there. There was opportunity to go into Calcutta and to catch a couple of movies—*Heaven Can Wait* and *Texas to Tokio* were showing—and on Sunday, 19 March, they heard on the radio that the 1st Air Commandos were in action. Shopping around for a newspaper, Roberts was able to find one that also included news of the unit. It had been two weeks since the launch of Operation Thursday, and news of the invasion had been largely kept out of the papers while it was ongoing.[4]

They left that afternoon for Lalaghat, towing a glider, and the next day made a series of short hops to pick up men and supplies—Lalaghat to Agartala, to Silchar, to Dohazari, to Jumchari, to Silchar, to Lalaghat. On Tuesday, 21 March, they learned that an Air Commando UC-64 had crashed in the mountains, killing 1st Lt. Frank Borowski and Sgt. Joseph "Tex" Kaplan.[5]

On the twenty-second, "Hairless Joe" was in the air continuously. They towed a glider with engineers to a new field northwest of Indaw, code-named Aberdeen, leaving Lalaghat at 3:00 a.m. The Japanese had not been idle while the British and Americans invaded Burma. Since the start of the war, India had been seen as the jewel in the crown of British colonialism. Taking India would not only knock China out of the war by closing down the Hump airlift, which was still going on, but also strike a very real blow to the heart of the global British Empire. While total conquest of India was no longer a realistic goal by 1944, certainly closing off the supply routes to Chabua and the other bases that marked the western terminus of the Hump supply route was feasible; additionally, this would provide a defensive line for the Japanese that was more viable. Thus, on 8 March, three days after Operation Thursday began the invasion of Burma, the Japanese launched their own attack against the Imphal Valley in Assam.

By 22 March, the situation was critical, and after delivering the glider to the field called Aberdeen, Cole and his flight crew spent the rest of the day shuttling back and forth between Lalaghat and various bases around Imphal. Roberts noted in his diary: "Evacuating Imphal Valley."[6] The following day, they continued with the evacuation flights, a continuous stream of C-47s into and out of Imphal and its surrounding towns. The Japanese attack eventually stalled and resulted in a resounding defeat for the enemy.

On the afternoon of the twenty-third, after a long morning of ferrying evacuees from Imphal, Cole and his crew were given another mission to Aberdeen. This time they carried British troops into the clearing on a rough strip constructed by the engineers they had dropped in by glider the day previously. Evidence of the close proximity of Japanese troops was startling. Roberts noted, "Saw natives with Jap clothes on."[7]

Since the invasion began on 5 March, Wingate had directed the operation from his headquarters at Sylhet while finding every excuse possible to visit Broadway and other clearings frequently. This was easily done by notifying Cochran, who then arranged for a B-25 to fly him to the stronghold at Broadway. Walter Radovich normally flew him in and then returned to Hailakandi so that the Mitchell would not be caught on the ground by attacking Japanese planes; the attacks were frequent. After a series of strikes had damaged or destroyed most of a group of RAF fighters stationed there as well as an Air Commando P-51, the fighters had been withdrawn. Wingate usually landed at Broadway and then was flown to other fields by light plane.

On 24 March, Radovich once again flew him to Broadway. He asked the British general when he wanted to leave, and Wingate replied he would be ready to go to Imphal at 1700, or 5:00 p.m. Radovich said he would return at that time. But that afternoon when he was preparing to leave Hailakandi, he was told by Alison, who had returned briefly to Hailakandi, that other pilots were unhappy that Radovich was hogging flight time, flying both fighters and bombers on combat missions as well as ferry flights for Wingate. Someone else would have to make the shuttle to Broadway to pick up the general. Lt. Brian Hodges was tapped, and he and his crew headed out from Hailakandi, arriving a few minutes past 5:00. Wingate, wearing his signature old-fashioned pith helmet and carrying a .303 rifle as usual, boarded the Mitchell along with his aide, Capt. George H. Borrow, and two press correspondents. The B-25H was fully armed with bombs, belts of ammunition for the .50-caliber machine guns, and 75mm shells for the nose cannon. They lifted off from Broadway and landed in Imphal, where Wingate conferred with Air Cmdr. S. F. Vincent about the deteriorating situation in the Imphal Valley.

That same evening, Cole and the crew of "Hairless Joe" lifted off from Lalaghat for a quick hop to Hailakandi to pick up radio equipment bound for the troops at Aberdeen. They had already made one flight into the new strip with a load of Chindits. Departing Hailakandi at 1740 (5:40 p.m.), they set course for Aberdeen at the time that Wingate was on his way to Imphal.[8]

Storms in northern Burma and eastern India were sudden and severe, as moisture-laden air was forced up over the mountains that were everywhere in the region. There the moisture cooled until it formed huge drops of rain; static electricity was released in jagged chains of lightning that could blind pilots for several seconds. Turbulence could be bone shaking, and rains could be so intense that visibility was reduced to less than a mile. When Cole arrived over Aberdeen (call sign Easy Easy Lazy) with the needed radio gear, it was dark and a storm was building. "Hairless Joe" was bouncing and shaking, while rain began to lash across the windscreen. As Cole set up his final approach, suddenly the runway lights shut off, and a red light signal indicated Do Not Land! Cole immediately aborted the landing, giving the transport full throttles and signaling to the copilot to raise the landing gear. The C-47 began to climb. Cole knew that a five-thousand-foot mountain was at the opposite end of the short runway, but in the darkness and the storm it was invisible. "Hairless Joe" strained, its engines at full power, and Cole held the nose high for the best angle of climb. The dark mass of the mountaintop passed just below them.

Roberts noted in his diary: "We just cleared 5,000 foot mountain on other end of runway, so we came right home. (Scared). Quite rough." They landed at Lalaghat at 2115 (9:15 p.m.).[9]

But the storm had claimed others. Wingate departed Imphal aboard Lieutenant Hodge's plane after his conference with Vincent; Imphal was just ninety miles east of Hailakandi, and it should have been a quick half-hour flight. But the time for his arrival came and went; concern turned to alarm, and when phone calls to Imphal confirmed the departure of Hodge's Mitchell, with Wingate aboard, alarm settled into gloom. Capt. Richard Benjamin, flying one of the first ACG C-47s, had radioed that he had seen a flash in the hills west of Imphal, adding that it appeared to him to be a plane crash. He was told to note the location on a map.

At first light on the twenty-fifth, planes were in the air, searching for the missing B-25, but the pilots were not told who was aboard. If Wingate was killed, the entire Chindit operation would suffer; he was the inspiration and the genius behind it. He was the driving force that had kept the idea of Long Range Penetration Groups alive in the face of fierce opposition in the British army. Cochran and Alison had worked closely with the British leader and had come to respect his intensity and accept his eccentricities. His bearded face and his topi, his beloved, antiquated pith helmet, had become symbols of the irregular warfare being waged by the joint force of Commonwealth and American forces.

S/Sgt. (Staff Sergeant) Lloyd I. Samp, an Air Commando light-plane pilot, was flying an L-1 in a grid pattern of his own invention; lacking any specific aerial search pattern, he reverted to his boyhood training on a farm and began flying a series of rows as though he were planting corn. After about an hour, he spotted wreckage in the center of a fire-blackened area on the western side of a mountain ridge, barely twenty miles from Imphal. Little was left, but a distinctive gull wing confirmed to Samp that the wreckage was that of a B-25. Noting the site on his map, he then returned to Hailakandi and reported his find to his commanding officer. Radio silence had been imposed on the search pilots; the sergeant-pilot returned to the area in an L-5 with his CO, who confirmed the wreckage was a B-25.

On the morning of 26 March, Samp with fellow pilot Bill Walters in the backseat as observer once more flew to the remote crash site in an L-5; they were to circle over the scene until a British search party in the area could see his plane and advance to the area. Samp and Walters continued to circle until the L-5 began to accumulate carburetor ice; the engine sputtered, and Samp made a rough landing near the crash site. Walters suffered a broken leg, but Samp was unscathed. He tended to Walters and then approached the wreckage of the Mitchell, where a group of Naga tribesmen were picking through the bits and pieces.

Then Samp spotted something. About thirty yards from the apparent point of impact, he bent and picked up a helmet. It was an outdated British pith helmet, the sort that only Wingate had been seen to wear.[10]

For several days, the news of the death of Maj. Gen. Orde Wingate, DSO and two bars, was kept under wraps for fear of the devastating effect it would have on morale of the Air Commandos and Chindits alike. When it was finally disclosed, encomiums and eulogies came from around the globe. It was truly a major blow; Walter Radovich said it "just took the wind out of our sails." It would seem strange now, knowing the small, intense leader with the dark beard and curious sun helmet, the brains and heart of the special operation, would no longer be seen climbing down from a Mitchell or an L-5 to conduct a lightning inspection of a unit in combat.

But as gut-wrenching as the violent death of Wingate and the other eight men aboard Hodge's B-25 was to the joint force, the mission was not over. The day-to-day supply and combat missions of the Americans went on, as did the guerrilla-style raids by the Chindits. Only with the coming of the monsoon rains would they be forced to stand down, and that was six to eight weeks away.

Samp and Walters, who crash-landed near the wreckage, faced several days of uncertainty, cold nights, headhunting Naga tribesmen, lack of provisions, and, for Walters, the agony of an untreated broken leg. A young Naga boy who spoke limited English acted as interpreter and guide; he organized a party that constructed a litter and began the long walk over the rugged hills back to Allied-controlled territory. A Naga runner delivered a note sent from the nearest British unit, along with tobacco, tea, sausages, Vegemite, and bully—with an apology that they didn't have more—and within a couple of days two British troops showed up and led them twenty-six miles to their primitive camp. They passed several villages that displayed human heads stuck on poles; none were European, but the American fliers were not reassured. Within two days after finally making it back to Hailakandi, Samp returned to flying duty, while Walters was flown back to the United States.[11]

For Cole, his crew, and the rest of the Air Commandos, the flights continued.

# CHAPTER 29

Aberdeen, because of its location in a small chain of mountains, was a much more hazardous destination than the relatively clear terrain of Broadway. On 25 March, without knowing that the Chindit commander had been killed the night before, Cole and his crew took off from Lalaghat at 4:15 a.m., carrying troops and mules to the new strip; the storm that claimed the life of Wingate and those with him was still raging around Imphal, and Cole steered "Hairless Joe" around the tumultuous weather. They made a second trip that evening, and only puffy white clouds marked the site of the previous violence in the atmosphere.[1]

For the next several days, Aberdeen was the focus of their flights. They ferried troops and matériel onto the short, dangerous strip, which had been discovered by the Japanese. On 28 March, the field was attacked by aircraft that bombed and strafed the Chindits, killing seven and wounding fourteen. A glider pilot was among the wounded, suffering a bullet through his leg.[2]

Storms continued to pound the region. The field at Aberdeen was too muddy to attempt a landing on 1 April, so Cole returned to Lalaghat. An RAF transport elected to land and crashed, but no one was injured. A TCC C-47 crashed the next day, again without injuries. On 3 April, Japanese aircraft once more bombed the jungle strip, tearing up the rough runway so that Cole was unable to land at midnight and again had to return to Lalaghat without delivering his cargo. Pelting rain closed down all operations for the next couple of days; the field at Lalaghat was too sloppy to attempt takeoffs. Going into Aberdeen on 6 April, a C-47 lost an engine; it landed safely but had to remain at the strip until equipment to repair it could be ferried in. Cole flew in that night, and five minutes

270

after he took off the field was again bombed and strafed by Japanese aircraft, which shot down an RAF transport. Mechanics changed engines on the TCC Gooney Bird, which was undamaged in the attack, and its pilots flew it out the next evening.

Adm. Louis Mountbatten flew in to Hailakandi on 9 April to talk to the Air Commandos about the loss of Wingate, to announce the appointment of Brig. Joe Lentaigne to head the Chindits, and to praise the Commandos for the job they were doing. He did not, as Roberts noted in his diary, say when they would be going home.[3]

It would not be for a while. Alison had been called back to Washington by Hap Arnold the week previously, with a stop in London to discuss with Gen. Dwight Eisenhower's staff any issues involved in glider operations. Gliders would be used extensively in the planned invasion at Normandy. But for the rest of the Commandos, they had more work to do.

Rain in Assam and northern Burma is often a violent event. Clouds don't gently release moisture onto the earth; they dump buckets of water in an unrelenting deluge, a waterfall of terrific intensity that soaks everything, turning fields into muddy swamps and making a mockery of walkways that quickly transform into slippery paths. Hard winds blow the rain sideways, dousing machines and people beneath sheltering porches and leaving everyone and everything sodden and miserable. For several days straight in early and mid-April, rain brought combat operations to a standstill. And the monsoon season was still a month away. Cole described one storm in a letter to his parents on 23 April: "*About a week ago we had a big wind and rain storm. The weather anemometer recorded winds up to 110 miles per hour then it went off the paper. All the trees round our camp kept our bashas from blowing down. All we lost was one—two men in it weren't hurt.*"[4]

By 15 April, flights into Taro, Aberdeen, Broadway, and other points in Burma had resumed. Air Commando pilots found yet another danger besides weather, terrain, and the Japanese: Transport 452, landing at Aberdeen, hit a water buffalo in the darkness. In the resulting crash, the pilot's arm was broken.[5]

Mail continued to frustrate the men in the Air Commandos; it seemed to take weeks to reach them, and then it arrived in batches. In his 23 April letter, Cole described the agony and the joy of the mail service: "*Boy! I really hit the jackpot two days ago. We didn't get any mail for a long time then finally it came. I got twenty letters, two from [sister] Mart Sr., one from Jo, and seventeen from Mart.*"[6]

The weather was turning hot—Cole described it in his letter as *"steaming"* and *"sultry,"* and expressed a desire for rain. It would come soon enough.

The Japanese were still active, and Lalaghat and Hailakandi were not immune to air attacks. On the twenty-sixth, Japanese fighters shot down a C-47; it crash-landed at Lalaghat with many wounded Indian troops and a Red Cross worker aboard. The fuselage and wings were riddled with bullet holes. Allied fighters downed one of the enemy planes ten miles east of the field.[7]

But the frenzied activity of the first few weeks of the Chindit campaign was beginning to resume a more normal pace. Fewer flights were made into Burma now, and the Japanese threat to the Imphal Valley had eased. Cole was circumspect about his activities, but wrote his parents enough that they might have read between the lines: *"We have been doing some more work, but not as much as we did a few weeks ago. In answer to Mart's question, Yep! I was der Charlie, me and Hairless Joe. Sure worked slick as you already know."*[8]

On 5 May, Cole and Bordley, with Roberts as crew chief, flew to Andol to pick up a glider, which they towed to Sylhet. On arriving back at Lalaghat, a throttle stuck, and "Hairless Joe" spun around on the runway, embarrassing the pilots but not causing any damage to the plane. Investigation by Roberts revealed a bird nest in the carburetor had blocked the linkage to the throttle.[9] Four days later, "Hairless Joe" suffered wing damage from an unlikely foe. A large bird—the pilots said it was a buzzard—collided with the wing of the transport and caused damage to the leading edge as well as several metal ribs in the wing. The plane was grounded for several days until it could be repaired.

The weather now in Assam was turning hot. It was difficult to sleep, and the men were red-eyed and weary. *"Here comes another note from torrid tropical India, and I mean torrid,"* Cole wrote his parents on 10 May. *"Last week has been terrible, up in the 120s and 30s. Tonight a big windstorm hit, no rain just wind, sort of cooled things off. Haven't slept well since it got so hot. Will have to get used to it all over again I guess. Ain't going to like it though."*

Cole then related an incident that revealed how dead-tired he was:

*Flew a good deal yesterday, got back late. Was tired, hot and sweaty, so just washed my face and went to bed. About five a.m. this morning we had an alert—the "Nips were on the prowl" so sleepy me gets out of bed. Someone had laid three letters on my desk after I'd gone to bed. Anyway I guess I picked them up and went out to my fox-*

*hole, read them, then came back and went to bed. When I got up the second time I couldn't ever remember of having read them and was trying to find out who'd been opening my mail. Some dope huh! Two were from Mart and one from her sis.*[10]

The rains were more frequent now; the monsoon season had arrived. Finally, in mid-May, the 1st Air Commandos began packing up their equipment and personal gear to move to a drier base at Asansol. The landing fields at the forward bases were often under several inches of water, and the coming monsoon winds promised to turn the base at Lalaghat into a semipermanent lake until October.

"Hairless Joe," after countless flights into the buzz saw of combat in Burma, suffered more indignity to add to the insult of the bird strike. Cole was not flying 19 May. On this day, the landing gear on the left side failed to lock. Cole was called to the tower and advised the pilots to fly over while men on the ground looked at the undercarriage through binoculars. The wheel was down but apparently not locked, so he advised the pilot to land but not to apply any brakes, which would cause the momentum of the heavy airplane to put additional strain on the gear.

The transport approached, touched down, and began its touchdown roll. But the pilot, perhaps thinking he was running out of runway, tapped his brakes. The left gear collapsed, dropping "Hairless Joe" onto the still-turning propeller and damaging the left propeller, engine, wing, strut, and wheel. It was a sad sight, sitting lopsided on the end of the runway.[11]

Jake Sartz and Bill Cherry, with previous tours in India flying the Hump, left for the States in early May. Cole was wistful when he wrote his parents: *"Haven't been doing much lately, a little work now and then. Bill and Jake have started home. Don't know if I'll get to come or not. 'Hairless Joe' has close to five-hundred hours on him now and still goin' strong."*[12]

But a couple of weeks later, Cole received orders to pack his gear and prepare for shipping home. He had been promoted to major in May, and he received a third Distinguished Flying Cross and another Air Medal for his work in the skies over Burma. In June he left India for the last time. He walked out of his room at Asansol carrying his B-4 bag and did not look back.

Dick Cole's war was over. He couldn't wait to see Mart again.

# EPILOGUE

Thirty-one-year-old Dick Cole ran his fingers through his hair and brushed out a small handful of sawdust. He was wearing a thick flannel shirt, grimy khakis, and government-issued high-top work boots; he carefully pushed another slab of pine log through the nine parallel blades of the huge saw, and again a shower of chips and sawdust flew over him, once more covering him in sticky, resin-soaked detritus. Splinters were a problem when handling the rough-sawn lumber, but Cole didn't wear gloves; they might snag on the saw blades and pull him in. It was noisy in the wooden building, and his ears rang with the high-pitched snarl of the coarse blades as they ripped through the aromatic wood. He was careful, extremely careful, to avoid the sharp teeth that would remove a finger or a hand before he knew what happened.

He had wanted to stay in the Army and continue to fly, but the war was over. More than sixteen million young men and women had been called to service; with the end of hostilities, and the signing of unconditional surrender documents by the Germans and the Japanese, the military was being scaled back drastically. Cole had been promoted to lieutenant colonel (reserve) before the ax fell. He was discharged in January 1947, "at the convenience of the government." The raid on Tokyo that had provided such a morale boost to Americans, the hazardous flights over the Hump, the audacious invasion of Burma didn't count for much in the winnowing; neither did the three Distinguished Flying Crosses, the Air Medals, the Chinese decorations, or any of the combat ribbons he had been awarded for his service in the air. Reserve officers had been invited to apply for a regular commission in the Army; Cole had done so but was not among those selected.

275

Instead, he had been discharged, and he and Mart and two-year-old Cindy had loaded into the family car and headed to Oregon. Cole had loved the area when he had been stationed at Pendleton and had determined to enroll at Oregon State University, in Corvallis, to complete his degree in forestry. They arrived after the semester started, so Dick sought a job, any job, to pay the bills for his young family. After a couple of weeks of fruitless searching, he landed the dangerous sawmill position, cutting down the rounded leftovers of pine logs into laths for use in plaster-wall construction. Mart found work at a bank; they were able to rent an apartment in a former Navy hospital that had been converted to housing for returning GIs.

When he returned from the Air Commando assignment in Burma, Dick Cole's war was over. The carnage in Europe and in the Pacific continued for another year, Fortress Europe was invaded at enormous cost in blood, and the grinding, island-hopping campaign to defeat the Japanese culminated in the dropping of the most destructive weapon ever released.

Cole's three combat assignments—as copilot of the first B-25 to leave the *Hornet* on its historic mission to Tokyo, as first pilot of a C-47 hauling vital matériel from Assam over the Himalayas to China, and as a tow pilot pulling gliders into Burma—had tested his courage, his devotion to duty, his skill as a pilot, and his stamina. He passed all those tests with highest marks. It was time to let others take up arms. Combat crews in bombers in Europe flew twenty-five to thirty-five missions—the number increased as the war continued and the men in Washington determined that the danger from the Luftwaffe was less—and then rotated home. Cole had placed himself in harm's way for nearly two years; he was ready to spend time with his new bride. Upon his return from the CBI, he was assigned as an acceptance test pilot at Wichita, Kansas, for the duration, flight-testing new aircraft as they rolled off the assembly line and settling into married life. It was time to think about love, about children, about a future with peace. For a year following the breakout of peace, he was in charge of training at Victorville Army Air Field, California. But then the assignments ended, and Cole was placed on terminal leave and discharged.

The war had spared Cole and both of his brothers. Mart's youngest brother, however, joined the Navy and died in the last year of the war.

Because the Army apparently had no room for Cole, his thoughts had returned to the outdoors. He remembered the rugged landscape, the bountiful game, the tens of thousands of acres of primal forest around Pendleton. So, one career in the air would close, and another in the outdoors would begin. Cole would become a forest ranger.

But before he could enroll in the fall semester at Oregon State, he received a telegram from the Army Air Forces. Would he accept a regular Army commission as a first lieutenant, as a staff officer at Wright-Patterson? It was a severe reduction in rank—four grades below his mustering-out position as lieutenant colonel—and he and Mart talked it over at length. The pay was not so great, but with additional allowances for flight duty, housing, and spousal and children stipends, it would be okay. In the end, the chance to continue flying was the deciding factor. Without waiting for official verification of his status, Dick and Mart and Cindy drove from Corvallis, Oregon, to Wright-Patterson, near Dayton. No insurance, no iron-clad assurance that it would work out, but the allure of continued flying was too strong to resist. Mart had known her man was a flier when she first met him on the ramp at the airport in Tulsa. She did not complain now.

Cole reported to Wright-Patterson to serve as a group staff officer; within three or four months, he was promoted to brevet, or temporary, major, and his pay increased substantially. It was needed, as the Cole family continued to grow. Daughter Christina was born in 1949 at Wright-Patterson; son Richard (Richie) was born three years later, when Cole was stationed at the Armed Forces Staff College in Norfolk, Virginia.

North Korea invaded their kinsmen to the south in 1950, and by September 1952 Cole was assigned to the Far East Air Force, stationed in Japan but with lengthy stays in Korea as a FEAF staff officer. He was awarded a Bronze Star medal for his work there, while the family lived in Japan. Base housing was scarce in postwar Japan; Dick and Mart rented a private residence in an area where they and their three children were the only Caucasians. It was just seven years after World War II, which saw the virtual destruction of many of Japan's major cities, but the Coles never experienced any animosity, not even a harsh look, and they welcomed the chance to interact with the Japanese. Two more sons were born to the Coles, Samuel in 1956 and Andrew two years later. Only Richie would follow his father's path; he became an F-15 pilot in the Air Force.

Other staff assignments continued over Cole's career in the Air Force (it became a separate branch of the armed forces in 1947). He served on

Air Force headquarters staff in the Pentagon from 1955 to 1958 and then attended an armed forces school to learn Spanish. He served three years as adviser to the Venezuelan Air Force in Caracas and when he returned Stateside served in assignments in North Carolina and California.

When Cole retired on the last day of 1966, he looked back on a fulfilling career. The young boy from Dayton who dreamed of flying was rated a command pilot, with more than five thousand flight hours in thirty different aircraft; he had flown more than 250 combat missions, and his log book recorded more than five hundred combat hours flown.

Dick and Mart and four of their children—Cindy had grown and was off to college in Ohio—had been eyeing the citrus farms in South Texas for a couple of years. They bought acreage in the Valley, as the region around the Rio Grande was called, and Dick had a four-thousand-square-foot house built, using twelve thousand bricks he purchased in Mexico. With no experience in business or in agriculture, Cole formed a partnership with Warren Reed, a former P-38 pilot he had known in the service. Reed grew grapefruit, Cole oranges, and together the former combat pilots sold their fruit to grocers in a loop from Boerne to Dallas to Sweetwater. They leased a packing shed, hired workers, and bought a truck. For fourteen years, R-C Farms produce was delivered personally by Cole or Reed, and it is doubtful that the store managers with whom they dealt ever knew anything about their military backgrounds.

Although Dick went through war unscathed, Cindy's fiancé was not so lucky. In 1966 Lt. Robert Gilchrist, an Air Force Academy graduate and son of Maj. Gen. Jack Gilchrist of the Air Force, was killed over North Vietnam on his ninety-ninth combat mission in an F-4 Phantom. Cindy later married James Chal and had two sons, Nathan and Elliot. Nathan became a tanker pilot in the Air Force and is still serving. Elliot will graduate from the US Military Academy at West Point in May 2015.

Cole continued his wartime reticence, preferring anonymity to fame. It was impossible to escape, however. Each year, the Doolittle Raiders held reunions at cities across the United States, many of which were eager for the legendary group to attract visitors and tourists who flocked to the sites. Doolittle himself attended until his death in 1993; each year, in the way of things, fewer members were able to attend. After 1959 roll was taken, and the sterling cups of those who had died during the year were carefully, respectfully, turned upside down in the mahogany case.

By April 2013, there were only four cups still upright. Just weeks before that year's reunion, Tom Griffin passed. Griffin, who survived the

Raid without a scratch, was later shot down in North Africa and became a prisoner of war of the Germans. He and Dick had been invited to China in 2005, part of a large contingent to be guests of the Chinese as they celebrated the sixtieth anniversary of the end of the war with Japan. Griffin had been perhaps Cole's closest friend among the Raiders in recent years, and it was a blow when he died so suddenly just before the final public reunion in Fort Walton Beach, Florida. Thousands of curious admirers attended the various activities, eager for a look at the last of the courageous band of eighty. Lt. Col. Edward Saylor flew in from Puyallup, Washington, and S/Sgt. (Staff Sergeant) David Thatcher was there from Missoula, Montana. Lt. Col. Dick Cole at ninety-seven was the oldest and the acknowledged unofficial leader. Lt. Col. Robert Hite, from Nashville, Tennessee, who had been captured by the Japanese and spent the war as a prisoner of the Japanese, was too ill to attend. The reunion included a public appearance, at which the Raiders signed autographs, answered questions, and held a news conference. Cole was taken for a flight in a B-25, where he took the controls for possibly the last time.

The Doolittle Raiders Association had established a scholarship fund; income from books, posters, and memorabilia sold at the reunions all went into scholarships for college students interested in a career in aviation. Thousands of dollars have been raised, and every penny has gone to the scholarships.

The spotlight continues to find him. Every year he is invited to dozens of air shows around the country. The biggest is Air Venture, in Oshkosh, Wisconsin, that draws up to a million visitors each August. He has been an honored guest there many times, and awed visitors always speak in quiet voices about the raid. Almost nothing is ever asked about his service flying the Hump, and few know anything about his time with the 1st Air Commandos. The Doolittle Raid. It is always about the raid, and at times Cole would prefer not to talk about it.

It grows increasingly difficult. As time goes on, and we realize that the remaining young men and women who marched off to fight fascism in the 1940s are now all in their nineties, there is an awareness, a poignant understanding, that these old warriors are leaving us rapidly. At one of America's darkest moments, eighty young men volunteered for one of the most daring—and dangerous—missions in our history and in doing so inspired a nation and possibly turned the course of the war in the Pacific. Accolades and awards have accumulated for the Raiders, and Cole has often been the one to accept them for the group. In January 2014, Cole was invited to Shreveport, Louisiana, as the representative of the Doolittle Raiders, to receive the Spirit of Independence Award. And in May 2014 he was in the Oval Office with President Barack Obama as the chief executive signed the bill approved by Congress awarding the Raiders the Congressional Gold Medal, America's highest civilian honor.

At nearly one hundred years old, Dick Cole has lived an extraordinary century, the century of flight, the century of the most destructive wars in history. He has lived long enough to know the pain of losing children, as first Christina and then Andy passed before him. His beloved Mart died in 2003; he still carries her photo in his wallet. These days he spends his time on his small ranch in the Texas hill country. He answers his own phone, signs books and memorabilia for the faithful, and continues to travel to events with his daughter Cindy. In May 2014, he attended a program near Waco to honor his old friend Charlie Turner, a glider pilot during the war. In early June 2014, he flew to Kansas City to appear with the author at a program about the 1st Air Commandos. The event drew more than six hundred who braved an early-summer rainstorm for a chance to see the famed pilot. It was the largest program ever presented by the Kansas City Public Library, officials said.

His mind remains sharp, and his wit sharper. In Kansas City, when asked by an audience member about the final-toast ceremony and the 117-year-old cognac, he responded: "Well, it was good, but I thought they were kind of chintzy. I would have liked more." And when asked what was his most memorable moment regarding the Tokyo Raid, he answered quickly: "When my parachute opened!"

In April 2015, Cole and the Doolittle Tokyo Raiders finally received the highest civilian honor that the Congress can bestow, the Congressional Gold Medal. It was specially designed, depicting a B-25 taking off from the *Hornet* on the obverse and three Mitchells and the insignia from the four squadrons of the 17th Bomb Group on the reverse. By now, time had answered Cole's jesting query from years before at a Raiders reunion toast to departed comrades: "I want to know who the other guy is going to be," in reference to the original plans for the final toast by the last two remaining Raiders. In January 2015, Lt. Col. Edward Saylor had died, and in March Lt. Col. Robert Hite had followed. It was now just Dick Cole and David Thatcher, the engineer-gunner on plane seven who had been awarded the Silver Star for rescuing his crew when their bomber flipped over and sank when it came down off the China coast.

The Congressional Gold Medal was a high honor, awarded only 158 times in the nation's history—the first one went to George Washington in 1776—but one both men declined to travel to Washington to accept.

"I don't know many people in Washington," Cole had said. "But I know a lot in Dayton. I'll be there." So Cole had declined to accept the medal in person, but opted to give it away instead, to the National Museum of the US Air Force for safekeeping and permanent display.

On 18 April 2015, the seventy-third anniversary of their famed raid, Cole and Thatcher were in Dayton to present the medal to the museum. Cole spoke briefly and displayed both his humility and his humor. After recounting the raid in a couple of minutes, he looked out over the audience gathered in one of the cavernous hangars that form the museum and mused that the time of evening was about that when he and Thatcher and the men of the other fourteen crews had made the decision to bail out or crash-land their bombers. He looked over at Thatcher.

"And while David was busy saving all of his crew, I was hanging from my parachute in a tree."

For all the hoopla over the raid, or even for the rest of his service in the CBI, he remains quietly insistent.

"I was just doing my job."

It was quite a job.

# NOTES

## CHAPTER 1

1. National Park Service Film, *On Great White Wings*.

2. *Dayton Daily News*, 7 September 1915 (extant copy in Dayton Public Library).

3. Mary Ann Johnson, *McCook Field, 1917–1927: The Force behind America's Golden Age of Flight*, 49–53.

4. Cole to the author, personal interview, Boerne, TX, 11–14 March 2013.

5. The photograph, probably cut from the pages of the *Daily News*, is carefully pasted into Cole's boyhood scrapbook. It is undated, but other dated articles before and after the photo place it at 1933. In just nine years, the boy who idolized Doolittle would be sitting beside him for a wartime mission that came to define both Doolittle and Cole.

6. Cole to the author, March 2013.

7. Ibid.

8. Undated memo from Cole to Ohio University, courtesy Ohio University Special Collections, Athens.

9. Cole to the author, March 2013.

10. Ibid.

11. Undated memo from Cole to Ohio University.

## CHAPTER 2

1. Cole, letter to his mother, 23 November 1940.

2. Cole, letter to his mother, 24 November 1940.

3. Ibid.

4. Cole, letter to his mother, 4 December 1940.

5. Ibid.

283

6. Ibid.
7. Cole to his mother, 18 December 1940.
8. Cole to his mother, 20 December 1940.
9. Cole to his mother, 11 February 1941.
10. Cole to his mother, 26 February 1941.
11. Cole to his mother, 16 February 1941.
12. Ibid.
13. Ibid.
14. Ibid.
15. Cole to his mother, 22 February 1941.
16. Cole to his mother, 15 March 1941.
17. Cole to the author, March 2013.
18. Cole to his mother, 23 June 1941.
19. Cole to his mother, 15 March 1941.
20. Ibid.
21. Cole to his mother, 2 April 1941.
22. Cole to the author, March 2013.
23. Cole to his mother, 15 April 1941.
24. Cole to the author, March 2013.
25. Cole to his mother, 15 April 1941.
26. Ibid.
27. Cole to his mother, 12 May 1941.
28. Ibid.
29. Cole to his mother, 3 June 1941.
30. Cole to his mother, 23 June 1941.

## CHAPTER 3

1. Cole to his mother, 28 August 1941.
2. Cole to the author, March 2013.
3. Cole to his mother, 4 September 1941.
4. Ibid.
5. Ibid.
6. Cole to his mother, 13 September 1941.
7. Cole to the author, March 2013.
8. G. Patrick Murray, "Louisiana Maneuvers: Practice for War."
9. Ted Lawson and Robert Considine, *Thirty Seconds over Tokyo*, 11.
10. Cole to his mother, 25 September 1941.
11. Cole to the author, March 2013.
12. Ibid.

13. Cole to his mother, 12 November 1941.

14. Cole to his mother, 15 November 1941.

15. Cole to his mother, 18 November 1941.

16. Cole to the author, March 2013.

17. Ibid.

18. Cole to his mother, 18 November 1941.

19. Ibid.

20. Cole to his mother, 25 November 1941.

21. Ibid.

## CHAPTER 4

1. Cole to his mother, 7 December 1941. Letter courtesy of Ohio University Special Collections.

2. Cole to the author, March 2013.

3. Cole to his mother, 7 December 1941.

4. Ibid.

5. Josh Sanburn, "Extra! Extra! How Did Journalists Cover Pearl Harbor the Day After?"

6. Cole to his mother, 10 December 1941.

7. Cole to his mother, 20 December 1941.

8. Ibid.

9. Lawson and Considine, *Thirty Seconds over Tokyo*, 19.

10. Ibid., 19–20.

11. Cole to his mother, 2 January 1942.

12. Ibid.

13. Cole to his mother, 25 January 1942.

14. Cole to his mother, 7 February 1942.

15. James H. Doolittle, *I Could Never Be So Lucky Again*, 224.

16. Cole to his mother, 22 February 1942.

17. Ibid.

## CHAPTER 5

1. Carroll V. Glines, *The Doolittle Raid: America's Daring First Strike against Japan*, 74.

2. "Born out of Pearl Harbor: Emotional Responses to Retaliate for Pearl Harbor—Early 1942."

3. Cooper, letter to unknown recipient, 22 May 1970; Reel 43812, Air Force Historical Research Agency, Maxwell Air Force Base, AL (hereafter referred to as AFHRA). At the time, Cooper was executive intelligence offi-

cer to Gen. Henry H. "Hap" Arnold. He had been an aviator in World War I, a founder of Pan American Airways, and a Hollywood film producer. His most famous film was *King Kong*.

4. Wesley Frank Craven and James Lea Cates, *Army Air Forces in World War II*, 1:341–42.

5. Glines, *Doolittle Raid*, 10–11.

6. Ibid., 14–15, 21–22.

7. Cole to his mother, undated but determined to be late March 1942.

8. Glines, *Doolittle Raid*, 30–31.

9. Cole to the author, March 2013.

10. Ibid.

11. Doolittle, *I Could Never Be So Lucky Again*, 226.

12. *B-25 Flight Operating Instructions*, 34.

13. Doolittle, *I Could Never Be So Lucky Again*, 226.

14. Charles R. Greening, "The First Joint Action: A Monograph Submitted to the Faculty of the Armed Forces Staff College, Norfolk, Virginia," 10.

15. Doolittle, *I Could Never Be So Lucky Again*, 227.

16. Greening, "First Joint Action," 11.

17. Ibid., 13.

18. Glines, *Doolittle Raid*, 33–34.

19. Greening, "First Joint Action," 13; Glines, *Doolittle Raid*, 34.

20. Greening, "First Joint Action," 15.

21. Ibid., 12–13.

22. Cole to the author, March 2013.

23. Ibid.

24. Doolittle, *I Could Never Be So Lucky Again*, 230.

25. Ibid., 231.

26. Cole to his mother, 1 April 1942.

## CHAPTER 6

1. Cole to the author, March 2013.

2. Doolittle, *I Could Never Be So Lucky Again*, 242.

3. Lawson and Considine, *Thirty Seconds over Tokyo*, 39–40.

4. Cole to the author, March 2013.

5. Ibid.

6. Doolittle, *I Could Never Be So Lucky Again*, 244–45.

7. Greening, "First Joint Action," 21.

8. Ibid., 18.

9. Doolittle, *I Could Never Be So Lucky Again*, 246.

10. Ibid., 250.

11. Ibid., 251.

12. Cole to the author, March 2013.

13. Cole, letter to surviving Raiders, 16 August 1955. Mitscher had died, and Cole was suggesting donations for a plaque to honor his role in the raid.

14. Cole to the author, March 2013.

15. Memo marked "Eisenhower papers, pp. 254–55, V. 1," on reel 43812, AFHRA. In a letter to Murray Green, head of the Air Force Historical Branch dated 26 November 1979, Brig. Gen. Edward H. Alexander (Ret.) says that Chiang's pique was "more apparent than real." Chiang was making decisions based on political, economic, and military considerations and was well aware that Stilwell was disdainful of him, according to Alexander. At the time of the raid, Alexander was sent to China from India to ensure that support for the Doolittle Raid was in place at the various airfields at which the crews were expected to land.

16. Glines, *Doolittle Raid*, 66.

17. Cole to the author, March 2013.

## CHAPTER 7

1. Doolittle, *I Could Never Be So Lucky Again*, 254.

2. Cole to the author, March 2013.

3. Ibid.

4. Ibid.

5. Ibid.

6. Glines, *Doolittle Raid*, 69–70.

7. Cole to the author, March 2013.

8. Glines, *Doolittle Raid*, 87.

9. Cole to the author, March 2013.

10. Ibid.

11. Ibid.

12. Ibid.

## CHAPTER 8

1. Arnold to King, stamped "Secret," 31 March 1942, microfilm reel 43812, AFHRA.

2. *B-25 Flight Manual*, 62–67.

3. Ibid., 65.

4. Cole to the author, March 2013.

5. Ibid.

6. Lt. Col. Jim Lunsford (Ret.) to the author, 15 April 2014. Lunsford was an officer in the 82nd Airborne Division and made 119 parachute jumps in a twenty-year career.

7. Cole to the author, March 2013. At the final public reunion of the Doolittle Raiders, April 2013, in Fort Walton Beach, FL, Cole, David Thatcher, and Ed Saylor appeared at a program that was opened to questions from the audience. They were asked, "What was the most exciting part of the mission for you?" Cole answered, "When my parachute opened!" It elicited much laughter, but he was quite serious. The question has been asked many times, and his answer never varies.

8. Cole to the author, March 2013.

## CHAPTER 9

1. Claire L. Chennault and Robert Hotz, *Way of a Fighter*, 168.

2. From an advertisement for Marble's outdoor equipment in *Hunting and Fishing*, 1929.

3. Cole to the author, March 2013.

4. "And she [Zipporah] bare him a son, and he [Moses] called his name Gershom: for he said, I have been a stranger in a strange land" (Exod. 2:22).

5. Cole to the author, March 2013. Cole carried the parachute all the way back to Chungking. He finally left it aboard the C-47 that carried him to India, expecting it to be inspected and reissued.

6. Doolittle, *I Could Never Be So Lucky Again*, 10.

7. Ibid., 255–56.

8. Ibid., 11.

9. Cole to the author, March 2013. This story was first related to the author by his friend Lee Lamar, a B-24 pilot in the war who was shot down. He became a POW with Doolittle Raider Ross Greening in 1944 in Stalag Luft I, in Barth, Germany. Greening had related the story to Lamar, who asked the author to verify or refute the story while interviewing Cole. Doolittle's copilot laughed when recalling the incident, adding that he had been just a few feet away when it occurred.

10. Copies of the AMMISCA cables were forwarded to the Doolittle Raiders on 4 April 1994 by Capt. Stephen L. Lea Vell of United Air Lines. Captain Lea Vell found the cables in the Library of Congress while doing research on the Doolittle Raid and made copies available to all of the surviving Raiders. Copies sent to Cole were generously made available to the author by Cole and his daughter Cindy Cole Chal.

11. Doolittle, *I Could Never Be So Lucky Again*, 256–58.

12. Alexander to Green, 26 November 1979.

13. AMMISCA cable, 4 May 1942.

14. Photographs of the boards can be found on microfilm reel 31233, AFHRA.

15. Microfilm reel 43812, AFHRA.

## CHAPTER 10

1. Cole to his mother, 4 May 1942.

2. Lucian Youngblood, unknown recipient, undated. Letter courtesy of Cindy Cole Chal.

3. Cole to his mother, 27 May 1942.

4. Cole to the author, Clifton, TX, 31 May 2014.

5. Doolittle to Cole's mother, 20 May 1942. Courtesy Ohio University Special Collections.

6. Cole to his mother, 27 May 1942.

7. Cole to his mother, 6 June 1942.

8. Cole to the author, 13 March 2013.

9. Cole to his sister, 12 September 1942.

## CHAPTER 11

1. Cole to the author, 13 March 2013.

2. Cole to his mother, 28 June 1942.

3. Of the eighty men who took part in the Doolittle Raid, nineteen would die during the war: Master Sgt. Edwin V. Bain, Lt. Robert S. Clever, Staff Sgt. William J. Dieter, Staff Sgt. Omer A. Duquette, Cpl. Leland D. Faktor, Lt. William G. Farrow, Sgt. William E. Fitzmaurice, Staff Sgt. Melvin J. Gardner, Capt. Robert M. Gray, Lt. Dean E. Hallmark, Staff Sgt. George E. Larkin, Master Sgt. Paul J. Leonard, Lt. Eugene F. McGurl, Lt. Robert J. Meder, Capt. Richard E. Miller, Lt. Kenneth E. Reddy, Capt. Donald G. Smith, Sgt. Harold A. Spatz, and Capt. Denver V. Truelove. Eight men were captured by the Japanese, and four were shot down in the European theater and captured by the Germans.

4. Cole to his mother, 15 July 1942.

5. Cole to his mother, 28 June 1942.

6. Cole to the author, 11 June 2014, Abilene, KS.

7. Herbert Weaver and Marvin A. Rapp, "The Tenth Air Force, 1942," 85–86; Glines, *Doolittle Raid*, 228–30.

8. Cole to the author, March 2013.

## CHAPTER 12

1. Theodore H. White and Annalee Jacoby, *Thunder Out of China*, 145.

2. Weaver and Rapp, "Tenth Air Force, 1942," 1.

3. William Koenig, *Over the Hump: Airlift to China*, 27.

4. Roger G. Miller, "A Pretty Damn Able Commander: Lewis Hyde Brereton."

5. Weaver and Rapp, "Tenth Air Force, 1942," 12.

6. Ibid., 19.

7. Ibid., 13.

8. Ibid., 15–16.

9. Koenig, *Over the Hump*, 27.

10. James P. Segel, *Riding the Hump*, 38.

11. Weaver and Rapp, "Tenth Air Force, 1942," 26.

12. Ibid., 27.

13. Ibid., 28.

14. Ibid., 29.

15. Ibid., 29.

16. Robert L. Willett, *An Airline at War: Pan Am's China National Aviation Corporation and Its Men*, 81–161.

17. Weaver and Rapp, "Tenth Air Force, 1942," 32.

18. Ibid., 35.

## CHAPTER 13

1. Cole to the author, March 2013.

2. William H. Tunner, *Over the Hump*, 73–75.

3. Cole to his sister Josephine, 12 September 1942.

4. Tunner, *Over the Hump*, 46.

5. Ibid., 81–82.

6. Antoine de Saint-Exupéry, *Flight to Arras*, 45–46.

7. John M. Davis, Harold G. Martin, and John A. Whittle, *Curtiss C-46 Commando*, 17–19.

8. Tunner, *Over the Hump*, 43.

9. Cole to the author, March 2013.

10. Ernest K. Gann, *Fate Is the Hunter*, 214.

11. Cole to the author, March 2013.

12. P. V. H. Weems, *Air Navigation*, 133–58.

13. Ibid., 260–93.

14. Carl Frey Constein, *Born to Fly . . . the Hump: A World War II Memoir*, 85.

15. Weaver and Rapp, "Tenth Air Force, 1942," 35–36.

16. Ibid., 43–44.

17. Robert L. Scott, *God Is My Co-Pilot*, 86–87.

18. Weaver and Rapp, "Tenth Air Force, 1942," 112–13.

19. Cole to the author, March 2013. He still has the shrapnel, mounted in a frame with his many military medals.

20. Segel, *Riding the Hump*, 141–42.

21. Cole to his mother, 11 January 1943.

## CHAPTER 14

1. Cole to his mother, 28 June 1942.

2. Cole to the author, March 2013.

3. Weaver and Rapp, "Tenth Air Force, 1942," 115.

4. Cole to the author, March 2013.

## CHAPTER 15

1. Cole to his mother, 15 July 1942.

2. Craven and Cates, *Army Air Forces in World War II*, 7:125.

3. Cole to the author, March 2013.

4. Scott, *God Is My Co-Pilot*, 123–34.

5. Weaver and Rapp, "Tenth Air Force, 1942," 93.

6. Cole to the author, March 2013.

7. *CBI Roundup*, 17 December 1942.

8. Scott, *God Is My Co-Pilot*, 110.

9. Cole to his parents, 5 August 1942.

10. John D. Plating, *The Hump: America's Strategy for Keeping China in World War II*, 73–104.

11. Cole to the author, March 2013; Glines, *Doolittle Raid*, 228. Cole was obviously deeply affected by this, clearly recalling the exact date and the circumstances as though the crash occurred quite recently.

## CHAPTER 16

1. Cole to his sister Josephine, 12 September 1942.

2. Scott, *God Is My Co-Pilot*, 113.

3. Ibid., 113.

4. Cole to the author, March 2013.

5. Scott, *God Is My Co-Pilot*, 115–21.

6. Gene Casey, "Wing Talk."

7. Segel, *Riding the Hump*, 127–31.

## CHAPTER 17

1. Cole to the author, March 2013.

2. Cole to his mother, jointly dated 5 and 17 December 1942. He makes a notation in the letter: "Trip—Gotta go."

3. Cole to his parents, 5 August 1942.

4. Segel, *Riding the Hump*, 140.

5. Ibid., 138.

6. Cole to the author, March 2013.

7. Ibid. Cole continued to wear the Navy-issue flight jacket throughout the war. His son owns it now.

8. Thorne, *The Hump*, 93.

9. Cole to his sister Josephine, 12 September 1942.

## CHAPTER 18

1. Cole to the author, March 2013.

2. Ibid.

3. The booklets were printed in a small size that enabled them to be carried in a flight-jacket or flight-suit pocket. They were general in nature, tending to attempt to cover all possible locations and scenarios.

4. Allied Air Forces, *Survival Hints*, 4–7.

5. Ibid., 66.

6. http://www.atlasobscura.com/articles/the-ramree-island-massacre.

7. Alan Leviton et al., "The Dangerously Venomous Snakes of Myanmar."

8. *CBI Roundup*, 31 December 1942.

9. Eric Severeid, *Not So Wild a Dream*, 250–301.

10. Segel, *Riding the Hump*, 182–84.

## CHAPTER 19

1. Cole to the author, March 2013. The veteran pilot expressed no bitterness or disbelief over this; he accepted it as necessary for the time and conditions, just as he accepted the loss of flight crews over the Hump and the apparent lack of assets or organization to locate and rescue downed airmen.

2. Ibid.

3. Army Air Forces, *Troop Carrier Airplanes: Cockpit Procedures*.

4. Cole to the author, March 2013. He chuckled as he said the words *exciting event*.

5. Ibid. Cole still has his original maps of the Hump route, clearly showing his penciled notations and course line.

6. Ibid.

## CHAPTER 20

1. Cole to his family, 5 and 17 December 1942.

2. Document courtesy of Richard E. Cole.

3. Cole to the author, March 2013.

4. Plating, *The Hump*, 65.

5. Ibid., 54.

## CHAPTER 21

1. Telegrams from Cole to his parents; copy to the author courtesy of Richard E. Cole.

2. Cole to the author, March 2013.

3. Cole to his mother, 19 June 1943.

4. Cole to his mother, 5 July 1943

5. Cole to his mother, 12 July 1943.

6. Telegram, Cole to his parents, 4 August 1943.

7. Cole to his mother, 13 September 1943.

8. Cole to the author, March 2013.

9. Ibid.

10. Ibid.

## CHAPTER 22

1. For further reading on the 1st Air Commandos, see Dennis Okerstrom, *Project 9: The Birth of the Air Commandos in World War II*; and R. D. Van Wagner, *Any Place, Any Time, Any Where: The 1st Air Commandos in World War II*. An older, out-of-print book is Lowell Thomas, *Back to Mandalay*. For information on the Chindits, see Sheldord Bidwell, *The Chindit War: Stilwell, Wingate, and the Campaign in Burma, 1944*; or Bernard Fergusson, *The Wild Green Earth*. Readers seeking additional background on Maj. Gen. Orde Wingate should consider John Bierman and Colin Smith, *Fire in the Night: Wingate of Burma, Ethiopia, and Zion*; or David Rooney, *Wingate and the Chindits: Redressing the Balance*.

2. Bierman and Smith, *Fire in the Night*, 59–237.

3. *Combined Chiefs of Staff, Conference Proceedings, 1941–1945*.

4. Henry H. "Hap" Arnold, "The Aerial Invasion of Burma."

5. For a more detailed discussion of the 1st Air Commandos and the men who were involved in Operation Thursday, the invasion of Burma by air, see my book *Project 9*.

6. Cole to the author, March 2013.

7. Headquarters, Army Air Forces, *Pilot Training Manual for the CG-4A Glider*, 21; Headquarters, Army Air Forces, *Pilot Training Manual for C-47*, 86–95.

8. Headquarters, Army Air Forces, *Pilot Training Manual for the CG-4A Glider*, 44–47.

9. Cole to the author, March 2013; Turner to the author, June 2014.

10. Cole to the author, March 2013

11. Ibid.

12. Ibid.

13. Philip G. Cochran, interview by Dr. James C. Hasdorff, 95–96.

14. Van Wagner, *Any Place, Any Time, Any Where*, 29.

## CHAPTER 23

1. Cole to the author, March 2013.

2. Cole to his mother, 13 December 1943.

3. Ibid. Cole still has the leather patch, a navy-blue question mark on a white background; it was never sewn onto his jacket.

4. Cole to his mother, 21 December 1943.

5. Ibid.

6. Turner to the author, March 2013.

7. Cole to his parents, 2 January 1944.

8. Ray Roberts, "India Diary, 1944." Maurice Ray Roberts was the assistant flight engineer for Cole aboard "Hairless Joe" throughout Cole's Air Commando deployment to India. He kept a detailed diary of each flight as well as daily life for the Air Commandos during his tour in the CBI. The diary was made available to the author through the kindness of his son, Keith Roberts.

9. Van Wagner, *Any Place, Any Time, Any Where*, 31, 33.

10. Cole to his mother, 26 January 1944.

11. Roberts, "India Diary, 1944."

12. This incident is related in detail in Okerstrom, *Project 9*. Documents relating to this were furnished to the author by James Miller, son of Donald "Red" Miller, one of the pilots shot down that day. The incident is also related in an interview of Cochran by Hasdorff.

## CHAPTER 24

1. Joint Intelligence Collecting Agency, "Report of Glider Operations," 18.

2. Turner to the author, 22 July 2014.

3. Ibid.

4. Van Wagner, *Any Place, Any Time, Any Where*, 37.

5. Turner to the author, 22 July 2014.

## CHAPTER 25

1. Turner to the author, March 2013; Chuck Baisden, *Flying Tiger to Air Commando*, 88.

2. John R. Alison, interview by Interrogation Branch of Assistant Chief of Air Staff, Intelligence.

3. Turner to the author, March 2013.

4. Ibid.

5. At least one World War II memoir declares that sentiment in its title: Mark Bagley's *The G Stands for Guts: A Glider Pilot Remembers WWII*.

6. Lewis's obituary, *Gaston (NC) Gazette*, 19 February 2011.

7. Turner to the author, March 2013.

8. Turner to the author, June 2014.

9. Photo provided to the author courtesy of John Bartlett, son of James "Mickey" Bartlett.

10. Van Wagner, *Any Place, Any Time, Any Where*, 57.

11. Today original jackets with theater-made decorative unit patches fetch thousands of dollars on the collectors' market.

12. Cole to his mother, 27 February 1944.

13. Harvey, *Meanwhile . . . : A Biography of Milton Caniff*, 448.

14. Cole to his mother, 27 February 1944.

15. James Eckert, interview by the author, October 2012.

16. Fergusson, *The Wild Green Earth*, 55–57; Van Wagner, *Any Place, Any Time, Any Where*, 39.

17. Roberts, "India Diary, 1944."

## CHAPTER 26

1. Joint Intelligence Collecting Agency, "Burma—Invasion of First Air Commando Force," 9.

2. Cochran interview, 394–98.

3. "Silent Wings: The American Glider Pilots of WWII," narrated by Hal Holbrook, 2007.

4. Cole to the author, June 2014.

5. Cochran interview, 20–21.

6. Ibid., 244–46.

7. Cole to the author, March 2013.

8. Roberts "India Diary, 1944"; Cole to the author, March 2013.

9. Cole to the author, March 2013.

10. Thomas, *Back to Mandalay*, 233–38.

11. Roberts, "India Diary, 1944."

12. Alison interview, 6.

13. Cochran interview, 261.

## CHAPTER 27

1. Alison interview, 7.

2. Roberts, "India Diary, 1944."

3. Ibid.

4. Turner to the author, March 2013.

5. Roberts, "India Diary, 1944."

6. Ibid.

7. Joint Intelligence Collecting Agency, "Report of Troop Carrier Command Participation in 'Thursday Operation' [*sic*]," 4.

## CHAPTER 28

1. Roberts, "India Diary, 1944."

2. Van Wagner, *Any Place, Any Time, Any Where*, 58.

3. Roberts, "India Diary, 1944."

4. Ibid.

5. Ibid.

6. Ibid.

7. Ibid.

8. Ibid.

9. Ibid.

10. Lloyd I. Samp, "Rescue Requested," 49. Among artifacts brought home by Sergeant Samp and still in possession of the Samp family is a burned rupee note picked up by the pilot at the site of Wingate's crash.

11. Ibid., 52.

## CHAPTER 29

1. Roberts, "India Diary, 1944."

2. Ibid.

3. Ibid.

4. Cole to his parents, 23 April 1944.

5. Roberts, "India Diary, 1944."

6. Cole to his parents, 23 April 1944.

7. Roberts, "India Diary, 1944."

8. Cole to his parents, 23 April 1944.

9. Roberts, "India Diary, 1944."

10. Cole to his parents, 10 May 1944.

11. Cole to the author, June 2014.

12. Cole to his parents, 10 May 1944.

# REFERENCES

Airlines War Training Institute. *Survival: A Manual for Aircraft Crews Forced Down in All Parts of the World*. Washington, DC: AWTI, 1943.

Alexander, Edward H. Letter to Murray Green, Air Force Historical Branch chief, 26 November 1979. Microfilm reel 43812, Air Force Historical Research Agency, Maxwell Air Force Base, AL. Hereafter referred to as AFHRA.

Alison, John R. Interview by Interrogation Branch of Assistant Chief of Air Staff, Intelligence, 25 April 1944. AFHRA, file 142.052.3.

———. Interview by Maj. Scottie S. Thompson, 22–28 April 1979. AFHRA, file K239.0512-1121.

Allied Air Forces. *Survival Hints*. Directorate of Intelligence: SWPA, 1943. Reprinted by SOA Books, 2013.

Army Air Forces. *Troop Carrier Airplanes: Cockpit Procedures*. Training Film TF 1-33, First Motion Picture Unit, Army Air Forces, US War Department. http://www.youtube.com/watch?v=1Mt-lOnfRyq4.

Arnold, Henry H., "Hap." "The Aerial Invasion of Burma." *National Geographic*, August 1944, 129–48.

Bagley, Mark. *The G Stands for Guts: A Glider Pilot Remembers WWII*. Ashland, OR: Hellgate Press, 2008.

Baisden, Chuck. *Flying Tiger to Air Commando*. Atglen, PA: Schiffer, 1999.

Bidwell, Shelford. *The Chindit War: Stilwell, Wingate, and the Campaign in Burma, 1944*. New York: Macmillan, 1979.

Bierman, John, and Colin Smith. *Fire in the Night: Wingate of Burma, Ethiopia, and Zion.* New York: Random House, 1999.

"Born Out of Pearl Harbor: Emotional Responses to Retaliate for Pearl Harbor—Early 1942." Microfilm reel 43812, AFHRA.

Caniff, Milton. *The Complete "Terry and the Pirates," 1943 to 1944.* Vol. 5. San Diego: IDW, 2008.

Casey, Gene. "Wing Talk." *Collier's,* 12 February 1944, 9. Copy courtesy of James Segel.

Chennault, Claire L., and Robert Hotz. *Way of a Fighter.* New York: Putnam, 1949.

Child, Robert. *Silent Wings: The American Glider Pilots of WWII.* Film produced, directed, and written by Child. Narrated by Hal Holbrook. Inecom Entertainment, 2007.

Cochran, Philip G. Interview by Dr. James C. Hasdorff, 20–21 October and 11 November 1975. AFHRA, file K239.0512-876.

Cole, Richard E. Collection. Mahn Center for Archives and Special Collections, Alden Library. Ohio University, Athens.

———. Correspondence, 1940–44. Letters to his parents and sisters. Copies made available to the author; originals in possession of Cole; some correspondence and letters in the Special Collections branch of Ohio University, Athens, and copies furnished by OU to the author.

———. Interviews by the author, Fort Walton Beach, FL, October 2012; Boerne, TX, March 2013; Clifton, TX, May 2014; Kansas City, MO, and Abilene, KS, June 2014. Tapes and notes in possession of the author.

*Combined Chiefs of Staff: Conference Proceedings, 1941–1945.* Vol. 2, *Quadrant Conference, August 1943.* Papers and minutes of meetings. Washington, DC: Office of the Combined Chiefs of Staff, 1943. Dwight D. Eisenhower Presidential Library, Abilene, KS.

Constein, Carl Frey. *Born to Fly . . . the Hump: A World War II Memoir.* N.p.: 1st Books Library, 2003.

Cooper, Merian C. Letter to unknown recipient, 22 May 1970. Microfilm reel 43812, AFHRA.

Craven, Wesley Frank, and James Lea Cate. *The Army Air Forces in World War II.* Vols. 1 and 7. Series online at http://www.ibiblio.org/hyperwar/AAF/I.

Davis, John M., Harold G. Martin, and John A. Whittle. *Curtiss C-46 Commando.* Kent, England: Air-Britain (Historians), 1978.

Doolittle, James H. *I Could Never Be So Lucky Again*. New York: Bantam, 1992.

Fergusson, Bernard. *The Wild Green Earth*. London: Fontana, 1956.

Gann, Ernest K. *Fate Is the Hunter*. New York: Simon and Schuster, 1961.

Glines, Carroll V. *The Doolittle Raid: America's Daring First Strike against Japan*. Atglen, PA: Schiffer, 1991.

Greening, Charles R. "The First Joint Action: A Monograph Submitted to the Faculty of the Armed Forces Staff College, Norfolk, Virginia." 1948. AFHRA, file 168.309-1.

Harvey, Robert C. *Meanwhile . . . : A Biography of Milton Caniff*. Seattle: Fantagraphics, 2007.

Headquarters, Army Air Forces, *Pilot Training Manual for C-47*. N.p.: Office of Flying Safety, n.d.

———. *Pilot Training Manual for the CG-4A Glider*. AAF Manual 50-17, March 1945. Reprinted by George A. Petersen, National Capitol Historic Sales. N.d.

Headquarters, India-China Wing, Air Transport Command. Special Order No. 72, 29 April 1943, Chabua, India. Pertaining to reassignment of Cole, Sartz, Segel, Grube, Boll, Walker, and other Hump pilots. Courtesy of James Segel.

Huston, John W., ed. *American Airpower Comes of Age: General Henry H. "Hap" Arnold's World War II Diaries*. Vol. 1. Maxwell Air Force Base, AL: Air University Press, 2002.

Johnson, Mary Ann. *McCook Field, 1917–1927: The Force behind America's Golden Age of Flight*. Dayton, OH: Landfall, 2002.

Joint Intelligence Collecting Agency. "Burma—Invasion of First Air Commando Force." China-Burma-India Report no. 1448 (29 March 1944). AFHRA.

———. "Burma—Supplemental Report on First Air Commando." China-Burma-India Report no. 1834, 15 April 1944. AFHRA.

———. "Report of Glider Operations." China-Burma-India Report no. 1449, 1 April 1944. AFHRA.

———. "Report of Troop Carrier Command Participation in 'Thursday Operation' [*sic*]." China-India-Burma Report no. 1579, 16 March, 1 April 1944. AFHRA.

Koenig, William. *Over the Hump: Airlift to China*. Ballantine's Illustrated History of the Violent Century, Campaign Book no. 23. New York: Ballantine, 1972.

Lawson, Ted, and Robert Considine. *Thirty Seconds over Tokyo.* New York: Random House, 1943.

Leviton, Alan, Guinevere O. U. Wogan, Michelle S. Koo, George R. Zug, Rhonda S. Lucas, and Jens V. Vindum. "The Dangerously Venomous Snakes of Myanmar." In *Proceedings of the California Academy of Science* 54, no. 24 (2003): 407–62.

Mason, Herbert A., Jr., Randy G. Bergeron, and James A. Renfrow Jr. *Operation Thursday: Birth of the Air Commandos.* Air Force History and Museums Program, 1994. Reprinted 2007.

Miller, Roger G. "A Pretty Damn Able Commander: Lewis Hyde Brereton." Pt. 1. *Air Power History,* no. 47 (22 December 2000). Online.

Mitter, Rana. *Forgotten Ally: China's World War II, 1937–1945.* Boston: Houghton Mifflin Harcourt, 2013.

Murray, G. Patrick. "The Louisiana Maneuvers: Practice for War." *Louisiana History: The Journal of the Louisiana Historical Association* 13, no. 2 (1972): 117–38.

National Park Service. *On Great White Wings.* Film. Dayton, OH: Dayton Aviation Heritage National Historic Park.

North American Aviation. *Handbook, Flight Operating Instructions, B-25J.* AN 01-60GE-1. Authority of the Secretary of the Air Force and Chief of Bureau of Aeronautics. 7 September 1949.

Office of Flying Safety, United States Army Air Forces. *Emergencies: Jungle, Desert, Arctic, Ocean.* No publication data, World War II era.

Okerstrom, Dennis. *Project 9: The Birth of the Air Commandos in World War II.* Columbia: University of Missouri Press, 2014.

Plating, John D. *The Hump: America's Strategy for Keeping China in World War II.* College Station: Texas A&M University Press, 2011.

Roberts, Maurice Ray. "India Diary, 1944." Private diary kept by Richard Cole's assistant flight engineer. Courtesy of Keith Roberts.

Rooney, David. *Wingate and the Chindits: Redressing the Balance.* London: Cassell, 1994.

Saint-Exupéry, Antoine de. *Flight to Arras.* New York: Reynal and Hitchcock, 1942.

Samp, Lloyd I. "Rescue Requested." *World War II,* May 1991, 46–52.

Sanburn, Josh. "Extra! Extra! How Did Journalists Cover Pearl Harbor the Day After?" -http://Newsfeed.time.com/2010/12/07/extra-extra-how-did-journalists-cover-pearl-harbor-the-day-after.

Scott, Robert L. *God Is My Co-Pilot*. Garden City, NY: Blue Ribbon Books, 1944.

Segel, James P. *Riding the Hump*. Unpublished memoir. Copy to the author courtesy of James Segel.

Severeid, Eric. *Not So Wild a Dream*. New York: Alfred A. Knopf, 1946.

Spencer, Otha C. *Flying the Hump: Memories of an Air War*. College Station: Texas A&M University Press, 1992.

Thomas, Lowell. *Back to Mandalay*. New York: Greystone, 1951.

Thorne, Bliss K. *The Hump: The Great Himalayan Airlift of World War II*. Philadelphia: Lippincott, 1965.

Trans-India Ferrying Command, 10th AAF. Special Order no. 10, 3 July 1942. Order pertaining to assignment of AMMISCA pilots. Courtesy of James Segel.

Tunner, William H. *Over the Hump*. Scott Air Force Base, IL: Military Airlift Command, 1991.

Turner, Charles. Personal interviews, March 2013, May 2014, July 2014. Notes in the author's possession.

Van Wagner, R. D. *Any Place, Any Time, Any Where: The 1st Air Commandos in World War II*. Atglen, PA: Schiffer, 1998.

Wagner, Ray. "The North American B-25A to G Mitchell." Leatherhead, Surrey (England): Profile Publications, 1965.

Weaver, Herbert, and Marvin A. Rapp. "The Tenth Air Force, 1942." US Air Force Historical Studies no. 12. AFHRA. Microfilm reel K1001; IRIS no. 467604. http://www.afhra.af.mil/studies/index.asp.

Weems, P. V. H. *Air Navigation*. New York: McGraw-Hill, 1931.

White, Theodore H., and Annalee Jacoby. *Thunder Out of China*. New York: William Sloan, 1946.

Willett, Robert L. *An Airline at War: Pan Am's China National Aviation Corporation and Its Men*. Privately published, 2008.